Ethics, Law and Justifying Targeted Killings

This book examines the normative debates surrounding the US use of targeted killings.

It questions whether the Obama administration's defence of its use of targeted killings is cohesive or hypocritical. In doing so, the book departs from the disciplinary purpose of international law, constitutional law and the just war tradition and instead examines discipline-specific defences of targeted killings to identify their requisite normative principles in order to compare these norms across disciplines. The methodology used in this book means that it argues that targeted killings are only defensible as acts of war, but it also highlights the normative role of accountability and responsibility in this defence. In doing so, it offers an argument that the use of 'pattern of life' killings by the CIA falls outside the defence offered by the Obama administration, but that this same type of targeting could be used by the military due to differing standards/mechanisms of responsibility assignment in these organisations. The book thus provides a way of investigating contemporary wars where the conduct of war lacks the traditional hallmarks of conventional warfare. Furthermore, by drawing attention to differing normative concepts that underpin competing interpretations of law and morality, it provides a way of analysing contemporary political violence in an interdisciplinary fashion without seeking to displace single disciplinary study.

This book will be of much interest to students of military studies, ethics of war, foreign policy, international security and IR.

Jack McDonald is a teaching and research fellow at the Centre for Science & Security Studies, part of the Department of War Studies at King's College London, and has a PhD in War Studies.

Contemporary Security Studies
Series Editors: James Gow and Rachel Kerr
King's College London

This series focuses on new research across the spectrum of international peace and security, in an era where each year throws up multiple examples of conflicts that present new security challenges in the world around them.

Mechanistic Realism and US Foreign Policy
A new framework for analysis
Johannes Gullestad Rø

Prosecuting War Crimes
Lessons and legacies of the International Criminal Tribunal for the former Yugoslavia
Edited by James Gow, Rachel Kerr and Zoran Pajić

The NATO Intervention in Libya
Lessons learned from the campaign
Edited by Kjell Engelbrekt, Marcus Mohlin and Charlotte Wagnsson

Truth Recovery and Transitional Justice
Deferring human rights issues
Iosif Kovras

Reconstructing Afghanistan
Civil-military experiences in comparative perspective
Edited by William Maley and Susanne Schmeidl

Strategic Narratives, Public Opinion and War
Winning domestic support for the Afghan War
Edited by Beatrice De Graaf, George Dimitriu and Jens Ringsmose

Liberal Wars
Anglo-American strategy, ideology, and practice
Edited by Alan Cromartie

Prosecuting Slobodan Milošević
The unfinished trial
Nevenka Tromp

Media Strategy and Military Operations in the 21st Century
Mediatizing the Israel Defence Force
Michal Shavit

Ethics, Law and Justifying Targeted Killings
The Obama administration at war
Jack McDonald

Ethics, Law and Justifying Targeted Killings
The Obama administration at war

Jack McDonald

LONDON AND NEW YORK

First published 2017
by Routledge
2 Park Square, Milton Park, Abingdon, Oxon OX14 4RN

and by Routledge
711 Third Avenue, New York, NY 10017

First issued in paperback 2018

Routledge is an imprint of the Taylor & Francis Group, an informa business

© 2017 Jack McDonald

The right of Jack McDonald to be identified as author of this work has
been asserted by him in accordance with sections 77 and 78 of the
Copyright, Designs and Patents Act 1988.

All rights reserved. No part of this book may be reprinted or reproduced or
utilised in any form or by any electronic, mechanical or other means, now
known or hereafter invented, including photocopying and recording, or in
any information storage or retrieval system, without permission in writing
from the publishers.

Trademark notice: Product or corporate names may be trademarks or
registered trademarks, and are used only for identification and explanation
without intent to infringe.

British Library Cataloguing-in-Publication Data
A catalogue record for this book is available from the British Library

Library of Congress Cataloging-in-Publication Data
Names: McDonald, Jack, Ph.D.
Title: Ethics, law and justifying targeted killings : the Obama
administration at war / Jack McDonald.
Description: Abingdon, Oxon ; New York, NY : Routledge, 2017. | Series:
Contemporary security studies | Includes bibliographical references and
index.
Identifiers: LCCN 2016007786| ISBN 9781138645790 (hardback) |
ISBN 9781315627953 (ebook)
Subjects: LCSH: Targeted killing (International law) | Targeted killing–
United States. | United States–Politics and government–2009–
Classification: LCC KZ6373.2 .M33 2017 | DDC 343.73/018414–dc23
LC record available at http://lccn.loc.gov/2016007786

Typeset in Times New Roman
by Wearset Ltd, Boldon, Tyne and Wear

ISBN 13: 978-1-138-58879-0 (pbk)
ISBN 13: 978-1-138-64579-0 (hbk)

To Maggie, for all the books.

Contents

	List of abbreviations	viii
	Acknowledgements	ix
1	Justifying targeted killings	1
2	American targeted killings	31
3	War and law enforcement	67
4	International law	97
5	Constitutional protections	123
6	Normative principles of war	154
7	Conclusion	179
	Bibliography	182
	Index	202

Abbreviations

ACLU   American Civil Liberties Union
AQAP   Al-Qaeda in the Arabian Peninsula
AUMF   Authorization for the Use of Military Force
CIA   Central Intelligence Agency
EO   Executive Order
FBI   Federal Bureau of Investigation
ICC   International Criminal Court
ICCPR International Covenant on Civil and Political Rights
ICJ   International Court of Justice
ICRC   International Committee of the Red Cross
IDF   Israel Defense Forces
IHL   international humanitarian law
IHRL   international human rights law
IPCC   Independent Police Complaints Commission
IRA   Irish Republican Army
ISR   Intelligence, Surveillance and Reconnaissance
JCS   Joint Chiefs of Staff
JSOC   Joint Special Operations Command
NGO   non-governmental organisation
NIAC   non-international armed conflict
NSA   National Security Agency
NSC   National Security Council
ROE   rule of engagement
SAS   Special Air Service
SCI   Supreme Court of Israel
UAV   unmanned aerial vehicle
UCMJ   Uniform Code of Military Justice
UN   United Nations
UNSC   United Nations Security Council
WPR   War Powers Resolution

Acknowledgements

This book, and any flaws that it may contain, are mine, but it would not exist without the support and help of my friends, family and colleagues. I would like to thank John Gearson and Michael Rainsborough, who supervised the thesis on which this book is built. Much of the time dedicated to transforming my PhD into a book was spent working with James Gow, Rachel Kerr and Guglielmo Verdirame on the ESRC-funded project SNT Really Makes Reality: Technological Innovation, Non-Obvious Warfare and the Challenges to International Law (ES/K011413/1), and so I would also like to thank the Economic and Social Research Council for funding the post that allowed me to engage with these ideas at length. Lastly, I would like to thank the staff at the Library of Congress, the Franklin D. Roosevelt Presidential Library and Museum, and the US Navy's Naval History and Heritage Command archive in Washington, DC. Thanks must also go to Ryan Evans, for letting me crash on his couch while rooting through archives, and to Yury Shats, for letting me do the same in New York City.

I would also like to thank Wyn Bowen, Chris Hobbs, Susan Martin, Matthew Moran, Heather Williams, Robert Downes, Dina Esfandiary, Daniel Salisbury, Hassan Elbahtimy, Jessica Marcos and my other colleagues at the Centre for Science and Security Studies for their friendship and support while I was completing this book. In addition, I would like to thank Kieran Mitton, Natasha Kuhrt, Thomas Rid, Frank Foley, David Betz, Rebecca Friedman, Walter Ladwig, Nicholas Michelsen, Ernst Djixhoorn, Brian Holden Reid, Jack Spence and the rest of my colleagues from the Department of War Studies, King's College London, who are too numerous to mention. I would also like to thank the students that I have had the privilege to teach in the past five years. Lastly, I have to thank my friends for all their support over the years, as I would never have made it this far without them.

1   Justifying targeted killings

I suppose that the arguments are more often prudential than moral, but I don't believe that the people sitting around the table are 'realists' who simply seize political opportunities or are driven by military necessities.

Michael Walzer[1]

My starting point is to take what Bush says at face value, and inquire how defensible the positions that he espouses are.

Peter Singer[2]

I took an oath to preserve, protect, and defend the Constitution as Commander-in-Chief, and as a citizen, I know that we must never, ever, turn our back on its enduring principles for expedience sake.... But I can say with certainty that my administration ... will do everything in our power to keep the American people safe.

President Obama[3]

Introduction

The use of targeted killings by the US government is highly contentious and raises many important legal and ethical questions. Central to this debate is the question of whether targeted killings are a legitimate means of disrupting terrorist networks. After 9/11, the George W. Bush administration argued that the transnational terrorist network responsible for the 9/11 attacks, al-Qaeda, posed a significant national security threat to the United States and its allies.[4] This perception of threat is mirrored in the statements made by the Obama administration.[5] Both the Bush and Obama administrations stated that they intended to eliminate al-Qaeda and associated terrorist networks. In doing so, both administrations have used a wide variety of counterterrorism methods. The Bush administration used targeted killings to attack al-Qaeda in a direct fashion, killing its operatives and network members with targeted killings in Afghanistan, Iraq, Pakistan, Somalia and Yemen.[6] This failed to defeat al-Qaeda, although its operations were disrupted. In *Leaderless Jihad*, Marc Sageman argues that its leadership was 'contained operationally'.[7]

2 *Justifying targeted killings*

In a set of key speeches the Obama administration has sought to portray itself as acting in accordance with the rule of law,[8] as a contrast to the George W. Bush administration's reshaping of legal parameters. Importantly the Obama administration, seeking to portray itself as an ethical alternative to the Bush administration, not only continued to use targeted killings, but also vastly increased their use against al-Qaeda and affiliates. This raises an important and highly contentious issue: the basis on which the US government internally legitimates the practice of targeted killings. The Obama administration has distanced itself from realist or amoral explanations for using force and instead explicitly seeks to legitimate the use of targeted killings as a legal and ethical means of using force against terrorist networks. These speeches, and the hidden legal rationale that they summarise, form a defence of targeted killings. This book examines the defence offered by the Obama administration for its use of targeted killings. In particular, I argue that a key feature of the Obama administration's defence hinges on the ability of the executive branch of government to define persons as enemies.

What are targeted killings?

Targeted killings – the use of violence by the state directed at individuals – are rare relative to other forms of warfare, but nonetheless important. In his authoritative book on the law relevant to targeted killings, Nils Melzer defines targeted killings as occurring within two legal paradigms but accepts that most states' targeted killing policies occur outside these legal regimes.[9] The definition of targeted killings is important, as well as being an essentially contested concept.[10] In this work, US 'targeted killings' refer to the activities that lead to the use of targeted killings by the US state against persons defined as enemies by the executive branch, with particular emphasis on such activities outside the context of US military activities in Iraq and Afghanistan. Many organisations – including the White House, the Central Intelligence Agency (CIA) and the Department of Defense – are involved in conducting targeted killings on behalf of the US state. One key feature of US targeted killings is that they have remilitarised the CIA. Many newspaper reports identify the CIA as using unmanned aerial vehicles (UAVs) to conduct targeted killings.[11] Despite its origins in World War II, the CIA, as George Tenet states, 'was built to gather intelligence, not conduct wars'.[12] Tenet admits that the CIA had an armed Predator UAV in 2001 but does not describe the use of such weapons outside Afghanistan.[13] Much is made of the bureaucratic overlap involved in US targeted killings, because it is often unclear whether the military or the CIA is in effective control of a given strike. Their use, however, derives from the legal authority afforded the executive branch of government by Congress in the form of the Authorization for the Use of Military Force (AUMF), and the president's political role in the US political system.[14] One implicit element of this is that the president has the right, as commander-in-chief, to define persons or organisations as enemies. In addition, this covers the use of targeted killings away from overt US military forces in Iraq and

Justifying targeted killings 3

Afghanistan. But it is in these areas that the use of lethal force raises serious questions of legality and ethics, particularly when the threat posed by terrorists or militants is not immediately obvious to observers.

The first confirmed US targeted killing outside of obvious war zones was conducted against Ali Qaed Sinan al-Harithi in 2002. He was killed by missiles fired from a UAV controlled by the CIA, a fact proclaimed by the Bush administration.[15] This killing posed a novel challenge and sparked considerable initial debate about its legality.[16] In particular, the killing raised questions about whether targeting persons outside a defined battlefield was legal, whether such acts could be defined as acts of war and whether the use of UAVs to conduct such strikes was ethical or legal.

The Bush administration continued to use targeted killings from 2004 onwards in Pakistan and, later, in Yemen and Somalia. An overview of reported strikes is available from the Bureau of Investigative Journalism.[17] Unlike the al-Harithi strike, these acts were not acknowledged. The use of these strikes was a semi-covert activity – while not acknowledged by the US government, the United States was the only state with the means and inclination to conduct them. What is clear from available evidence is that the Bush administration increased the use of targeted killings, and that the Obama administration increased the use of this method further, numbering more than one hundred in 2010. This provoked renewed criticism from long-time critics such as Mary Ellen O'Connell, as well as considerable further debate of this practice.[18]

The Obama administration increased the use of targeted killings, but it is often unclear what immediate purpose they serve. The US use of targeted killings, particularly in Pakistan, is linked to the wider conflict in Afghanistan. The tribal areas where these targeted killings occur border Afghanistan and, as such, form staging areas for insurgent forces who cross over to Afghanistan to fight. Targeted killings are used on both sides of the border. The two conflicts overlap; for example, the killing of Mullah Dadullah in Afghanistan was possible due to tracking insurgents in Pakistan.[19] Pakistan presents a different set of legal challenges to Afghanistan or Iraq, because it is not a defined war zone, and US strikes in the country have largely gone unavowed.

As important as the expansion in the number of targeted killings, the Obama administration also conducted one that was qualitatively different from previous strikes – the killing of Anwar al-Awlaki. An American-Yemeni, al-Awlaki held dual citizenship, and therefore the Obama administration's premeditated use of lethal force against him transgressed the normal constitutional restrictions on the use of force by the state against its citizens. The use of violence against US citizens is important, since in the US case targeted killings are only used beyond the territorial boundaries of the United States, or in US-controlled territories such as US military bases and other places of US extraterritorial authority. Targeted killings have been used in war zones in which US forces are present, such as Iraq and Afghanistan. Most of the people targeted and killed are not members of the US political community. However, the targeting and killing of Anwar al-Awlaki sparked legal cases in the United States and refocused the debate on

4 Justifying targeted killings

the legality of targeted killings in constitutional law. This debate centres around the legitimacy of using targeted killings against US citizens.[20] Targeting citizens raises due process concerns, which refer to the respect that the US state must have for the legal rights of US citizens.[21] The killing of citizens by the state is a tightly controlled practice in democratic societies, and the prospect of the US government killing al-Awlaki led to significant court cases, such as *Al-Aulaqi* v. *Obama*, which was dismissed by a district court and failed in its attempt to force the government to desist from targeting al-Awlaki.[22]

The use of targeted killings represents a continuation of one of the key, contentious authorities used by the Bush administration – the ability to define persons as enemies and place them outside the US legal system. The Bush administration's use of such discursive authority in Guantanamo Bay was one of the most contentious elements of its post-9/11 counterterrorism policy. Furthermore, targeted killings are by definition an extreme practice – the debates about due process for Guantanamo Bay detainees would matter little to the subject of a successful targeted killing. Therefore even though the legal controversy of targeted killings is intimately related to that of military detention, it is qualitatively different due to their intended lethality. For these reasons, the US use of targeted killings drew widespread criticism from a diverse array of commentators, journalists, lawyers, activists and academics during both the Bush and Obama administrations. Philip Alston, former UN Human Rights Council Special Rapporteur, is a trenchant critic of the practice,[23] as are academic critics such as Mary Ellen O'Connell,[24] Philip Dore,[25] Vincent-Joël Proulx[26] and Karl Meessen.[27] Leading journalists such as Glenn Greenwald[28] and Jeremy Scahill[29] are staunchly opposed to the practice. For most of the Bush administration, the executive remained silent on the issue. Initially a similar silence on the issue prevailed in the Obama administration. But in recent years, leading figures such as John Brennan,[30] Jeh Johnson,[31] Leon Panetta,[32] President Obama, Harold Koh[33] and Attorney General Eric Holder[34] have made public speeches and statements defending and supporting the activity.

The key problem with the targeted killings debate is its fractious nature, as it covers a number of highly contested areas of politics, law and ethics. Other countries that use targeted killings have also faced criticism. The most notable country to adopt targeted killing policies is Israel. Daniel Byman charts the development of these methods in his book, *A High Price*.[35] The Israeli use of targeted killings led to a lawsuit which resulted in a judgment from the Supreme Court of Israel (SCI) that legitimated the practice in the specific Israeli context.[36] Other states have used targeted killings; however, the scale of their use by both Israel and the United States dwarfs these other examples. The developing defence offered by the Obama administration relies on two key principles: (1) that the use of targeted killings is both legal and ethical, and (2) that their use relies on normal aspects of the president's authority. In the words of John Brennan: 'we will continue to work to safeguard this Nation and its citizens responsibly, adhering to the laws of this land and staying true to the values that define us as Americans'.[37] The second element of this defence, however, is that this is a normal element of the president's authority – as the Obama administration has studiously worked to reverse the perceived overreach of presidential authority during the Bush administration. Whether this is actually true is open to question. Many critics point out that the standardisation of targeted killings under Obama is because there is more continuity than change between the two administrations.[38]

Analysing this issue is difficult because the debate surrounding targeted killings is characterised by the fact that the different sides to this debate (to the extent that they exist) take quite different starting positions on the topic. This includes the use of language, where targeted killings are sometimes termed 'assassinations'[39] and 'extrajudicial executions'.[40] This book uses the term 'targeted killing' as it is as neutral a term as can be ascribed. 'Assassination', a term commonly used to refer to these killings, confers an inherently negative viewpoint and is an attempt to link these killings with Executive Order 12333, which prohibits them. Nils Melzer notes that definitions 'may suit the context in which they are discussed'.[41] The commonly used phrase 'drone strikes' is too limited, because current US policy does not necessarily restrict itself to these means. The basic definition of targeted killings, as outlined by Melzer, is that they are premeditated uses of lethal force with the intentional targeting of an individual by a subject of international law.[42] Defining them in this manner is, however, a semi-legitimising act from the viewpoint of a person who considers such acts to be assassinations. Consequent to this, different sides to the debate also interpret available evidence in a different manner. Disagreements regarding linguistics point to a larger issue, one that is key to the Obama administration's attempt to defend its conduct through public speeches: the legitimisation of targeted killings as acts of war.

Justifying violence

Targeted killings are an example of political violence. War, as a phenomenon, legitimises destructive and lethal acts of violence that are widely considered unethical and illegal in times of peace. The precise manner in which war, as well as destructive acts within its context, is legitimated differs between societies. The Obama administration's defence of targeted killings seeks to legitimise the use of this practice during war by using the frameworks of legitimation that are shared between states – international law and just war ethics. Therefore, the Obama administration's defence attempts to define these acts as legitimate in the context of what Russell Weigley termed the 'American way of war', as well as in the normative practices of warfare.[43] The practice of warfare is intimately linked to the culture of the society that conducts it and the manner in which this society considers war.[44] It is important to distinguish between how US society legitimates warfare and how societies in the wider 'West' do so. This book focuses on the former, although because the United States and other Western states use common legal and ethical frameworks, any legitimisation of these acts by the United States will imply their wider legitimacy within Western cultures.

6 *Justifying targeted killings*

In order to examine the attempts at legitimating the practice of targeted killings in the United States, it is necessary to examine how the phenomenon of war relates to US culture. In the social sciences, '[T]he widely held view ... is that a discourse is a set of ideas, beliefs and practices that provide ways of representing knowledge'.[45] In this sense, war is a form of discourse, and the use of language specific to war is a way of defining actions in this context. Targeted killings are defined in international law as the use of premeditated lethal force by the state against persons not in custody.[46] This does not, however, explain targeted killings in their entirety; to do so requires reference to the manner in which these acts are justified and legitimised. In effect, a discourse of war is the framework within which acts and events within a war are given meaning, providing the basis for judgement.

The examination of the Bush and Obama defences of targeted killings is therefore examining attempts to legitimise these acts within the particular context of the US discourse of war. The discourse of war cannot be separated from the culture from which it emanates, but prior to exploring the US example, it is necessary to denote two primary methods of examining war in terms of discourse. First, there is the integral characteristic of war, noted by Clausewitz – that it is itself a discourse, where the use of violence forms a language between two groups in a state of war within one another.[47] In this analytical use of the term, violent acts, and the way in which they communicate political goals, form a grammar of violence created by two societies at war. Absent the direct interaction between two warring groups, the 'discourse of war' relates to the wider cultural context of war and a given society. In this sense, cultural discourse alters the manner in which war is perceived or thought of by society at large, or by significant political actors within it. Analysis on this level gives rise to the concepts of an 'American way of war' or a 'western way of war'.[48] It is important to note, however, that these two levels of discourse analysis cannot be separated from one another, and that the grammar of killing noted by Clausewitz is, in a sense, the result of two discourses of war interacting. The conduct of war is a dialectical process between two cultural discourses. Where these discourses share large similarities, this dialectic is constrained by sets of commonly assumed, or held, rules. This is a key component of conventional warfare. Where two sides to a conflict have differing ideas about the purpose or legitimacy of violent acts, such conventions are absent. Western conventions include key legal and ethical frameworks that are examined later in this book, such as international humanitarian law (IHL) and just war ethics. However, these do not comprise the totality of Western, or US, discourse.

Understanding the role of war within a culture is key to understanding a culture's discourse of war. The purpose of war is not fixed; rather, cultures perceive war in different ways and thus conduct it differently. The US discourse of war considers the phenomenon to be instrumental – that is, war is to a certain degree a rational act that can be used to achieve a set of defined goals. Fundamentally, the US discourse depoliticises the conduct of war itself, separating its practice from the political goals sought.

Justifying targeted killings 7

The key problem of discourse analysis is that it necessarily encompasses a culture and, in the case of discourses of war, also requires the study of competing discourses. The discourse of war in the United States considers war in instrumental terms as a rational rather than expressive act. Yet this does not, in itself, legitimise the use of force and violent acts in the conduct of such wars. Although this book takes the United States, not 'the West', as its focus, violent acts within wars are legitimated in the United States in part via legal and ethical frameworks – international law and just war ethics – that are common also in the West.

Western, and US, militaries typically regard their conduct as both ethical and subject to the rule of law.[49] In particular, much attention is placed on adherence to the international legal codes that form IHL. With regards to targeted killings, both the Bush and Obama discourses that legitimised these uses of force did so within the framework of this wider US discourse. Both presidents made a claim on US values, but their definitions of what these values entailed differed, as did their identification of other practices as legitimate or illegitimate. The key claims common to both administrations' statements are that targeted killings are useful, legal and ethical. Furthermore, the targeting of Anwar al-Awlaki, a US citizen, during the Obama administration introduced a fourth claim: that the use of targeted killings against US citizens could be constitutional in certain circumstances. Where the administrations differ is in the grounds on which these acts are legitimated. In particular, the Bush administration sought to extend the boundaries of these legal and ethical frameworks after 9/11.[50] In contrast, the Obama administration attempts to define targeted killings as legal and ethical within the normal scope of these frameworks.

Competing discourses that seek to legitimise or delegitimise war and the violent acts that occur within it do not restrict themselves to questions of law and ethics. What is notable about the Obama administration's defence of the practice of targeted killings is that it seeks to justify their use in these terms, not in terms of politics. Targeted killings are, in this discourse, presented as an essentially functional act, and this in itself presents them as part of the wider US discourse of war, in which war itself is a depoliticised, functional tool. The Obama administration's defence of targeted killings also calls on values, but it does so as an object to be protected, rather than analysing the values that allow for the use of targeted killings. In this sense, the Obama administration's defence of targeted killings relies heavily upon legitimising them as 'normal' within the common frameworks of law and ethics, while avoiding their political nature and the fundamental questions of values that they raise.

Two important dimensions that require consideration are the changing nature of the discourse of war in the United States and the manner in which targeted killings, as a particular practice, are legitimated by this discourse itself. The evaluation of the legal and ethical claims made by the Obama administration is important despite the changing discourse of war in US culture and, furthermore, despite the technological changes that have enabled the widespread use of targeted killings as currently practised by the United States.

8 *Justifying targeted killings*

The development of precision warfare enables the use of targeted killings, but these acts are selected for use within the shifting discourse of war in the United States. The key question is why the Obama administration would choose to use targeted killings as opposed to other, less contentious forms of violence. One of the key changes noted by authors is the introduction of the element of risk into US society, and thereby into discourse regarding war. Christopher Coker identifies risk as one of the key defining characteristics of US discourse regarding war, and war, and the use of force, thereby become a policy tool for risk management.[51] Within this risk management discourse, the use of targeted killings becomes a means of reducing the risks of terrorist acts. However, key to this is the transfer of risk from Western states such as the United States to those states directly affected by targeted killings. Martin Shaw defines this as part of a trend in Western democracies towards 'risk transfer war'.[52] But this in itself does not quite account for the precise selection of targeted killings. It is when viewed through the lens of 'post-heroic' warfare[53] that one can perceive the particular utility of targeted killings for policymakers. In *The New American Way of War*, Benjamin Buley argues that the US way of war is changing to 'immaculate destruction', which combines both the utilitarian and apolitical tendencies that Weigley identified, as well as the idea of clean, bloodless warfare: '[I]n the prevailing discourse that now conditions the US public's understanding of war, warfare is no longer Hell – but potentially immaculate'.[54] Although there are differences between these authors on the limits and outcomes of the changing discourse of war in the United States, the commonalities – risk management, the use of force to transfer risk to an opponent and the need for an 'immaculate' manner of waging war – all legitimate the use of targeted killings.

Targeted killings are a technology, one used in an instrumental manner by the US state in accordance with the US discourse of war. However, the relationship between technology and warfare is complex, and is debated by many authors. First, it is important to recognise that technology, culture and warfare are interrelated; as outlined by Martin Van Creveld: '[W]ar is permeated by technology to the point that every single element is either governed by or at least linked to it'.[55] This definition is, however, too broad to serve a functional use in this context. What Van Creveld warns against is the chicken-and-egg paradox when thinking of war and technology. Indeed, the use of technology is, to a large extent, governed by cultural attitudes and assumptions. As John Ellis outlines in *The Social History of the Machine Gun*, cultural perceptions of war can dominate the use of a technology, as happened with the early development of the machine gun.[56] In this model, discourse governs the use of a weapons technology. Yet John Lynn identifies a feedback loop between discourse and reality – the plain facts of combat eventually alter or change the discourse of war.[57] This can be seen in the history of the machine gun, and in the manner in which the machine gun's use eventually altered the discourse regarding war despite strong resistance from military cultures that sought to preserve it.[58] Some critics of targeted killings lay the blame for their use with the technology of UAVs and the manner in which it routinely enables these acts.[59] Mary Ellen O'Connell states that drones are 'seductive'. What she is in fact referring to is a combination of two technologies – targeted killings and UAVs – and their relationship to the US discourse of war.[60] UAV technology is, in effect, a subsidiary technology of targeted killings, which is in itself used due to the dominant discourse of war in the United States. UAVs are not required to conduct targeted killings, but the use of UAVs makes such activities significantly easier. Once the policy of using targeted killings was put into effect, Lynn's feedback loop from reality echoes O'Connell's reasoning of 'seduction', but neither fully explains the choice to employ targeted killings. As Mahnken states, '[I]f before September 11 nobody wanted control of (and responsibility for) the armed Predator [UAV], after the attacks everyone wanted it'.[61] In order to examine why the United States now uses targeted killings, and why the Obama administration attempts to legitimise their use, it is necessary to place them into a wider context of states targeting individuals with lethal force.

The state practice of targeting individuals

The Obama administration's defence of targeted killings relies on the legitimacy of targeting and killing individuals as a normal aspect of warfare. As Eric Holder stated:

> it is entirely lawful – under both United States law and applicable law of war principles – to target specific senior operational leaders of al Qaeda and associated forces. This is not a novel concept. In fact, during World War II, the United States tracked the plane flying Admiral Isoroku Yamamoto – the commander of Japanese forces in the attack on Pearl Harbor and the Battle of Midway – and shot it down specifically because he was on board. As I explained to the Senate Judiciary Committee following the operation that killed Osama bin Laden, the same rules apply today.[62]

Critics argue that this practice is unethical and illegal when used against persons who are not members of a conventional military force. In particular, the legality and ethics of targeted killing terrorists, or those suspected of terrorism, is the key issue.[63] This is compounded by groups such as al-Qaeda working alongside or with armed insurgent groups, particularly in Pakistan.

The Obama administration's defence of targeted killings is predicated on the idea that they are necessary and have military utility. Without utility, the use of force, in Western discourse, is illegitimate – purely expressive violence does not fulfil the necessity requirements of either IHL or just war ethics.[64] Conversely, a key criticism of the US use of targeted killings is that these acts are either useless or counterproductive.[65] Targeted killings work by applying lethal force to individual persons identified as enemies, often on a case-by-case basis. Critics of targeted killings argue that the use of military force against individuals in this manner is illegal, unethical and illegitimate.[66] Arguing from a legal perspective, Chris Downes points to the central problem of targeting individuals – the way in

10 *Justifying targeted killings*

which they are categorised: '[A] further disturbing trend in the international response to terrorism is the tendency to view suspected terrorists, as individuals, as acceptable military targets'.[67]

Central to this point is the relationship between the use of violence against a person and the reason for its use. This is the difference between strategic and tactical targeting – the use of force is always directed at a person or target, but the strategic use of force differs between conventional warfare and targeted killings. A common assumption made in support of these acts is that the use of force by the military against individuals in this manner is legitimate, and has always been legitimate. This is not necessarily the case. Even though combatants and participants are subject to violence in war, warfare has not typically involved targeting individuals on a case-by-case basis through bureaucratic process. The traditional object of warfare, land warfare in particular, is an opposing army or mass. This is discernible in the fact that even when the reason to engage an opposing force changed over time, massed forces tended to remain the focus.[68] Different ways of fighting change the process by which individuals are defined as part of a group and, ultimately, become the subject of strategic uses of force. The Obama administration's defence of targeted killings is predicated on this operational means being legitimate; therefore, it is necessary to examine the legitimacy of using military force against individuals.

One important difference for states is the variance in practice between the conduct of 'small wars'[69] and conventional war. The conduct of small wars, particularly of those that place emphasis on policing and targeting small groups, is in many respects law enforcement by military means. Above all, the central question of targeting is how individuals are identified by the state or its agents as legitimate targets of attack.

The legitimacy of the use of force against individuals who are part of a military force forms the core of the Obama administration's defence. The basis of IHL is that military necessity allows for the use of force by an individual. However, conventional warfare is anonymous – opponents are identified as a mass, not as individuals. The generic nature of the opponent is a function of the type of battle fought at the time of the first formal treaty governing the conduct of land warfare, the 1864 Geneva Convention.[70] Since then, the practice of warfare has changed; importantly, the targeting of specific individuals within a military hierarchy has become a legitimate strategy. Fundamentally, it is important to differentiate between the tactical targeting of individuals and the strategy of targeting individuals. Here, it is instructive to consider the difference between snipers and regular soldiers. The methodology of sniper attacks is important, as persons armed with long-range, accurate rifles can identify targets more accurately than others can. Snipers can be used to conduct targeted killings, but are also used tactically in conventional warfare. There are examples of targeting individuals prior to Yamamoto, but these were tactical and, importantly, not rooted in the identity, or strategic effect, of killing the individual target. In the first Battle of Saratoga of the American Revolution, US marksmen picked off British officers to cause chaos. This was, however, a tactic, not a strategy or operational method.

Justifying targeted killings 11

Irregular wars are important because the use of military force against individuals is not restricted to states. These policies form an important part of asymmetric warfare. The Anglo-Irish War (or War of Irish Independence) provides a good example. During this conflict, a group of British intelligence agents, the 'Cairo Gang', were targeted and killed by an Irish Republican Army (IRA) unit known as 'the squad'.[71] This tactic, a hallmark of urban guerrilla warfare, differs from the general tactic of killing members of the security forces. The 'Cairo Gang' were targeted because of their specific activities rather than because of their membership of the British Establishment. Anne Dolan notes, however, that this tactic was seen as illegitimate by some of the men conducting the operation:

> In many of the statements there is a sense of knowing that it was wrong, that there was something in it that was just not fair. War was about ambushes, a fair fight; it was not supposed to be about killing a man in his bed.[72]

Asymmetric opponents often adapt a policy of targeted killing; however, their opponents, state authorities (should they consider themselves to be subject to the rule of law), are less able to pursue such activities. By definition, terrorists and insurgents ignore legal restrictions and do not derive their legitimacy from strict adherence to the law of armed conflict (even though some seek recognition as belligerents under its auspices). The matter at hand, however, is the Obama administration's defence; therefore, such questions are important to consider, but state practice is our current focus.

A number of case studies trace the turn towards legitimating the strategic targeting of individuals on the basis of their identity. For example, the killing of Admiral Yamamoto is commonly held to justify the targeting of known individuals in a war. This forms part of the Obama administration's defence of the practice of targeting individuals, as Harold Koh uses the example in his speech.[73] Also, John Yoo bases his argument on the targeting of individuals in part on the targeting of Admiral Yamamoto.[74] Furthermore, the Obama administration refers to him. Admiral Yamamoto is the most famous example of individual targeting, but the reticence with which he was targeted underlines the change in attitudes towards the targeting of individuals. World War II provides a number of examples of targeting individuals. Yamamoto is used here because it was a successful operation. Other significant targets included Erwin Rommel (Operation Flipper), Reinhard Heydrich (Operation Anthropoid) and Adolf Hitler. Only the attempt on Heydrich was successful. Of the three, the British attempt on Rommel in 1941 is significant, as it was the first attempt to kill an enemy general, but it ended in failure. Heydrich was targeted in a political role, as was Hitler, and therefore they are less applicable to this section, which focuses on military targets for military purposes.

Admiral Yamamoto was in command of Japan's Pacific Fleet during World War II. He was a significant figure, although historians do not consider his death as having changed the outcome of the war, because the United States had already won at the Battle of Midway. US officers understood that killing Yamamoto

12 *Justifying targeted killings*

would have an effect on morale,[75] although Japan's comprehensive defeat at the Battle of Midway meant that their eventual defeat, although not certain, was far more likely at that stage in the war. However, the US military targeted Yamamoto as a one-off, because Naval Intelligence was able to identify and verify his location. However, prior to authorising the operation to kill Yamamoto, the commanders responsible for the war in the Pacific first consulted with the White House, and the relative unease with which the operation was put into effect underlines the moral and ethical restraints on killing someone, even a significant military figure in time of war, on an individual basis.[76]

The Yamamoto case is important for two reasons: first, it demonstrates that there is state practice in targeting individuals within military organisations; and second, it demonstrates that this is a development not axiomatic to the general conduct of military operations. Yamamoto could only be targeted due to advances in intelligence-gathering capabilities. Furthermore, the targeting of Yamamoto in this manner indicates the widening interpretations of IHL when compared to its origins in physically contested battlefields – Yamamoto was a direct (tactical) threat to no one at the time of his death, but the Americans considered him a legitimate target due to his significant role in the Japanese navy's command structure.

The targeting of individuals such as Yamamoto and Rommel was the product of the increased importance of intelligence in warfare. Since World War II, the weapons available to military forces have achieved steadily greater precision. This has led to changing conceptions of the proper use of these weapons. Importantly, the ability to target individuals was both legitimised and incorporated into military targeting strategies. In 1951 the US military targeted and killed a large number of North Korean military officials and communist party members in a single strike.[77] Singling out the command structure of an armed force had by then become a legitimate practice in warfare. Command and control is an important concept in military operations. Without it, large-scale contemporary military forces are unable to function as a cohesive whole, and are therefore far less effective. Attacking command-and-control networks therefore forms an important part of contemporary warfare. The legitimisation of targeting command-and-control networks (rather than formations or units of military) necessitates a different basis for targeting, one that ultimately leads to the targeting of soldiers as individuals.

Network-centric warfare is the logical extension of this targeting process. In this way of thinking about warfare, military planners are advised to consider opponents as networks, focus their targeting on individuals and platforms most likely to disrupt the network, and achieve 'full spectrum dominance'.[78] The network-centric warfare concept arose from discussions on the so-called 'revolution in military affairs'[79] where Admiral William Owens wrote a paper on the emerging 'system-of-systems' that documented the convergence of Intelligence, Surveillance and Reconnaissance (ISR), Command, Control, Communications, Computers and Intelligence (C4I) and precision capabilities.[80] In introducing the concept of network-centric warfare based on Owens' work, Arthur Cebrowki and John Garstka envisioned targeting to the level that separated the individual from their weapon platform.[81] John Arquilla and David Ronfeldt built on this theory, incorporating ideas of 'fourth-generation warfare'[82] into their own theory of 'netwar'.[83] Netwar depicts an opposing military force as a network where key individual nodes are the important targets.[84] In effect, an opposing military force is no longer considered a cohesive body, but is instead considered a connected web of individuals. In this model, individual targeting is not only legitimate, but also near-axiomatic to the conduct of successful operations. One can therefore see how the conventional targeting method, where targeting is predicated on conditions on contested battlefields, gives way to the strategic targeting of individuals as part of military organisations.

The Obama administration's defence of targeted killings is predicated on the rule of law and the applicability of IHL. In this context it is difficult to see how it could legitimate the targeting of civilians. Yet some states have resorted to targeting individual civilians – for their connections to states or terrorist networks – in a manner that is nearly indistinguishable from targeted killings. Again, a key point for our consideration is that the definition of these persons as enemies by the states in question, by dint of their posing a military threat, was integral to the legitimation of their targeting as individuals by the state.

A good example of this targeting was Operation Damocles, an Israeli targeted killing programme directed at civilian scientists. Egypt employed a number of European scientists to develop long-range surface-to-surface missiles, testing them on 21 July 1962. Israel considered this to be a significant threat, since these rockets would alter the military balance in the region. Michael Bar-Zohar quotes the then Deputy Defence Minister Shimon Peres as saying '[T]he advent of these modern weapons has radically changed the nature of the danger that lies in wait for us and the measures that we have to take to protect ourselves from it'.[85] As this was prior to the outcome of the 1967 and 1973 Arab–Israeli Wars, which stabilised the region somewhat, Israel still considered itself threatened by its neighbours, a situation that remains to a certain extent today. In order to counter the threat that the missiles were thought to pose, Mossad – Israel's intelligence arm – began a campaign of targeted killing directed at the non-Egyptian elements of the rocket plan. This involved letter bombs, kidnappings and presumed killings – one scientist, Dr Heinz Krug, was never found.[86] The aim of the campaign was to dissuade European scientists from participating in the Egyptian missile programme, thus starving it of both the required technical knowledge, and material support. Mossad lacked an effective operational wing at the time, instead requiring the support of Shin Bet, Israel's internal security agency.

The operation was a qualified success. On a tactical level, the targeted killings were mostly ineffective: a scientist's secretary was injured, five Egyptian factory workers were killed and one scientist was abducted and probably killed. Thus the means available to target these individuals was relatively poor, and also indiscriminate. The political fallout from the campaign led to the resignation of Isser Harel, Mossad's director, under pressure from the prime minister. However, despite the relative ineffectiveness of the killing, and the political fallout, which

14 *Justifying targeted killings*

rendered it unsustainable, the operation had the requisite effect – German and other European scientists were dissuaded from becoming involved in the project.

Operation Damocles fell apart after the capture of an Israeli agent, Yoseph Ben-Gal, in Switzerland. Ben-Gal was arrested relaying a warning to the daughter of Professor Paul Goerke, who was part of the Egyptian rocket programme. The question of pressing Germany on extradition caused Isser Harel and Ben-Gurion to fall out, and Isser began to brief the media to pressure the government and try to convince the public of the legitimacy of actions taken against the German scientists. This point is important, because although the operation existed in the grey area of international law (since it was internally justified on military necessity and self-defence), it caused significant political problems, and the government was unwilling to admit to these actions. The targeting was legitimated on the grounds that the scientists' work would pose a military threat to Israel, but the policy was itself divisive within government. Since these actions drew firm legitimacy from neither the population nor the government, they were unsustainable. Isser resigned over the operation, and Ben-Gurion resigned soon after.

States often resort to force, both legal and paralegal, against criminal networks. As I will show in Chapter 3, however, the conduct of targeted killing campaigns against criminals is generally held to be incompatible with the rule of law and norms of law enforcement. The use of force against criminal networks is best demonstrated in the destruction of the Cali and Medellín Cartels in Colombia. Many types of state force were used here, including capture and arrest, extradition and killing. Pablo Escobar was killed by three bullets during his arrest,[87] and Mark Bowden questions whether this may have been carried out by US forces aiding the Colombian 'Search Block' that was hunting him at the time.[88] In this case, the rule of law effectively broke down – the state combined its forces and targeted persons external to the rule of law. Even so, the United States sought to deal with these networks primarily through the rule of law, putting extraordinary pressure on President Manuel Uribe to ensure the extradition of Gilberto Rodríguez Orejuela, one of the key figures in the Cali Cartel.[89] Despite the US discourse of the 'war on drugs' and the militarisation of counternarcotics operations, the United States' targeting of these traffickers was still in line with the rule of law paradigm. This was despite the lack of such delineation in its partner state, Colombia. Targeting civilians with military force can be internally legitimated, but it is difficult to legitimate externally. Furthermore, this legitimation is only possible by depicting civilians as posing a military threat. What differentiates these criminal networks from the terrorist organisations is the direct threat posed by terrorist networks.

Terrorists and insurgents lie between the strict division of civilians and military persons as a form of liminal identity or categorisation. States are, in certain circumstances, quite capable of legitimating the targeting of individuals for their involvement in terrorist or guerrilla networks, but terrorists are usually dealt with by law enforcement authorities rather than by military force. Furthermore, there is custom and practice of states targeting these liminal individuals in both war and situations not covered by IHL, both inside and beyond their territorial borders.

Terrorists and insurgents are liminal actors because, as political opponents of states, they are subject to the law enforcement paradigm (prosecution for treason or related political offences against the state itself), but states also turn to the use of armed force if they pose a military threat. Four examples demonstrate state legitimation of the use of lethal force against terrorist networks and the controversy that this generates. The first example, Israel's 'Operation Wrath of God', targeting Black September, used lethal force against a terrorist network that had committed an atrocity at the 1972 Summer Olympics in Munich, but did not enter into direct hostilities. The second, the United States' Phoenix Program, partly consisted of targeting civilians (defined as enemies) with lethal force during the Vietnam War. Both were highly controversial. The third, Britain's targeting of the IRA with lethal force, demonstrates the interchangeability of the law enforcement and hostilities paradigms – arguably they coexist in some situations, and the British forces, by choice of challenge context, effectively selected the hostilities paradigm, in which force could be used legitimately. Last, the example of Israel's use of targeted killings in the Second Intifada demonstrates that this coexistence of paradigms can be managed in a different manner, showing that the selection of paradigms is not universal among states.

Israel's 'Operation Wrath of God', conducted in the wake of the Munich killings, provides a good case study of the lethal targeting of individuals for participation in a network. Daniel Byman argues that Operation Wrath of God was Israel's first targeted killing campaign.[90] It was the first counterterrorist campaign, but not the first campaign predicated on the targeting of individuals with lethal force. Similar to the United States' current campaign, it was not fervently disavowed. Israel's motive in conducting these attacks was a mix of revenge for Black September's killing of Israeli athletes, and deterrence.

The operation itself was internally legitimated to the highest political level by the inclusion of Prime Minister Meir in the X Committee, which directed its operations and selected targets.[91] It is a problematic topic, because there is much controversy over its effectiveness and the validity of its targets. In particular, the relative merit, or connections to terrorism, of some targets was questionable at best. Aaron Klein notes that the core perpetrators escaped targeting by hiding in non-European countries, where Mossad was unable to attack them.[92] There is evidence to suggest that the operatives involved went beyond their orders in a matter of revenge, although the response to this underlines the basis on which these operations were considered legitimate – revenge for Munich. Operation Wrath of God is a good example of the flexibility of targeting, but also one that many would consider to be illegitimate. Israel's use of cut-outs and plausible deniability serves to underline that its actions were not promoting targeted killings as a normal action of states.

Individuals that either support or participate in insurgencies represent an important liminal category. In the Vietnam War, the civilian population were originally conceived as being persons that required shielding from the coercive

16 *Justifying targeted killings*

apparatus of the Vietcong.[93] In 1967 the CIA developed a plan for unifying the disparate local intelligence-gathering organisations responsible for rooting out the Vietcong as part of the pacification programme.[94] After the Tet Offensive, this plan was put into operation, resulting in a large number of deaths because persons were killed during capture, despite the obvious benefit in keeping them alive for intelligence-collection purposes.

The United States' targeting of the Vietcong support network with the Phoenix Program demonstrates the method by which states typically identify network participants and then target them on this participation. The Phoenix Program is the name commonly assigned to a CIA-assisted programme that resulted in the deaths of many Vietcong, and probably non-Vietcong, in the latter phases of the Vietnam War. Ronald Spector notes that 'national police were nominally in charge of the Phoenix program, but massive support came from the CIA, which also armed and trained special paramilitary forces'.[95] Phoenix itself consisted of two separate lines of operation: (1) an intelligence-collection operation that improved the intelligence-collection capability of the CIA regarding Vietcong networks in South Vietnam, and (2) the neutralisation of identified persons. The Phoenix Program was arguably a success, although its exact level of success is disputed by historians of the conflict. Stanley Karnow states that it played a role in badly damaging the Vietcong's rural machinery, but that this was also in part due to mass flight to the cities in response to violence.[96] The strategic result of this mass urbanisation is also noted by David Elliott.[97] As a result of these issues, precise analysis of the effect of Phoenix is difficult, if not impossible. In tracking and destroying the Vietcong networks, the Phoenix Program was operationally successful but strategically indecisive – the United States would go on to lose the war regardless. It is therefore difficult to assess the utility of this operation, both operationally and strategically. What is clear from the programme is that it was considered illegitimate. Conducted in relative secret, and with considerable problems of verification, this programme was depicted as a barbaric assassination campaign. It is hard, however, to disentangle the antipathy towards the Phoenix Program from the public disgust with the war itself. The Phoenix Program took place at a stage when public opinion had turned against the war itself. It is therefore difficult to judge whether it would have been considered a legitimate method by the public prior to this.

The use of lethal force is a political act, and this act can alter the political context of a conflict. Harold Wilson publicly deployed the British Special Air Service (SAS) to Northern Ireland in 1976, and they quickly became involved in activities that transgressed the border with the Republic of Ireland.[98] In 1978 the SAS shot three IRA men who were in the act of firebombing a post office. The circumstances were controversial because no guns were found[99] and because a fourth, civilian, person was also killed. A further two killings added to the political storm, and the SAS did not kill anyone for five years. This did not stop killings in Northern Ireland. Special Branch officers and the Det (a military intelligence unit of the British Army) combined to continue targeting terrorists. After the British established Tasking and Co-ordinating Groups, which effectively

Justifying targeted killings 17

combined the security forces into a single, armed targeting entity,[100] police efforts resulted in six controversial killings in the autumn of 1982.

The use of force in these circumstances is important because it outlines the problems of reconciling targeted killings, ethics and international law. In particular, the targeting of persons picking up weapons from secret hiding places displays the liminality of terrorist suspects in these circumstances. On 4 December 1983, the SAS killed two IRA members, Brian Campbell and Colm McGirr. They were killed after retrieving weapons from a cache known to the security forces.[101] Even if they were challenged, as the SAS assert, they were challenged in a way that led to their deaths. The authorities had the opportunity to lift their weapons cache prior to them arriving, but chose not to do so. These men could not be considered an immediate threat until they picked up the weapons and turned to face the challenge, but the authorities chose to challenge them in this way.

Accounts of the activity of the SAS vary depending on viewpoints. They were accused of executing a wounded IRA member, Seamus McElwine. Importantly, regardless of accounts, the SAS and the Det appear to have retained the civilian/combatant division of these persons, despite targeting them with the intent to kill. In contrast to the later Israeli case study, the British forces chose to engage these persons in a manner likely to involve lethal force, rather than do so in a manner that was likely to lead to their arrest and possible release on lack of evidence.

This is demonstrated in the 1987 Loughall Ambush that killed eight men from the IRA's East Tyrone Brigade during an attack on the Loughall Royal Ulster Constabulary station. With a three-to-one disadvantage,[102] the IRA members stood no chance. Ed Moloney noted that the last time such losses had been inflicted in a single day had been in 1921.[103] Unlike the current US campaign, the SAS waited in ambush until the individuals concerned commenced violent actions, thus legitimating the use of force against them. The British campaign was legal in text but not in spirit, because their choice of challenge locations probably ensured the deaths of many that died. Does this count as a targeted killing campaign? Although different in character to others noted here, opting to use lethal force or to confront situations using force rather than disruptive police raids seems to err towards classifying it as such.

The Second Intifada, or uprising, began in 2000. As a matter of policy, Israel began to target the leadership of militias and Palestinian groups. This differs from the targeted killings of the preceding decade because it represents a coherent policy of targeted killing with the strategic aim of preventing the uprising from being successful. The Second Intifada targeted killing campaign is important because it resulted in one of the few instances of (national) case law on the subject. This is what differentiates this targeted killing programme from previous acts of (lethal) espionage and military force. In making such a programme subject to the rule of law, and with the ruling in fact legitimising this programme, the targeted killing programme was internally legitimated, and openly so. Israel's Second Intifada targeted killing programme contains the key

18 *Justifying targeted killings*

ingredients required to fulfil a targeted killing programme as part of a containment policy. The programme was not intended to destroy Palestinian groups, but it was intended to disrupt them. In this, it succeeded:

> [G]iven all the drawbacks, why does Israel continue with targeted killings? The reason is simple: targeted killings work. The strikes have disrupted Hamas, PIJ, the al-Aqsa Martyrs Brigade, and other Palestinian terrorist groups; they have depleted the number of skilled operatives; and they have forced the remaining militants to spend more time in hiding than in plotting future attacks.[104]

Byman lists many drawbacks and moral quandaries that are particularly important in contextualising the programme.[105] Therefore, the legitimation of this programme, and the legal quandaries surrounding its conduct, are important context for the US case study. There are, however, key differences; for example, Israel was operating internally (on contested areas such as the West Bank and Gaza Strip) and in external territories (such as Lebanon). The US campaign is extraterritorial – taking place halfway around the world.

The judgment of the SCI in the matter is important. The court's verdict held that harming civilians that take a direct part in hostilities 'even if the result is death, is permitted, on the condition that there is no other means which harms them less, and on condition that innocent civilians nearby are not harmed'.[106] This requirement to find other, less-than-lethal means would classify significant British operations as illegal if retroactively applied. It does, however, rely on the good faith of the Israel Defense Forces (IDF) in identifying less lethal means, which has drawn criticism. The decision was highly contentious in general, primarily revolving around the use of membership as a criterion for assessing direct participation in conflict. Kristen Eichensehr criticised the 'membership model' implicit in the judgment's widening of criteria for 'direct participation', but her commentary is flawed by its explicit rejection of the function of custom in law: 'states must not be allowed to change the law in order to comply with it'.[107] Blum and Heymann note that the judgment did not label terrorists combatants in total, which would have legitimised their targeting at any point.[108] Furthermore, while the decision calls for the balancing of security needs and human rights, it does not consider the political aspect: the risk involved to IDF personnel in conducting capture operations rather than targeted killings. This is significant, and the political dimension of this book's primary case study explores this risk-balance. Importantly, the decision leaves the question of legality open and interpretable (liminal) and, furthermore, ascribes primary importance to customary international law rather than to strict treaty law. This custom can be moulded by the actions of states such as Israel and the United States.

From these case studies, it is clear that states sometimes consider the targeting of individuals with military (lethal) force to be acceptable and routine in times of war. In this sense, the Obama administration's use of force is not contentious, but legitimation – both internal and external – is predicated on an opposing force being considered a legitimate target of attack by the military. Key to this is its depiction as a military threat. The case of Operation Damocles demonstrates, however, that democratic populations do not consider targeted attacks on civilians to be legitimate. Because populations are the ultimate arbiter of legitimacy in democratic states, legitimate targeting can only occur against military targets or liminal categories of persons. The latter category is especially important, because it has (by definition) no fixed boundaries. In this, the changing threat that terrorists are thought to pose is essential to understanding how these persons are perceived and classified by states.

Research scope

The speeches on targeted killings by senior policy figures in the Obama administration, alongside the leaked memos and published legal reasoning, allow for a greater depth of analysis of the Obama administration's defence of targeted killings than was possible when such a defence was only elaborated in anonymous leaks to the press. The key feature of the debate surrounding the US use of targeted killings is the lack of agreement on the interpretation of available data. Quite simply, much of the inner workings of the US use of targeted killings, as well as its effects, are unknown quantities. In the absence of such data, discourse and interpretation play key roles in analysis. Because of this, critics and supporters of targeted killings disagree over the way in which the evidence that exists in the public realm should be interpreted, including the relative weight that should be given to leaked details. Furthermore, critics and supporters disagree on the meaning and implications of this lack of evidence. Philip Alston argues that in the absence of evidence the United States is required to demonstrate that its actions conform with international law: '[T]o the extent that the United States genuinely believes it is currently acting within the scope of those rules it needs to provide the evidence'.[109] Conversely, writers such as Gregory McNeal clearly believe that it is the responsibility of the critics to demonstrate evidence to disprove the assertions of the Obama administration.[110] At issue is the definition of objectivity in relation to targeted killings. Each defence and criticism of targeted killings contains its own normative assumptions of objectivity, and normative assumptions as to how subjective ideas and information should be interpreted. Given the nature of the topic, and the lack of data, absolute objectivity is an unattainable goal, but this in itself does not preclude investigation of the use of targeted killings.

The Obama administration seeks to present targeted killings as a legitimate means of warfare, citing their legality and adherence to ethical principles.[111] Integral to this is the notion that the president is not overstepping their authority in the constitutional system of government by conducting targeted killings. US politics and the rule of law are therefore important to the Obama administration's defence, because they provide the framework within which the administration's discourse is judged.[112] This book separates out these concepts to analyse them, but does not seek to challenge this conception. The tripartite structure of

20 *Justifying targeted killings*

the US system at the federal level means that domestic politics is important in the realm of foreign policy and that the relationship between Congress and the executive is neither stable nor assured.[113] To construct this defence, however, the use of targeted killings must serve some kind of purpose. Therefore the strategy (in relation to war: 'the use of armed force to achieve the military objectives and, by extension, the political purpose of the war') that requires targeted killings and the utility of these acts are also important to the Obama administration's defence.[114] The question of whether the Obama administration's various positions are defensible against the arguments of its critics – based on the evidence available – as well as internally consistent is of paramount importance. If the Obama administration's arguments are indefensible in the areas listed above, then its defence is inconsistent. If so, it is difficult to differentiate the use of targeted killings by the Obama administration from the legal realism of the Bush administration. The difference in context can be seen from Leon Panetta's speech that argued that targeted killings were 'the only game in town'. This can be taken as a call to use blunt force, regardless of other concerns, but cannot be taken as such within the wider discourse offered by Obama, Holder, Koh and Brennan. In context, it refers to the need to use such methods in specific circumstances.[115] After all, the key question in the debate is not whether the United States can perform targeted killings, but whether the Obama administration can legitimate them in a manner consistent with the rule of law.

The Obama administration makes one overarching claim (that its use of targeted killings is legitimate), which is supported by two subsidiary claims (that the use of such methods is both legal and ethical). How is one to test these propositions without evidence? The lack of a statistical basis on which to base analysis presents a problem of proof. Without the evidence to disprove a hypothesis, the results are unscientific, regardless of method. Furthermore, given the varying normative frameworks that interact in the debate surrounding the US use of targeted killings, the selection of any neutral value will, arguably, impart bias to the study. This book seeks to circumvent this shortcoming in qualitative research by using the method used by Peter Singer[116] in his analysis of the ethics of President George W. Bush.[117]

In *The President of Good and Evil*, Singer investigates the ethical framework of then President George W. Bush by 'taking him seriously'. In effect, by giving his subject the benefit of the doubt, Singer argues that his ethical principles were inconsistent, independent of conjecture as to Bush's internal motivations. This is an approach that allows for the examination of important questions for which evidence is unlikely to be available, and therefore appropriate for the examination of targeted killings. The use of targeted killings relies on the authority to define individuals as enemies, and as legitimate targets of attack, at the intersection of law and politics, of internal and external divisions and of interlocking regions of national and international law. Key areas of law have inherently interpretable, liminal spaces and concepts – such as the concept of military necessity within IHL. Investigations of discourse and these areas are highly susceptible to the employment of 'straw man' arguments and other logical fallacies. To

Justifying targeted killings 21

circumvent this, it is necessary to allow discursive leeway. In short, if the Obama administration's argument cannot be certainly disproved, then it functions as a workable defence.

Giving the Obama administration such leeway is, depending on one's perspective, a sensible approach to national security or a facile exercise in accepting power. It is neither. In order to be secure, the Obama administration's position has to be both defensible and consistent. Furthermore, an analysis of the Obama administration's position provides an understanding of a particular mode of thought regarding a form of warfare that is likely to be used increasingly in the near future. The debate about whether targeted killings constitute widespread murder is important, but the examination of the emergence of a mode, strategy and philosophy of warfare in which such acts are wholly legitimate and defensible is equally important.

The administration purportedly holds data that its supporters claim prove their arguments. Public data are not available. Tracking the changes that occur in 'dark networks'[118] such as al-Qaeda as a result of targeted killings is problematic because these networks are highly fluid. Such information would be required in order to make definitive claims regarding the efficacy of targeted killings. However, change over time is observable. There is enough secondary-source information on its network structures to enable long-term analysis of the effects of the US targeted killings of members of its target, al-Qaeda.[119]

The Obama administration's defence covers a wide range of academic fields and makes an expansive set of claims. It is important to recognise that defences and criticisms of this practice have different disciplinary standards. Ethical claims are usually judged by logical argument, whereas legal claims rely on authority and precedent, and are subject to the political authorities passing new laws. Furthermore, since the defence offered by the Obama administration must be consistent, these different sets of standards must also work together. It is, for instance, pointless to outline a manner in which the Obama administration's defence could be argued legitimate in constitutional terms that is a priori illegal in international law. US constitutional law relating to the authority of the president to authorise the use of force[120] is the first primary field of analysis within this book. This includes military law[121] and politics relevant to the relationship between the constitutional authority of the president and the rights of US citizens. The second major field is international law and the United States' interaction with it. International law referred to within this book is public international law, which regards the system as a whole, rather than disputes within the system.[122] Key to international law is the lack of a sovereign authority, which makes final arbitration impossible without state consent (or coercive action by other states). Law does exist within the international 'anarchical society' of states, but the nature of international law does differ from national legal systems due to the blunt fact of sovereignty.[123] The important sources for consideration are custom and practice, treaty and *opinio juris* – legal opinion – as this book examines *opinio juris*, state practice and treaty law in reference to targeted killing policies. There exists little in the form of *opinio juris* specific to targeted

22 *Justifying targeted killings*

killings as a practice, although there are plenty of leading opinions on the subject, ranging from the Church Committee's findings on assassination to assessments of Israel's use of targeted killings.[124] The Judge Advocate General's *Operational Law Handbook* is an important source of targeting conduct and US interpretation of IHL.[125] The United Nations (UN) is the most powerful international body and source of law. The United States is a permanent member of the UN Security Council (UNSC), which effectively renders it immune from legalised intervention, because this body legitimises intervention in international law under Articles 6 and 7 of the Charter of the UN. The judicial organ of the UN, the International Court of Justice (ICJ), is an important source of law; however, the United States withdrew from its compulsory jurisdiction in 1986 (following *Nicaragua* v. *United States*). The major bodies of international law relevant to this book are IHL and international human rights law (IHRL). IHL governs the conduct of war, or non-state violent conflict, whereas IHRL governs the relationship between states and citizens. IHRL technically applies at all times, with exceptions made for IHL, where applicable. In line with Habermas' theories, derogation from these laws creates norms of state conduct, particularly important since the United States is a superpower.

The United States' use of targeted killings sets a precedent for the acceptance of such activity as customary in international law – an example of norm creation. Mervyn Frost defines a norm 'as settled where it is generally recognized that any argument denying the norm (or which appears to override the norm) requires special justification'. The openness with which these killings are conducted, in contrast to the secrecy with which extraterritorial killings are usually conducted (with plausible deniability), is therefore important.[126] Lastly, since the Obama administration relies on ethical claims, the ethical frameworks in which war is waged are an issue, thus necessitating the study of just war theory. Just war theory provides the most important body of ethics in Western conceptions of war and also underpins the strict legality of IHL.[127] This book does not seek to argue that such an activity should, or should not, be used. Instead, the purpose is to test both the criticisms and defences of the US targeted killing programme, to create a framework of analysis and an individual assessment of the Obama administration's discourse. Where appropriate, this book notes the possible and plausible side effects, or consequences, of the Obama administration's defence, but these will not disprove it.

Outline

This book will first examine the US context of targeted killings, to provide context for the Obama administration's defence of the practice. It will then turn to four core questions concerning this defence: does the president have the authority or right to use military counterterrorism (in the form of targeted killings) over law enforcement methods? Does the president have the right to define people, even US citizens, as legitimate targets for the purpose of targeted killing? Are US targeted killings in accordance with the principles of IHL? Do US targeted killings contravene the moral principles of the just war tradition? The ultimate issue that this book seeks to address is whether these four questions can be answered in a cohesive manner. If they can, then the defence offered by the Obama administration seems defensible, even if it is unlikely to be accepted by a range of domestic and international critics. If not, then such a defence is hypocritical from the outset.

It would be impossible to assess the Obama administration's defence of targeted killings without reference to the particularities of the US case study. Chapter 2 will lay out these issues in full. For present purposes the important elements of the US use of targeted killings is how and why they came to be defined as necessary, and why the Obama administration defended them in such a public manner. The particular character of the Obama administration's defence is important, and Chapter 2 examines the way in which the Obama administration sought to distance itself from the Bush administration. Nonetheless, there is far more continuity than change in the role of law and legal arguments in the defence of contentious counterterrorism policies. This is particularly important for the US case study, because one of the principle issues at hand is the role of the CIA, an intelligence organisation, in the conduct of US targeted killings. For this reason, the Obama administration's defence of targeted killings has to defend the conduct of the same action by both the US military and the CIA. In particular, this means that the Obama administration's justification for targeted killings must cover the use of signature strikes by the CIA. As will be explained in detail in Chapter 6, this poses a key problem for the Obama administration's defence.

Chapter 3 addresses the question of whether the president and the US government have the right to treat their targeted killings as acts of war, or even resort to their use in the first place. The chapter examines the arguments of those who would prefer the United States to treat al-Qaeda as a law enforcement problem, and those who argue that the use of lethal force against al-Qaeda is unnecessary, counterproductive and/or illegal. Since a core component of the Obama administration's defence of targeted killings is that it is necessary to take action in this way, these claims must be addressed. The chapter argues that the balance of evidence is not enough to undermine the argument of the Obama administration that lethal action is necessary at the edges of the state system, where states lack the ability to treat al-Qaeda as common criminals. This is not enough to provide a complete justification for the use of targeted killings. A central element of the Obama administration's defence is that these actions have some form of utility. Here the available data do not serve to conclusively disprove the Obama administration's argument that targeted killings are useful. That said, the data do not support the idea that targeted killings can eliminate al-Qaeda as a functional organisation, only that they can serve to disrupt the organisation itself. This more limited claim fits within the overall justification of targeted killings made by the Obama administration.

The language of international law is an important element of the Obama administration's justification of targeted killings. Chapter 4 examines the role of

24 *Justifying targeted killings*

international law in the defence of targeted killings. The principle argument of the chapter is that the Obama administration seeks to preserve the non-illegality of targeted killings: that it interprets international law in such a way that it is impossible to define these actions as illegal from first principles. Most importantly, the US state is free from the mechanisms of judgment in international law, notably the jurisdiction of the ICJ and the International Criminal Court (ICC), and sanction by the UNSC. This does not free the United States from judgement by a range of persons and non-governmental organisations (NGOs), but it means that its legal arguments are likely to be tested in US courts only. Therefore, even if the Obama administration's justification cannot be ruled unlawful, it has important consequences for international law and the United States. The chapter outlines some of these consequences, notably the idea that states might seek to wage war across territorial boundaries. The consequence for the United States of this activity is that maintaining these positions means that it will continue to be isolated from more progressive or cosmopolitan states and organisations within the international community, many of which are its closest allies.

The ultimate authority of the president to authorise targeted killings is examined in Chapter 5. As seen in Chapter 4, the ability and authority to define persons in law (as persons taking 'direct participation' in hostilities) is central to the conduct of targeted killings. However, the constitutional protections afforded citizens of the United States are intended to prevent the unilateral use of force against citizens by the state. This issue came to the fore with the court cases surrounding the targeted killing of al-Awlaki. The Obama administration's justification of targeted killings is framed such that the targeted killing of a US citizen is as permissible as that of a non-citizen, even though it is far more of a political issue in the United States. Chapter 5 details the legal authority of the president to order the use of force, again noting that it is predicated on the country being at war or, in legal terms, engaged in an armed conflict. The key argument of the chapter is that the president is neither overreaching his authority nor stripping citizens of their legal rights. Rather, what the use of targeted killings highlights is the way in which people are defined in relation to coexisting bodies of law, and the permission that the existence of armed conflict gives for the president to define citizens as lawful targets in relation to IHL. That this is lawful should not, therefore, be the end of the discussion; rather, it reflects on the political system of the United States.

The final substantive chapter of this book, Chapter 6, examines the moral claims made by the Obama administration. The chapter focuses on the concept of responsibility in the use of force, which underpins the normative framework of just war theory. In this sense, one of the key challenges to the Obama administration's defence of targeted killings is the use of force where no one can be held accountable. This runs deeper than the criticisms of US targeted killings as lacking political accountability. In this chapter, I identify signature strikes as posing a particular moral problem, due to the disaggregated nature of information collection leading to targeting. A counterargument to this is that military organisations rely on the distribution of intelligence collection in many forms of targeting. I argue that the principles and norms of command responsibility inherent in military organisations (and in the US military in particular) are what permits them to use force in this manner. This is not an account that would satisfy a moral philosopher seeking a wholly rational account of human action, because certain understandings of command responsibility are inherently unfair to the commander held liable for the actions of subordinates. However, it reflects the manner in which human societies have negotiated the ethical problems that war and warfare pose. This issue poses a fundamental problem for the Obama administration because although the Obama administration's defence of targeted killings is coherent for the use of 'personality' strikes by the CIA and the military (and signature strikes by the military), it does not remain coherent for the use of signature strikes by the CIA, because these raise the possibility of systematic non-voluntary uses of force in war and armed conflict.

Notes

1 Michael Walzer, 'Terrorism and Just War' *Philosophia* 34 (2006): 7.
2 Peter Singer, *The President of Good and Evil: The Ethics of George W. Bush* (London: Dutton, 2004): 6.
3 Barack Obama, 'Remarks by the President on National Security' (Speech, National Archives, Washington, DC, 21 May 2009).
4 Bruce Hoffman, 'The Changing Face of Al Qaeda and the Global War on Terrorism', *Studies in Conflict and Terrorism* 27(6) (2004); Lawrence Wright, *The Looming Tower: Al-Qaeda and the Road to 9/11* (New York: Knopf, 2006).
5 See, for example, Barack Obama, 'Remarks by the President in Address to the Nation on the Way Forward in Afghanistan and Pakistan' (Speech, United States Military Academy, West Point, NY, 1 December 2009); Harold Hongju Koh, 'The Obama Administration and International Law' (Speech, Annual Meeting of the American Society of International Law, Washington, DC, 25 March 2010); John O. Brennan, 'Strengthening Our Security by Adhering to Our Values and Laws' (Speech, Harvard Law School, Cambridge, MA, 16 September 2011).
6 Avery Plaw, *Targeting Terrorists: A License to Kill?* (Aldershot, England and Burlington, VT: Ashgate, 2008): 116–19.
7 Marc Sageman, *Leaderless Jihad: Terror Networks in the Twenty-First Century* (Philadelphia: University of Pennsylvania Press, 2008): 132.
8 For key speeches, see Obama, 'Remarks by the President on National Security'; Koh, 'Obama Administration'; Jeh Johnson, 'Speech to the Heritage Foundation' (Speech, Heritage Foundation, Washington, DC, 18 October 2011); Jeh Johnson, 'National Security Law, Lawyers and Lawyering in the Obama Administration' (Speech, Yale Law School, New Haven, CT, 22 February 2012); Brennan, 'Strengthening Our Security'; John O. Brennan, 'The Ethics and Efficacy of the President's Counterterrorism Strategy' (Speech, Woodrow Wilson International Center for Scholars, Washington, DC, 30 April 2012).
9 Nils Melzer, *Targeted Killing in International Law* (Oxford University Press, 2008): 435.
10 Walter B. Gallie, 'Essentially Contested Concepts', *Proceedings of the Aristotelian Society* (Harrison & Sons, 1955).
11 Greg Miller, 'Under Obama: An Emerging Global Apparatus for Drone Killing', *Washington Post*, 27 December 2011.

26 *Justifying targeted killings*

12 George Tenet, *At the Center of the Storm: My Years at the CIA* (London: Harper Press, 2007): 211.
13 Tenet, *At the Center of the Storm*: 218.
14 Authorization for the Use of Military Force (2001).
15 Claire Downes, '"Targeted Killings" in an Age of Terror: The Legality of the Yemen Strike', *Journal of Conflict and Security Law* 9(2) (2004).
16 See Joshua Raines, 'Osama, Augustine, and Assassination: The Just War Doctrine and Targeted Killings', *Transnational Law and Contemporary Problems* 12 (2002); William C. Banks and Peter Raven-Hansen, 'Targeted Killing and Assassination: The US Legal Framework', *University of Richmond Law Review* 37 (2002); Daniel Statman, 'Targeted Killing', *Theoretical Inquiries in Law* 5 (2004); Downes, '"Targeted Killings"'; Jonathan Ulrich, 'The Gloves Were Never On: Defining the President's Authority to Order Targeted Killing in the War against Terrorism', *The Virginia Journal of International Law* 45 (2004); Vincent-Joël Proulx, 'If the Hat Fits, Wear It, If the Turban Fits, Run for Your Life: Reflections on the Indefinite Detention and Targeted Killing of Suspected Terrorists', *Hastings Law Journal* 56(5) (2005).
17 Bureau of Investigative Journalism, 'Covert War on Terror: The Data', *Bureau of Investigative Journalism* (2015).
18 See Mary Ellen O'Connell, 'Unlawful Killing with Combat Drones: A Case Study of Pakistan, 2004–2009', in *Shooting to Kill: Socio-Legal Perspectives on the Use of Lethal Force*, edited by Simon Bronitt *et al.* (Oxford and Portland, Oregon: Hart, 2012); Thomas Hunter, *Targeted Killing: Self-Defense, Preemption, and the War on Terrorism* (Booksurge, 2009); Afsheen Radsan and Richard Murphy, 'Due Process and Targeted Killing of Terrorists', *Cardozo Law Review* 31 (2009): 405; Kenneth Anderson, 'Targeted Killing in US Counterterrorism Strategy and Law', in *Legislating the War on Terror*, edited by Benjamin Wittes (Washington, DC: Brookings Institution Press, 2009); Gabriella Blum and Philip Heymann, 'Law and Policy of Targeted Killing', *Harvard National Security Journal* 1 (2010); Robert Chesney, 'Who May Be Killed? Anwar Al-Awlaki as a Case Study in the International Legal Regulation of Lethal Force', *Yearbook of International Humanitarian Law* 13 (2010); Cheri Kramer, 'The Legality of Targeted Drone Attacks as U.S. Policy', *Santa Clara Journal of International Law* 9 (2011): 375.
19 See Alex S. Wilner, 'Targeted Killings in Afghanistan: Measuring Coercion and Deterrence in Counterterrorism and Counterinsurgency', *Studies in Conflict and Terrorism* 33(4) (2010): 308–9.
20 See Chesney, 'Who May Be Killed?'; Jeremy Scahill, 'Speech at the International Drone Summit' (Speech, Washington, DC, 29 April 2012).
21 Charlie Savage, 'Secret US Memo Made Legal Case to Kill a Citizen', *New York Times*, 8 October 2011.
22 *Al-Aulaqi* v. *Obama*, 727 F. Supp. 2d 1 (DDC, 2010).
23 Philip Alston, 'Report of the Special Rapporteur on Extrajudicial, Summary or Arbitrary Executions' (UN General Assembly, Human Rights Council, 2010); Philip Alston, 'The CIA and Targeted Killings Beyond Borders', *Harvard National Security Journal* 2 (2011): 283.
24 Mary Ellen O'Connell, 'To Kill or Capture Suspects in the Global War on Terror', *Case Western Reserve Journal of International Law* 35 (2003); O'Connell, 'Unlawful Killing'; Mary Ellen O'Connell, 'Seductive Drones: Learning from a Decade of Lethal Operations', *Journal of Law, Information and Science* 21(2) (2011/2012).
25 Philip Dore, 'Greenlighting American Citizens: Proceed with Caution', *Louisiana Law Review* 72 (2011).
26 Proulx, 'If the Hat Fits, Wear It': 801–900.
27 Karl M. Meessen, 'Unilateral Recourse to Military Force against Terrorist Attacks', *Yale Journal of International Law* 28 (2003).

Justifying targeted killings   27

28 Glenn Greenwald, 'America's Drone Sickness', *Salon*, 19 April 2012.
29 Jeremy Scahill, *Dirty Wars: The World is a Battlefield* (London: Serpent's Tail, 2013).
30 Brennan, 'Strengthening Our Security'; Brennan, 'Ethics and Efficacy'.
31 Jeh Johnson, 'Speech to the Heritage Foundation'; Jeh Johnson, 'National Security Law'.
32 Leon Panetta, 'Director's Remarks at the Pacific Council on International Policy' (Speech, Pacific Council on International Policy, Los Angeles, CA, 18 May 2009).
33 Koh, 'Obama Administration'.
34 Eric Holder, 'Northwestern University Speech' (Speech, Northwestern University School of Law, Chicago, IL, 5 March 2012).
35 Daniel Byman, *A High Price: The Triumphs and Failures of Israeli Counterterrorism* (New York: Oxford University Press, 2011).
36 *Public Committee against Torture in Israel* v. *Government of Israel* (2006).
37 Brennan, 'Ethics and Efficacy'.
38 Trevor McCrisken, 'Ten Years On: Obama's War on Terrorism in Rhetoric and Practice', *International Affairs* 87(4) (2011): 793–7.
39 Scahill, *Dirty Wars*: 24–5.
40 Alston, 'Report of the Special Rapporteur'.
41 Melzer, *Targeted Killing*: 7.
42 Melzer, *Targeted Killing*: Ch.1.
43 Russell F. Weigley, *The American Way of War: A History of United States Military Strategy and Policy* (Bloomington: Indiana University Press, 1977).
44 Theo Farrell, *The Norms of War: Cultural Beliefs and Modern Conflict* (Boulder, CO: Lynne Rienner Publishers, 2005): 173.
45 Christopher Coker, *Ethics and War in the 21st Century* (London: Routledge, 2008): 30.
46 Melzer, *Targeted Killing*: 3–4.
47 Carl von Clausewitz, *On War* (Oxford University Press, 2007).
48 The concept of a particularly American way of warfare is the result of Russell Weigley's book on the subject. See Weigley, *American Way of War*.
49 David Whetham, 'Ethics, Law and Conflict', in *Ethics, Law and Military Operations*, edited by David Whetham (Basingstoke, UK: Palgrave Macmillan, 2011): 10–12.
50 Coker, *Ethics and War*: 143.
51 Christopher Coker, *War in an Age of Risk* (Cambridge, UK: Polity Press, 2009): 26–7.
52 Martin Shaw, *The New Western Way of War: Risk-Transfer War and Its Crisis in Iraq* (Cambridge, UK: Polity Press, 2005): 94–5.
53 Edward Luttwak, 'A Post-Heroic Military Policy: The New Season of Bellicosity', *Foreign Affairs* 75(4) (1996).
54 Benjamin Buley, *The New American Way of War: Military Culture and the Political Utility of Force* (Abingdon, UK: Routledge, 2007): 88.
55 Martin Van Creveld, *Technology and War: From 2000 BC to the Present* (New York, NY: Free Press, 1991): 311.
56 John Ellis, *The Social History of the Machine Gun* (Baltimore, MD: Johns Hopkins University Press, 1986).
57 John A. Lynn, 'Discourse, Reality, and the Culture of Combat', *International History Review* 27(3) (2005).
58 Ellis, *Social History*: 17.
59 Grégoire Chamayou, *A Theory of the Drone* (New York: The New Press, 2014).
60 O'Connell, 'Seductive Drones'.
61 Thomas G. Mahnken, *Technology and the American Way of War* (New York, NY: Columbia University Press, 2008): 202.

28   *Justifying targeted killings*

62 Holder, 'Northwestern University Speech'.
63 Plaw, *Targeting Terrorists*:143–4.
64 Coker, *Ethics and War*: 32–5.
65 See Jeremy Scahill, 'Washington's War in Yemen Backfires', *The Nation*, 5 March 2012; Medea Benjamin, *Drone Warfare: Killing by Remote Control* (New York and London: OR Books, 2012); O'Connell, 'Seductive Drones'.
66 Yale Stein, 'Any Name Illegal and Immoral', *Ethics and International Affairs* 17(1) (2003).
67 Downes, '"Targeted Killings"': 293.
68 Beatrice Heuser, *The Evolution of Strategy* (Cambridge University Press, 2010): 145–6.
69 This term derives from the work of Colonel C. E. Callwell. See Charles E. Callwell, *Small Wars: Their Principles and Practice*, 3rd edn (Lincoln: University of Nebraska Press, 1996); also, United States Marine Corps, *Marine Corps Manual* (Washington, DC: U.S. Govt. Printing Office, 1940).
70 Geneva Convention for the Amelioration of the Condition of the Wounded on the Field of Battle (Geneva, 22 August 1864).
71 Tim Carey and Marcus de Búrca, 'Bloody Sunday 1920: New Evidence', *History Ireland* 11(2) (2003).
72 Anne Dolan, 'Killing and Bloody Sunday, November 1920', *Historical Journal* 49(3) (2006): 810.
73 Koh, 'Obama Administration'. See also Paul W. Staeheli, 'Collapsing Insurgent Organizations through Leadership Decapitation: A Comparison of Targeted Killing and Targeted Incarceration in Insurgent Organizations' (Thesis, Naval Postgraduate School, Monterey, CA, 2010); Blum and Heymann, 'Law and Policy'; Afsheen Radsan and Richard Murphy, 'The Evolution of Law and Policy for CIA Targeted Killing', *Journal of National Security Law and Policy* 5 (2012).
74 John Yoo, 'Assassination or Targeted Killings after 9/11', *New York Law School Law Review* 56 (2011): 64.
75 David Kahn, *The Codebreakers: The Story of Secret Writing* (New York: Macmillan, 1967): 598–9.
76 Kahn, *Codebreakers*: 598–9. John Costello, *The Pacific War* (New York: Quill, 1982): 401. E. B. Potter, *Nimitz* (Annapolis, MD: Naval Institute Press, 1976): 233.
77 Paul M. Edwards, *Korean War Almanac* (New York: Facts On File, 2008): 253.
78 John M. Shalikashvili, *Joint Vision 2010* (Washington, DC: Chairman of the Joint Chiefs of Staff, 1995).
79 Jeffrey McKitrick *et al.*, 'The Revolution in Military Affairs', *Air War College Studies in National Security: Battlefield of the Future* 3 (1995): 65–97.
80 William A. Owens, 'The Emerging U.S. System-of-Systems', *Strategic Forum* 63 February (1996).
81 Arthur K. Cebrowski and John J. Garstka, 'Network-Centric Warfare: Its Origin and Future', *US Naval Institute Proceedings* (1998).
82 William S. Lind *et al.*, 'The Changing Face of War: Into the Fourth Generation', *Marine Corps Gazette* (1989): 22–6.
83 John Arquilla and David Ronfeldt, 'Cyberwar Is Coming!', *Comparative Strategy* 12(2) (1993); John Arquilla and David Ronfeldt, *The Advent of Netwar* (Santa Monica, CA: RAND, 1996); John Arquilla and David Ronfeldt, *Networks and Netwars: The Future of Terror, Crime, and Militancy* (Santa Monica, CA: RAND, 2001).
84 Arquilla and Ronfeldt, *Advent of Netwar*: 95.
85 Michael Bar-Zohar, *Spies in the Promised Land: Iser Harel and the Israeli Secret Service* (Boston: Houghton Mifflin, 1972): 258.
86 Ephraim Kahana, *Historical Dictionary of Israeli Intelligence* (Lanham, MD: Scarecrow Press, 2006): 73.

Justifying targeted killings 29

87 Ron Chepesiuk, *The Bullet or the Bribe: Taking Down Colombia's Cali Drug Cartel* (Westport, CT: Praeger, 2003): 144.
88 Mark Bowden, *Killing Pablo: The Hunt for the World's Greatest Outlaw* (2002).
89 Chepesiuk, *Bullet or the Bribe*.
90 Daniel Byman, 'Do Targeted Killings Work?', *Foreign Affairs* 85 (2006): 52.
91 Byman, 'Do targeted killings work?': 53.
92 Aaron J. Klein, *Striking Back: The 1972 Munich Olympics Massacre and Israel's Deadly Response* (New York: Random House, 2005).
93 David W. P. Elliott, *The Vietnamese War: Revolution and Social Change in the Mekong Delta, 1930–1975* (Armonk, NY: M. E. Sharpe, 2003): 860.
94 Stanley Karnow, *Vietnam: A History* (New York, NY: Viking, 1991): 616.
95 Ronald H. Spector, *After Tet: The Bloodiest Year in Vietnam* (New York, NY: Free Press, 1993).
96 Karnow, *Vietnam*: 618.
97 Elliott, *Vietnamese War*: 1139.
98 Peter Taylor, *Brits: The War against the IRA* (London: Bloomsbury, 2001): 190–1.
99 Taylor, *Brits*: 213.
100 Taylor, *Brits*: 242.
101 Taylor, *Brits*: 255.
102 Taylor, *Brits*: 271.
103 Ed Moloney, *A Secret History of the IRA* (2002): 305.
104 Byman, *A High Price*: 312.
105 Byman, *A High Price*: 309–10.
106 *Public Committee against Torture in Israel* v. *Government of Israel* (2006): para 60.
107 Kristen Eichensehr, 'On Target? The Israeli Supreme Court and the Expansion of Targeted Killings', *Yale Law Journal* 116 (2007): 1881.
108 Blum and Heymann, 'Law and Policy': 157.
109 Alston, 'CIA and Targeted Killings': 445.
110 Gregory S. McNeal, 'Are Targeted Killings Unlawful? A Case Study in Empirical Claims without Empirical Evidence', in *Targeted Killings: Law and Morality in an Asymmetrical World*, edited by Claire Finkelstein, Jens D. Ohlin and Andrew Altman (Oxford University Press, 2012): 328.
111 For ethical principles, see Holder, 'Northwestern University Speech'.
112 For more on political/legal discourse, see Jurgen Habermas, *Legitimation Crisis* (Boston: Beacon Press, 1975).
113 Robert Zoellick, 'Congress and the Making of US Foreign Policy', *Survival* 41(4) (1999).
114 Peter Paret, Gordon Alexander Craig and Felix Gilbert, *Makers of Modern Strategy from Machiavelli to the Nuclear Age* (Oxford: Clarendon, 1986): 3.
115 Panetta, 'Director's Remarks'.
116 Not to be confused with P. W. Singer, who also features in this book due to his work on robotics and UAVs.
117 Singer, *President of Good and Evil*.
118 Jörg Raab and H. Brinton Milward, 'Dark Networks as Problems', *Journal of Public Administration Research and Theory* 13(4) (2003).
119 For change over time, see the Hoffman/Sageman debate and Rohan Gunaratna and Aviv Oreg, 'Al Qaeda's Organizational Structure and Its Evolution', *Studies in Conflict and Terrorism* 33(12) (2010). See also recent work on al-Qaeda's franchising – Barak Mendelsohn, 'Al-Qaeda's Franchising Strategy', *Survival* 53(3) (2011); revisionist accounts of its formation – Peter Bergen and Paul Cruickshank, 'Revisiting the Early Al Qaeda: An Updated Account of Its Formative Years', *Studies in Conflict & Terrorism* 35(1) (2012); as well as, on key types of operative in current operations – Peter Neumann, Ryan Evans and Rafaello Pantucci, 'Locating Al Qaeda's Center of Gravity: The Role of Middle Managers', *Studies in Conflict & Terrorism* 34(11) (2011).

30 *Justifying targeted killings*

120 Key here are the debates about authority of the state to use violence against citizens. See *Al-Aulaqi* v. *Obama*, as well as the key detention debates about due process. The second debate is whether the president has the authority to conduct targeted killings. The key area of debate is the president's authority to define a person as an enemy, and the president's authority in war time. Congress technically acts as a check on presidential authority, although this has been ceded in both the George W. Bush and Barack Obama presidencies. See Ryan Hendrickson, 'War Powers in the Obama Administration', *Contemporary Security Policy* 31(2) (2010).

121 The Uniform Code of Military Justice, 64 Stat. 109, 10 U.S.3. Chapter 47.

122 Malcolm N. Shaw, *International Law,* 5th edn (Cambridge University Press, 2003): 2.

123 Hedley Bull, *The Anarchical Society: A Study of Order in World Politics,* 3rd edn (Basingstoke: Palgrave, 2002).

124 See *Al-Aulaqi* v. *Obama*; Church Committee, 'United States Senate Select Committee to Study Governmental Operations with Respect to Intelligence Activities', *AARC* (Assassination Archives and Research Center, 1975); *Public Committee against Torture in Israel* v. *Government of Israel* (2006); Antonio Cassese, 'Expert Opinion on Whether Israel's Targeted Killing of Palestinian Terrorists Is Consonant with International Humanitarian Law', *Public Committee Against Torture* et al. v. *Government of Israel* et al. (Israeli High Court of Justice, 2007).

125 Sean Condron, *Operational Law Handbook* (Charlottesville, VA: The Judge Advocate General's Legal Center and School, US Army, 2011).

126 Mervyn Frost, *Towards a Normative Theory of International Relations: A Critical Analysis of the Philosophical and Methodological Assumptions in the Discipline with Proposals Towards a Substantive Normative Theory* (New York: Cambridge University Press, 1986): 121.

127 Walzer, *Just and Unjust Wars*; Saint Augustine, tr. Marcus Dods, *The City of God* (Peabody, MA: Hendrickson Publishers, 2009); Saint Thomas Aquinas, tr. Kenneth E. Comp Alrutz, *War and Peace* (Washington, DC: University Press of America, 1982); Hugo Grotius, *On the Law of War and Peace* (Whitefish, MT: Kessinger, 2004); Jeff McMahan, *Killing in War* (Oxford University Press, 2009).

2 American targeted killings

'You've taken an agency that was chugging along and turned it into one hell of a killing machine,' said the former official.... Blanching at his choice of words, he quickly offered a revision: 'Instead, say "one hell of an operational tool."'[1]

Anonymous official

Introduction

It is impossible to understand the Obama administration's defence of targeted killings without taking into account the particularities of the US context. For example, a key criticism of US targeted killings is that they contradict the rule of law established by executive orders (EOs), which effectively outlawed the use of assassination in the wake of the Church Committee.[2] In the US system, it is for the executive to decide and define political enemies, as well as to take executive action. However, Congress plays an important role in authorising the use of the United States' military (one that also legitimises the use of force), as demonstrated in the 2001 AUMF.[3] The text of the AUMF specifically allows the president to target individuals, thus legitimising (within the US system of legitimacy) a form of individuated warfare between the United States and al-Qaeda.[4]

The power inherent in the ability to define enemies is one of the reasons that this exercise of executive authority is such a divisive topic. One of the strengths of John Yoo's work on the legal and political authority of the president is that it recognises the relationship between law and politics, even if his critics point out that his interpretation of this relationship is somewhat extreme.[5] The central problem with the legal arguments that surround the debate about targeted killings is that the interpretability of law is in itself a tool used by both sides in the debate. On one side, human rights activists and prominent legal scholars such as Mary Ellen O'Connell consider any interpretation of law that expands, or allows for the expansion of, state authority to use force to be illegitimate. Others such as Kenneth Anderson point to the fact that the wording of many legal precedents is exceedingly woolly and that the hard ban on targeted killings does not exist.[6] At its limits, these arguments can produce exceedingly illogical premises, such as the fact that because transnational conflict between a state and a non-state

32 *American targeted killings*

actor is not recognised in international law, it cannot exist in fact.[7] Jens Ohlin's criticism of this approach is insightful:

> If, on the other hand, one sticks with the definition of NIAC [non-international armed conflict] as being an armed conflict that does not cross state boundaries, then I find little support for the conclusion that IAC [international armed conflict] and NIAC occupy the entire field of armed conflicts. When the two concepts are not defined in opposition to each other, the warrant for concluding that together they exhaust the notion of armed conflict seems rather thin.[8]

These legal discussions matter because law, and legal interpretation, form an important element of the Obama administration's attempt to differentiate and distance itself from the Bush administration that preceded it, but they are not the only basis for the Obama administration's defence of its activities. From the outset, the Obama administration categorically rejected the use of a number of methods and practices used by the Bush administration against al-Qaeda. On taking office, Obama banned the use of 'enhanced interrogation techniques' and ordered the closure of detention facilities at Guantanamo Bay. Congressional opposition to the closure of Guantanamo Bay has stalled the process indefinitely.[9] The character of this attempt at distancing is important because the practice of targeted killings is a key method of the Bush administration that was not rejected by the Obama administration. Instead, the Obama administration increased the use of targeted killings and subsequently defended them in public. Many of the issues raised by the use of contentious methods by the Bush administration are inextricably linked to the use of targeted killings. Therefore, the decision to reject a large number of these methods yet retain the use of targeted killings is important to understanding both the issues raised by targeted killings and the Obama administration's defence of this policy. Ultimately, the Obama administration's defence of targeted killings rests on defining them as lawful and moral uses of force. This masks, however, a web of nested points. One is that the United States can lawfully use military force against al-Qaeda and that the president has the authority to select military or lethal options in lieu of approaches rooted in law enforcement. A second point that requires defending is that the president has the authority to define people – even US citizens – as participants in this political conflict. Third and fourth: any violence used is in accordance with IHL and the just war tradition. In order to understand why these questions are important, however, it is first necessary to explain the threat to the United States that al-Qaeda was thought to pose in the wake of 9/11.

The changing threat of terrorist networks

Underlying the use of targeted killings against al-Qaeda and associated groups by both the Bush and Obama administrations is a change in the perception of the threat that these networks pose to the United States. The September 11 attacks shocked both Americans and the US government, and provoked a militarised response that was fundamentally different to US responses to prior attacks. The 9/11 Commission Report goes into detail on this matter. It is critical of the fact that 'the United States did not, before 9/11, adopt as a clear strategic objective the elimination of al Qaeda'.[10] Nonetheless, the US had previously resorted to the use of force against the organisation. In response to the 1998 embassy bombings, a principals meeting at the White House agreed to a missile strike aimed at killing Osama bin Laden and his chief lieutenants. This stands in direct contrast to the government's attitude earlier in the year, and the authority to kill was later reversed by President Clinton.[11]

The Bush administration responded to 9/11 by declaring a 'war on terror' where President Bush proclaimed that '[O]ur enemy is a radical network of terrorists, and every government that supports them'.[12] Barry Buzan argued that, in this sense, the War on Terror represented 'macro-securitisation' – an overarching security concept, although one that was unlikely to be as dominant as the Cold War.[13] The Bush administration discarded reactive policies in favour of pre-emptive ones.[14] However, such a response was not universal, as states responded differently to al-Qaeda after 9/11. Stuart Croft points out that the British establishment, the United States' close ally, self-consciously underplayed the threat of al-Qaeda in public until the July 7 bombings.[15] Such differences aside, on 9/11 terrorist networks entered the Western public consciousness as an existential threat – although quite how big, immediate or dangerous a threat was entirely debatable, usually on a very thin evidential basis in the early years of the War on Terror. For example, the assertion of increased terrorist willingness to cause mass casualties was based on a small sample of attacks over the previous decade.[16]

The significance of non-state actors and terrorist networks

The Bush administration considered that al-Qaeda posed a significant enough threat that it invaded Afghanistan in an attempt to root out and destroy the organisation in order to 'disrupt the use of Afghanistan as a terrorist base of operations, and to attack the military capability of the Taliban regime'.[17] The Obama administration considers that the network represents such a threat that it continues to use targeted killings to attack and disrupt the network. How, one wonders, did a relatively small terrorist network became significant enough to trigger such a response from the most powerful state in the world?

Non-state actors such as al-Qaeda were not always as significant in international politics. Charles Tilly's classic work on the formation of states charts the process by which they became the primary actors of political import in the international system by the twentieth century.[18] Yet Tilly does not argue that this outcome was teleological or preordained. In contrast, Francis Fukuyama argued that liberal democratic states formed something of an end-state; in Fukuyama's words their triumph represented 'the end of history'.[19] Yet subsequent to such statements the post-Cold War period saw the reintroduction of non-state actors

34 *American targeted killings*

as significant entities in global politics – between 1989 and 2001 there were 115 armed conflicts, many involving non-state actors.[20] Intrastate violence and civil conflict were the dominant forms of warfare in the decade following the collapse of the Soviet Union. Mary Kaldor identified significant numbers of non-state actors as important actors in 'globalised war economies'.[21] The Correlates of War Project, which provides the staple data sets for war and conflict, recently included 'non-state wars' in their data sets.[22] In addition, transnational organised crime became a significant subject of international debate.[23] The rise of non-state actors is important because criminal, terrorist and insurgent groups now use new communications technology, global financial regimes and areas of weak state authority to form durable transnational networks. These communications technologies and correlated processes of globalisation enable them to withstand pressure from state actors.[24] Al-Qaeda's core remains a threat because it is able to use these global connections to leverage local conflicts to acquire new recruits and transmit technical knowledge to persons in the West.

The emblem of this rise in importance is the September 11 attacks by al-Qaeda on the United States. These attacks were the most significant attacks on the US homeland since the nineteenth century. From this point onwards, the Bush administration committed itself to eliminating al-Qaeda and affiliated networks.[25] There were two important shifts that occurred. One was that the law enforcement paradigm, which had governed US conduct towards these terrorist networks, was rejected by the Bush administration in favour of a war paradigm, which legitimised the widespread use of militarised and lethal force against members of these networks.[26] Importantly, this legitimised the general use of force against individual terrorists, which would be key to the adoption of targeted killing operations as an operational method of achieving the goal of eliminating al-Qaeda. Up to 1998, this was not US policy, and even then the use of force was restricted to figureheads such as Osama bin Laden.[27]

Defining the threat of al-Qaeda

The shift from law enforcement to militarised counterterrorism was not automatic – the Bush administration's words framed the discourse of the War on Terror. This term was itself derived from then President George W. Bush's speech to a joint session of Congress.[28] The Bush administration justified and legitimised the use of military force against al-Qaeda by defining al-Qaeda as a political enemy and an existential threat. The State Department had defined al-Qaeda as a terrorist group prior to 9/11: al-Qaeda was added to the State Department's list of designated 'Foreign Terrorist Organizations' as of 8 October 1999 by the then Secretary of State Madeleine Albright. In the aftermath of 9/11 the Bush administration argued that since this network had demonstrated the ability and coordination to kill almost 3,000 people in a simultaneous attack, it required a forceful response. Securitisation is the process of bringing a concept into the security domain by defining it in terms of security, which is a prerequisite to the identification of security threats. This, according to Barry Buzan, legitimates 'exceptional measures' in response.[29] Ole Wæver argues that the act of naming a concept in terms of security moves it into the security domain. He identifies this action ('utterance') as a speech act, in reference to linguistic theories.[30] Although the very act of considering something in terms of security is part of securitisation, it is when this 'speech act' has a significant effect on policy that a securitisation process can be considered important outside of academic debates. The critical Copenhagen School of theorists – Barry Buzan, Ole Wæver and their collaborators – defined security 'not as an objective condition, but the outcome of a specific social process'.[31] Therefore because this act is subjective, it is unsurprising that the exact effects of the 9/11 attacks are debated, especially the degree to which the world 'changed'. In political discourse, the 9/11 attacks were taken to represent a decisive break with history. In Freedman's words it was 'an event so traumatic in its impact that a reference to "9/11" is normally sufficient in itself to infer a turning point in international affairs'.[32] Michael Howard refers to it as 'the close of an epoch', the Westphalian state system itself.[33]

In the discourse of the War on Terror, the securitisation of al-Qaeda enabled the use of military methods outside the 'normal' law enforcement paradigm. Security concepts are no longer considered limited to traditional criminal and military spheres – securitisation now encompasses a wide variety of issues. This widening of security studies occurred during the 1980s and early 1990s, with theorists such as Ullman, Brown, Wæver and others widening the scope of security studies beyond its traditional subjects.[34] The primary tension in the field is between those that consider that security should have a narrow definition and those that wish to widen the concept to apply to other fields, such as environmental security.[35] Some theorists consider that these definitions produce axiomatic responses.[36] What is important, however, is that despite both the Bush administration and the Obama administration depicting al-Qaeda as an existential threat, the Obama administration has chosen to use different means to target the group, explicitly rejecting many of the practices, such as enhanced interrogation, of the Bush administration.[37]

Key to understanding the different responses of the Bush and Obama administrations is legitimacy. Legitimacy is a key concept that is 'essentially contested', such that by definition it can have no singular meaning.[38] In democratic societies, the conferring of legitimacy on government by the governed is typically conceived as the primary legitimating factor. Some critics, such as Sofia Näsström, argue that 'the people' are hard to define.[39] Others, such as Edward Herman and Noam Chomsky, also point out that this legitimacy can be altered or created by governing power structures and the media.[40] Such criticism invariably relates back to the role of the media in society, building on the work of Walter Lippmann and others.[41] Theorists of legitimacy tend either to the normative conception of legitimacy (what ought to be obeyed) and the descriptive conception (what those within a political system believe should be obeyed). This book uses the hybrid model of Habermas, in which legitimacy is a normative concept, where the claim to legitimacy by an actor is matched by the acceptance (or lack

36 *American targeted killings*

thereof) of the person(s) on whom such a claim is made.[42] The importance of legitimacy is that the legal claims made by both the Bush and Obama administrations were claims made within this framing. Thus law is a claim by the issuing authority, and its legitimacy is also related to the extent to which it is upheld.

The importance of law is that Ole Wæver argues that the structure of a speech act requires that the 'securitising actor' must have social legitimacy for it to change social constructions. Both the Bush and Obama administrations sought to frame their actions as legitimate, but their discursive legitimacy claims differed. The Bush administration framed the threat posed by al-Qaeda as exceptional and used it as a basis to legitimate policy responses to it that derogated from key international treaties. Conversely, the Obama administration seeks to legitimate the continued and expanded use of one of these policy responses – targeted killings – by arguing that it is a legal and ethical means of warfare.

The use of targeted killings is a means of conducting policy – a choice – of both the Bush and Obama administrations. President Bush's address to the nation on the evening of the 9/11 attacks, and the subsequent congressional approval for the AUMF, enabled the use of an expanded range of policy options against al-Qaeda, authorising the president:

> to use all necessary and appropriate force against those nations, organizations, or persons he determines planned, authorized, committed, or aided the terrorist attacks that occurred on September 11, 2001, or harbored such organizations or persons, in order to prevent any future acts of international terrorism against the United States by such nations, organizations or persons.[43]

The Bush administration used this authority to legitimate a wide variety of policy responses predicated on the exceptional threat posed by al-Qaeda. The use of such methods is impossible without supporting bureaucratic structures – the United States' national security apparatus. These bureaucratic entities, primarily federal, are responsible for the security of the state and its populace. They derive from the post-World War II structures and arrangements outlined in the National Security Act of 1947. This created the post of the Secretary of Defense, in charge of a newly created Department of Defense, and also created the National Security Council (NSC), the Joint Chiefs of Staff (JCS) and the CIA. Significant alterations to this structure are rare – the 1986 Goldwater–Nicholls Act removed the JCS from the operational command chain; and the Department of Homeland Security was created in 2002. Considerable effort went into improving inter-agency cooperation in the United States after 9/11.[44] The Bush administration significantly expanded and integrated the agencies responsible for national security. President Bush created the Office of Homeland Security, under Tom Ridge. The formation of the Department of Homeland Security after the passage of the 2002 Homeland Security Act collated considerable numbers of federal agencies into one, although notably not the Federal Bureau of Investigation (FBI), nor the CIA. These agencies were given more domestic powers with the passage of the Patriot Act in 2001.[45] Importantly, although the Obama administration repudiated many of the policies used by the Bush administration, it did not reject these structures or alter them in a fundamental manner. This lack of significant structural change demonstrates that the policy responses to al-Qaeda are choices rather than an inherent characteristic of the security structures.

The Obama administration inherited the national security apparatus extant at the end of the Bush administration. Its continued use of targeted killings demonstrates that it is willing to use this contentious practice. However, the Obama administration argued that it was qualitatively different from the Bush administration, in part by criticising the basis for the Bush administration's policy: 'the decisions that were made over the last eight years established an ad hoc legal approach for fighting terrorism that was neither effective nor sustainable'.[46] Unlike the Bush administration, the Obama administration has not significantly altered the structure of the national security apparatus. Instead, it has made two claims: first, that it will use its power in a qualitatively different manner; and second, that because of this it will not use certain policies of the Bush administration. To examine this claim, it is necessary to examine these policies in depth and the reasons why they were considered to be against the rule of law (or are depicted as such by the Obama administration). The next section examines the Bush administration's contentious policies in the War on Terror, why they were rejected by the Obama administration and why it is fundamentally important that the Obama administration has retained the use of one of them – targeted killings.

The Obama administration's defence

The Obama administration explicitly sought to distinguish itself and its national security policy from the Bush administration, but simultaneously increased the use of targeted killings, as well as the use of these methods directly against US citizens. The importance of the Obama administration's defence of targeted killings is that it seeks to normalise this activity. This defence is explicitly different from the rationale of realist self-defence offered by the George W. Bush administration for the use of extreme measures during his presidency. The Bush administration's justification predicated itself on legality but also on overriding emergency and exceptionality; in contrast, the Obama administration's defence predicates itself on legality and ethics irrespective of emergency. The Obama administration considers war to exist between the United States and al-Qaeda, but argues that its responses are legal and ethical in the face of such emergency. This is outlined in recent official admissions and defences of the programme by officials from the Obama administration such as then Head of the CIA Leon Panetta,[47] Attorney General Eric Holder,[48] General Counsel of the Department of Defense Jeh Johnson,[49] General Counsel of the CIA Stephen Preston,[50] Legal Adviser of the Department of State Harold Koh[51] and the chief counterterrorism advisor to the President, John Brennan.[52] Taken together, these speeches form a public defence of the US use of targeted killings, and President Obama has also publicly admitted in an online discussion to the use of UAV strikes in the semi-autonomous FATA region in northwestern Pakistan.[53]

38 *American targeted killings*

President Obama's initial speech on national security argued that the Bush administration had treated principles 'as luxuries that we could no longer afford' despite being 'motivated by a sincere desire to protect the American people'.[54] Obama characterised his approach as negotiating a path between two poles, neither of which he deemed satisfactory:

> On the one side of the spectrum, there are those who make little allowance for the unique challenges posed by terrorism, and would almost never put national security over transparency. And on the other end of the spectrum, there are those who embrace a view that can be summarized in two words: 'Anything goes.' Their arguments suggest that the ends of fighting terrorism can be used to justify any means, and that the President should have blanket authority to do whatever he wants – provided it is a President with whom they agree.

Obama argued that 'we need not sacrifice our security for our values, nor sacrifice our values for our security, so long as we approach difficult questions with honesty and care and a dose of common sense', and at core this first speech argued that the way forward lay in abiding by the rule of law. For Obama, this means acting in accordance with the Constitution and its 'principles that have been the source of our strength and a beacon to the world'. This was echoed in Obama's later speech at West Point:

> And finally, we must draw on the strength of our values – for the challenges that we face may have changed, but the things that we believe in must not. That's why we must promote our values by living them at home – which is why I have prohibited torture and will close the prison at Guantanamo Bay. And we must make it clear to every man, woman and child around the world who lives under the dark cloud of tyranny that America will speak out on behalf of their human rights, and tend to the light of freedom and justice and opportunity and respect for the dignity of all peoples. That is who we are. That is the source, the moral source, of America's authority.[55]

Obama outlined the moral character of his national security policy in his speech accepting the Nobel Peace Prize.[56] This speech directly referenced the just war tradition and noted that 'no matter how justified, war promises human tragedy ... war itself is never glorious, and we must never trumpet it as such'. Obama publicly reaffirmed the limits to the use of force:

> I believe that all nations – strong and weak alike – must adhere to standards that govern the use of force. I – like any head of state – reserve the right to act unilaterally if necessary to defend my nation. Nevertheless, I am convinced that adhering to standards, international standards, strengthens those who do, and isolates and weakens those who don't.... Where force is necessary, we have a moral and strategic interest in binding ourselves to certain

rules of conduct. And even as we confront a vicious adversary that abides by no rules, I believe the United States of America must remain a standard bearer in the conduct of war. That is what makes us different from those whom we fight. That is a source of our strength.

In these early speeches, it is clear that the defence of *any* conduct has to be justifiable in terms of constitutional law and international law, and has to be in accordance with the moral principles of the just war tradition. The specific linking of these ideas to a public defence of targeted killings was made by a series of significant figures in the Obama administration. The State Department legal advisor Harold Koh reiterated Obama's points in a major speech to the American Society of International Law, stating that '[L]et there be no doubt: the Obama Administration is firmly committed to complying with all applicable law, including the laws of war, in all aspects of these ongoing armed conflicts'.[57] Noting that the United States must comport itself with both international and domestic law, Koh then specifically referred to the use of force and stated that

in this ongoing armed conflict, the United States has the authority under international law, and the responsibility to its citizens, to use force, including lethal force, to defend itself, including by targeting persons such as high-level al-Qaeda leaders who are planning attacks.

Koh stated that the United States had reviewed 'the rules governing targeting operations' to ensure conduct consistent with law of war principles that include the core principles of distinction and proportionality:

[I]n U.S. operations against al-Qaeda and its associated forces – including lethal operations conducted with the use of unmanned aerial vehicles – great care is taken to adhere to these principles in both planning and execution, to ensure that only legitimate objectives are targeted and that collateral damage is kept to a minimum.

Koh's defence of targeted killings is clear, since he argued that 'individuals who are part of such an armed group are belligerents and, therefore, lawful targets under international law' and that they do not constitute 'unlawful extrajudicial killing', since 'a state that is engaged in an armed conflict or in legitimate self-defence is not required to provide targets with legal process before the state may use lethal force'. Subsequent to the killing of Osama bin Laden, Koh reiterated this argument in a post to *Opinio Juris* to defend the killing, and state that '[I]n sum, the United States acted lawfully in carrying out its mission against Osama bin Laden'.[58]

Later speeches outlined specific points of the defence. John Brennan pointed out that '[T]he United States does not view our authority to use military force against al-Qa'ida as being restricted solely to "hot" battlefields like Afghanistan'.[59] This is an important element of the Obama administration's defence since:

40   *American targeted killings*

[O]thers in the international community – including some of our closest allies and partners – take a different view of the geographic scope of the conflict, limiting it only to the 'hot' battlefields. As such, they argue that, outside of these two active theatres, the United States can only act in self-defence against al-Qa'ida when they are planning, engaging in, or threatening an armed attack against U.S. interests if it amounts to an 'imminent' threat.

Pointedly, Brennan defined a criterion for targeting persons beyond Afghanistan and Iraq: 'individuals who are a threat to the United States, whose removal would cause a significant – even if only temporary – disruption of the plans and capabilities of al-Qa'ida and its associated forces'. This extends to US citizens, as Jeh Johnson made clear: 'belligerents who also happen to be U.S. citizens do not enjoy immunity where non-citizen belligerents are valid military objectives'. Reiterating principles from *Ex Parte Quirin* in 1942, the Supreme Court in 2004, in *Hamdi* v. *Rumsfeld*, stated that '[a] citizen, no less than an alien, can be "part of or supporting forces hostile to the United States or coalition partners" and "engaged in an armed conflict against the United States" '.[60] This point was reiterated by Eric Holder, the Attorney General, who argued that the Fifth Amendment's due process clause did not protect citizens from lawful uses of force in war, so long as:

> [L]et me be clear: an operation using lethal force in a foreign country, targeted against a U.S. citizen who is a senior operational leader of al Qaeda or associated forces, and who is actively engaged in planning to kill Americans, would be lawful at least in the following circumstances: First, the U.S. government has determined, after a thorough and careful review, that the individual poses an imminent threat of violent attack against the United States; second, capture is not feasible; and third, the operation would be conducted in a manner consistent with applicable law of war principles.[61]

The final element of the defence was given by Stephen Preston, the CIA's General Counsel.[62] Preston argued that the CIA could lawfully use force within the framework set out above. This argument is rooted in the fact that, as Preston defines it, the CIA has the legal authority to act, and does so in compliance with relevant law. Preston argues that the CIA has the authority to act where

> the contemplated activity is authorized by the President in the exercise of his powers under Article II of the U.S. Constitution, for example, the President's responsibility as Chief Executive and Commander-in-Chief to protect the country from an imminent threat of violent attack

and that this is 'in accordance with the covert action procedures of the National Security Act of 1947, such that Congress is properly notified by means of a Presidential Finding'. In international law, Preston argues that the CIA has the authority to act due to the inherent right of self-defence, and the 'existence of an armed conflict might also provide an additional justification for the use of force under international law'. Key to Preston's argument is that the CIA acts in compliance with the principles of international law, and that on a lawful operation:

> the Agency would implement its authorities in a manner consistent with the four basic principles in the law of armed conflict governing the use of force: Necessity, Distinction, Proportionality, and Humanity. Great care would be taken in the planning and execution of actions to satisfy these four principles and, in the process, to minimize civilian casualties.

In essence, therefore, the Obama administration's defence of targeted killings must cover both military and CIA action, and do so in a manner consistent with constitutional law, international law and the just war tradition. The salient question, which transcends the policies of both administrations, is the manner in which a terrorist network can be eliminated. Audrey Cronin models the end of terrorist campaigns as occurring in six ways: success, failure, reorientation, repression, decapitation and negotiation.[63] Al-Qaeda have neither succeeded in their goals, nor have they failed, since they still exist. Although the operational role of al-Qaeda's core has changed,[64] their purpose has not, and therefore the group cannot be said to have reoriented themselves. As al-Qaeda are a global movement, they cannot be repressed in the manner that Cronin describes.[65] The fact that al-Qaeda still exist despite the deaths of important leadership figures, including Osama bin Laden and Abu Musab al-Zarqawi, demonstrates that decapitation is not a viable option for defeating them, and states are determined not to negotiate with the group.

Forcing al-Qaeda's 'failure' appears to be the only method of defeating them. The past 11 years have been mixed in this regard. Al-Qaeda rely on spectacular attacks to sustain themselves. Preventing such attacks therefore serves a dual purpose: providing security and depriving al-Qaeda of their required sustenance. Cronin argues that terrorist networks are likely to fail once they move beyond the initial generation, particularly when the movement enters the second or third generation.[66] Therefore, Cronin argues, in order to force al-Qaeda's defeat, states need to reduce their relevance and wait for the group to crumble.

The disrupting effect of measures taken against al-Qaeda by states appears to have reduced their operational ability over the past 11 years, but not to the point of irrelevance; significant attacks that are linked to al-Qaeda include the March 11 Madrid train bombings (in 2004), the July 7 London attacks (in 2005) and the October 12 Bali bombings (in 2002), among others. The United States has suffered a number of attacks, but none of the same order of magnitude of 9/11. The result, it appears, is stalemate. Self-starting, or self-radicalising, terrorists pose a threat, one that could undoubtedly be increased by contact with 'middle managers', who Peter Neumann argues are responsible for attacks such as Madrid.[67] Domestic law enforcement measures give states such as the United States considerable options to disrupt middle managers operating within their jurisdiction. Yet such methods do not appear to eliminate al-Qaeda as an entity.

42　*American targeted killings*

The Obama administration's continued defence of targeted killings in the face of uncertain results draws widespread criticism from a range of public figures and organisations. Within academia, the practice has vocal critics from academics and international lawyers, as well as from senior figures from international organisations, such as Philip Alston.[68] The nature of these acts led important non-governmental organisations (NGOs) within the United States to mount lawsuits against the government.[69] Many leading newspapers have published editorials either critical of, or questioning, the practice.[70] Individually and collectively, these persons and organisations criticise different facets of targeted killings. Many critics of the US use of targeted killings share similar positions, but there is no 'unified' focus. Critics variously assert that these strikes are in breach of international legal regimes;[71] or that they are counterproductive, stoking grievances and radicalism; or that the United States should seek alternate methods to combat al-Qaeda, such as state-building.[72]

Just as critics of targeted killings differ, so too do those who consider elements of the practice to be legitimate. Such views on targeted killings are drawn from academia, lawyers, policymakers and journalists.[73] Many differ in their reasons for supporting these acts. Key to understanding the Obama administration's defence of targeted killings is that it seeks to define these acts as possible within the boundaries of law and ethics. This is in contrast to 'expansionist' supporters of this practice, who argue that the president should (or does) have the right to expand their authority in time of emergency.[74] Therefore, in many senses the Obama administration's defence needs to prove itself against not only the critics of targeted killings, but also many of its would-be supporters. The nature of targeted killings is such that analysts and scholars often wish to draw definitive conclusions – are these acts legal or illegal? Are they moral or immoral? The binary nature of such conclusions is in some ways a reaction to initial biases for or against such acts, but is also a function of the dominance of legal scholarship on the debate. Law, however, is clearly important to all persons concerned, and therefore it is necessary to examine the interplay of law and politics in US uses of force.

Law and war

After 9/11, the methods used by the Bush administration took full advantage of both law enforcement agencies and military force. In the domestic sphere, this took the form of considerable change in domestic agencies, as well as the granting of legal authority for a wide variety of domestic surveillance activities. This included controversial activities that were not standard practice in 2001; for instance, data mining.[75] This is perhaps unsurprising: surveillance is closely linked to state power and the modern state.[76] The Bush administration's strategy of pre-emption led it into two wars: Afghanistan (2001) and Iraq (2003). It also conducted a militarised counterterrorism campaign in many other countries. The Obama administration continued this use of militarised counterterrorism – expanding the use of targeted killings – and retained many of the domestic security powers and capabilities developed by the Bush administration. Importantly, the Obama administration retained the use of targeted killings while rejecting a number of contentious practices used by the Bush administration – enhanced interrogation, extraordinary rendition and extrajudicial detention.

Why were the methods adopted by the Bush administration contentious? At its core, there is the essential argument – that certain practices, such as torture, are ethically (and legally) wrong regardless of circumstance. But detention is not essentially wrong – states can, and do, detain persons routinely, with high levels of public satisfaction and legitimacy, although the exact structure of penal and criminal justice systems varies from society to society.[77] The methods used by the Bush administration were considered problematic by critics, who argued that these methods had significant political effects; furthermore, they were widely perceived to be in contravention of the rule of law.[78] This perception was fuelled by the Bush administration's position, which sought in many cases to legitimate its activities on the exceptional threat posed by al-Qaeda.

The Obama administration rejected the use of practices such as enhanced interrogation (torture),[79] extraordinary rendition and extrajudicial detention on moral grounds, and argued that these practices did not conform to the rule of law.[80] There are good reasons for argument: torture, for example, is illegal in US law.[81] In 2002, John Yoo and Jay Bybee drafted and signed legal opinions that differentiated 'enhanced interrogation techniques' from torture.[82] These memos internally legitimated many practices that critics considered torture.[83] Rule of law considerations also played a part in extraordinary rendition. There are two components to extraordinary rendition. The first is the transfer of a suspect to a third-party state, on the understanding that legal protections afforded them there are lesser. The second component is US custody of these suspects.[84] James D. Boys charts the rise of the first component under Clinton but, importantly, while the United States increasingly used extradition procedures, it did not take custody of key suspects prior to their being transferred to third-party states. Boys attributes this to military insubordination.[85] After 9/11, the CIA's reported rendition programme has involved the kidnapping of individuals directly, prior to transferring them to third-party jurisdictions. In 2006 President Bush formally acknowledged the existence of the CIA programme that involved the detention of terrorist suspects in third-party states.[86] The practice was investigated and substantiated by a key report from the European Union parliament.[87] After 9/11 the United States resorted to what critics term extrajudicial detention, as well as to the military detention of civilians. Key areas of contention are the rendition practices described above and the internment at Guantanamo Bay of 'unlawful combatants', who were held without access to courts.[88]

For its part, the Bush administration consistently argued that its methods were legal, or that the law needed to be reinterpreted to conform to the reality of fighting al-Qaeda.[89] Key to understanding the Bush administration's attitude towards the law is its realist conception of legality – in particular, an attitude that dismisses or derides the applicability of international law. The American Civil Liberties Union traced the legal developments in secret legal memos and opinions

44 *American targeted killings*

that determined detainees were not protected by the Geneva Conventions.[90] Political realism often derides the applicability of international law and places great emphasis on retaining freedom of action for states to defend themselves and their citizens at any cost against political enemies. The rejection of naked political realism by the Obama administration is important – it seeks to defend the practices that it conducts without reference to the exceptionality of the threat posed.[91] Importantly, even though the Obama administration refers to the exceptionality of al-Qaeda, it also binds itself, by self-proclamation, to following the rule of law. The next subsection examines three key practices rejected by the Obama administration as being inconsistent with its ethical and legal concept of national security.

The key problem with the policies of the Bush administration is the intersection of warfare with domestic legal systems. 'Lawfare' refers to the interaction between war and law (notably civil codes), although Charles Dunlap Jr espouses its neutrality as an analytical tool for examining the intersection of law and war.[92] The 'lawfare' debate therefore contains two areas of overlap: first, an overlap between national-level legal systems and international law that governs the conduct of war; and second, an overlap between war and law itself. Critics of the concept argue that it is formed of 'a disturbing pattern of manoeuvres by politicians, jurists and conservative litigators to degrade the capacity of progressive public interest lawyers to bring cases'.[93] The manner in which law is analysed in Dunlap Jr's originating essay on the subject differs from the notion of a truly analytical concept. His bias for effective conduct is clear from his asking '[I]s international law undercutting the ability of the U.S. to conduct effective military operations?'[94] Terrorism is central to this debate, because terrorists and insurgents can either be tackled by law enforcement or military means. Furthermore, the competing attitudes to law are perhaps reflective of the legal traditions (IHL, constitutional) from which each side of the debate originates. Critically, Dunlap Jr is talking of the use of law as a weapon *by* enemies, whereas critics such as Luban assert that this same process is being used by the US government *against* detainees.[95] David Scheffer argues that the view of law in terms of pure military affairs is 'exceptionally myopic, oblivious to how other nations view international justice, and disingenuous regarding the United States' own aggressive use of the law to confront perpetrators of atrocity crimes'.[96]

Notable critics of US targeted killings, such as Mary Ellen O'Connell and Philip Alston, argue that law enforcement methods should always take precedence over military means.[97] The expansion and reordering of the United States' national security organisations did not implicitly lead to the use of particular methods in the name of counterterrorism, although it did enable them. The contemporary contours of the lawfare debate are the result of the policies implemented by the Bush administration concurrent with and subsequent to this reordering – notably, extrajudicial detention, extraordinary rendition, enhanced interrogations and targeted killings. Some of these policies – for example, enhanced interrogations – were possible prior to the reordering of the United States' national security apparatus. The Bush administration justified the use of

American targeted killings 45

such practices in realist terms, but also argued that they were legal. Importantly, all three practices triggered considerable constitutional and legal battles that went all the way to the Supreme Court.

The salient feature of the Bush administration's approach to detention is that it chose to place the majority of captured persons beyond the reach of US courts, and also derogate from the detention standards and practices of IHL. This was pursuant to the Presidential Military Order issued on 13 November 2001, according to which the US government determined that al-Qaeda had 'created a state of armed conflict'.[98] The military was authorised to detain these individuals and prosecute them with military commissions. Early in the War on Terror, the Bush administration chose to detain captured terrorists outside the United States. 'Guantanamo Bay' is the typical name referring to the military detention and interrogation facility located within the United State's Guantanamo Bay naval base in Cuba. The United States leased the base from Cuba in 1903. The Supreme Court ruling *Johnson* v. *Eisentrager* held that non-citizens held offshore were not entitled to the protection of the courts when outside the territorial jurisdiction of the United States.[99] Furthermore, the detention order identifies persons held as 'detainees', not prisoners of war, which the Bush administration used to deny them protections afforded by the Geneva Conventions. Instead, it defined them as 'illegal enemy combatants'.[100] This involved two separate identifications: first, that persons detained were combatants and therefore outside the law enforcement paradigm; and second, that in breaking the laws of war, these persons could be denied protections afforded combatants by the Geneva Conventions and IHL. The Bush administration's ability to define these individuals as such was key to this practice and was predicated on their preliminary identification as enemies (by purportedly being part of al-Qaeda). Furthermore, by detaining persons abroad, US courts lacked automatic jurisdiction, although considerable legal and political struggles occurred to gain and deny access to the US courts.[101] Criticism of this practice came from many corners.[102] Related to this was the later discovery of so-called CIA 'Black Sites', where persons were reportedly detained by the CIA in third-party states.[103] Both types of detention drastically reduced the judicial remedies available to detainees, including those with dual citizenship, to review their situation.[104] Furthermore, the treatment of these detainees fell short of that required by the Geneva Conventions.[105] The key criticism of the practice of detention is that it was, in effect, arbitrary. Scott Michaelson and Scott Shershow argue that the United States has consistently sought to exclude 'its current enemies [al-Qaeda] from the protections of the Geneva accords, but does so specifically with reference to these same accords'.[106] This masks an important point: the Bush administration's definition of these persons as enemies, although external to the United States, is always an arbitrary act – no law prevents the president from labelling external persons as enemies. The choice of how to deal with these persons was, however, arbitrary, in the sense that the Bush administration chose to externalise them from the US legal system and not to apply provisions of the Geneva Conventions to them, on the basis of their supposed behaviour prior to capture. In this sense, the actions of

46 American targeted killings

the Bush administration were arbitrary, and persons were placed into legal grey areas. In contrast, the Obama administration has consistently attempted to close Guantanamo Bay and deal with these persons in three manners: trial by federal court, military commission or transfer to the authority of a third-party state. Obama's EO 13492 Section 4 (4) states that:

> [W]ith respect to any individuals currently detained at Guantánamo whose disposition is not achieved under paragraphs (2)[transfer] or (3)[prosecution] of this subsection, the Review shall select lawful means, consistent with the national security and foreign policy interests of the United States and the interests of justice, for the disposition of such individuals. The appropriate authorities shall promptly implement such dispositions.[107]

These practices, although the use of military courts is contentious, place the persons detained at Guantanamo Bay into a defined legal system. Persons are to be either transferred to the US court system or a foreign judicial system, or prosecuted by military commission for breaches of the laws of war.[108]

The second contentious practice, supposedly rejected by the Obama administration, is that of extraordinary rendition. Again, persons thought to be terrorists were detained in covert operations and transferred to third-party states for interrogation.[109] Where this differs from the example of detention is that the Bush administration clearly manipulated differing legal systems in order to avoid the US court system. Furthermore, protections available to these persons in third-party countries were significantly worse than those afforded to persons detained in the United States. In particular, credible accusations were levelled at the US government for its part in transferring persons to places where such practices were routine.[110]

The last contentious practice specifically rejected by the Obama administration is the use of 'enhanced interrogation' methods. Critics argued that the use of methods such as waterboarding constituted torture and clearly contravened both the rule of law and ethical barriers to the use of these methods.[111] Conversely, the Bush administration sought to portray such methods as extreme but legal forms of interrogation.[112] Cheney's 2009 defence of the practice argued that '[T]he interrogations were used on hardened terrorists after other efforts failed. They were legal, essential, justified, successful, and the right thing to do'.[113] The Obama administration discontinued this practice as a matter of principle, restricting the use of interrogation methods to standards applied for standard military interrogations. President Obama's unequivocal statement on the subject leaves little room for manoeuvre: 'I can stand here today ... and say without exception or equivocation that we do not torture'.[114]

In examining the contentious practices of the Bush administration, it is possible to define three key areas of contention: (1) the ability of the president to define a person as an 'enemy', (2) the manipulation of legal regimes to strip persons of legal protection or standing and (3) the use of methods that are ethically problematic by definition. Crucial to the Obama administration's rejection of the Bush administration's methods is the rejection of the second and third processes but not the first – the executive's ability to define persons as enemies.

In conventional warfare, there is no such thing as a 'suspected soldier', yet in law enforcement there is no such thing as a 'terrorist' until a court has tried a person for terrorist offences and found him or her guilty of a crime. This difference is not as tautological as it first seems when one considers the idea of using military measures against 'terrorist suspects'. A parallel to this process can be found in the definition of persons as 'enemies'. Persons identified as soldiers of an opposing army are, axiomatically, enemies, as are persons who are defined as traitors. One must exercise caution in the use of 'enemy' – Carl Schmitt argues that the distinction between 'friend' and 'enemy' is the root of politics.[115] Schmitt also differentiates between public and private enemies, observing the difference in Latin between *hostis* and *inimicus*. Thus an 'enemy' was a public enemy (*hostis*), not a person disliked on a private level (*inimicus*). In later work, however, Schmitt introduces the concept of enmity, differentiating between 'enemies' and 'real enemies', the latter being applied to politicised forms of warfare involving partisans or 'real' hatred.[116] In conventional warfare, the anonymous soldier of an opposing army is therefore an enemy by definition, but not a 'real' enemy; furthermore, the feeling towards them is supposed to be public (*hostis*). What links these concepts to treason is political crime. As Schmitt states, '[T]he political unity of a people has its concrete form in the constitution. Infractions like high treason or treason in a Land protect political existence'[117]. The concept of treason therefore axiomatically implies that a person becomes a 'real' enemy by nature of the crime – it is a political attack on the polity. This book uses 'political enemy' to denote 'real' enemies, as it links both internal and external enemies. Chapter 5 argues that the anonymity that Schmitt implies in the concept of public enemies cannot exist in the context of targeting non-conventional opponents.

There exists a considerable gap between the processes by which a person can be defined a traitor or an external enemy, even though the result, as demonstrated in the practices used by the Bush and Obama administrations, is the same. Defining a person as a terrorist (political enemy) while using targeted killings can be a death sentence. This is in part because 'terrorist' is a liminal category – persons can either be dealt with via law enforcement or military means, and it is impossible to precisely define the limits of either regime.[118] Liminality is used in connection with terrorists by a number of authors, such as Saniotis, who casts terrorists as 'liminal beings'.[119] Saniotis, however, uses this term regarding the terrorists' internal perceptions/role. It is used here to denote a status between two identities. Terrorists, guerrillas and other subjectively identified individuals are liminal in that they are between the common understanding of combatant and non-combatant. This mirrors Menjívar's concept of 'liminal legality' regarding the predicament of Guatemalan and Salvadorean immigrants to the United States.[120]

Larson highlights the problem of internal political enemies – traitors.[121] The US Constitution (Article 3.3) contains specific provisions that prevent the executive branch from unilaterally defining a US citizen as a traitor, yet contains no

48 *American targeted killings*

such bar to the executive defining a foreign soldier as an enemy. Specifically, the Constitution requires that a person be convicted of treason, thereby necessitating due process concerns:

> Treason against the United States, shall consist only in levying War against them, or in adhering to their Enemies, giving them Aid and Comfort. No Person shall be convicted of Treason unless on the testimony of two Witnesses to the same overt Act, or on Confession in open court.

Indeed, as commander-in-chief, the president is invested with the ability both to define enemies as they see fit and to use force against them, pursuant to congressional authorisation. War powers are divided in the US Constitution. Article 1, Section 8 defines Congress' powers to declare war and to raise armies. Article 2, Section 2 states that '[T]he President shall be Commander in Chief of the Army and Navy of the United States, and of the Militia of the several States, when called into the actual Service of the United States'. The traditional tension between these two is essentially unresolvable. John Yoo argues that it is an essential feature of the constitutional system.[122] Nonetheless, the president's authority to define enemies is relatively clear – the president had a clear limit placed on their ability to define persons internal to the constitutional political system as enemies (Citizens), but no limit to define persons external to this system as such.

From this perspective, it is clear that all four contentious practices rely on the externalisation of persons from the constitutional system. By defining persons as part of an external threat (al-Qaeda), the Bush administration legitimated the use of methods against persons who would otherwise have been subject to due process constraints defined in the Constitution.[123] By physically placing persons outside the continental United States, the Bush administration restricted the US courts' jurisdiction over their persons. The Obama administration's response to this has been twofold: attempting to put as many persons through the federal courts system as possible (using military commissions to provide due process where not possible) and transferring persons to another system entirely. Therefore it theoretically satisfies the rule of law questions by defining a legal regime under which an individual is processed.

The use of targeted killings against US citizens abroad does, however, demonstrate that the Obama administration retains, and considers proper, the authority to unilaterally define a person as part of al-Qaeda, and therefore as an enemy. The legality, constitutionality and legitimacy of this authority is central to the US use of targeted killings. It is unclear what due process is possible when, in defining persons physically external to the United States, the executive branch concurrently decides that they are a political enemy. Whether there could, or should, be legal restrictions on the US president's ability to determine this about a person is central to the restraint, or lack thereof, of its ability to conduct targeted killings against US citizens. The key question remains: why does the Obama administration consider it illegal and/or immoral to indefinitely detain persons, manipulate legal regimes by transferring them physically, or subject them to enhanced interrogation methods, but use targeted killings against them? The principal answer to this question is that killing, while arguably worse than detention, is justifiable under IHL. Moreover, under the 1947 National Security Act, the president can authorise the CIA to undertake covert action: '[A]n activity or activities of the United States Government to influence political, economic, or military conditions abroad, where it is intended that the role of the United States Government will not be apparent or acknowledged publicly'.[124] The authority to use military force, or to authorise the CIA to use force, must, however, be put into recent historical context.

The US context of targeting

The legal and political authority to order acts of public violence relies on socially sanctioned organisations to carry them out. In the United States, critics have decried the fact that both the CIA and the military carry out targeted killings on behalf of the state, often in close cooperation. Critics of the US use of targeted killings argue that the CIA is an illegitimate actor to conduct targeted killings. In 2011, Human Rights Watch, an NGO, wrote to President Obama outlining a set of problems, which are common to other critics, such as Alston:

> The CIA, like all US government agencies, is bound by international human rights and humanitarian law. Unlike the US armed forces, the CIA provides little or no information regarding the training and composition of its drone teams, or the procedures and rules it follows in conducting targeted killings. Nor has the government provided information as to whether the CIA has conducted any investigations into possible international law violations and their outcomes ... so long as the US government cannot demonstrate a readiness to hold the CIA to international legal requirements for accountability and redress, the use of drones in targeted killings should be exclusively within the command responsibility of the US armed forces.[125]

However, the question of which organisation should conduct the use of force on behalf of the US government is secondary to the question of who (or what) has the authority within the US government to legitimise the use of force. Who defines a political enemy, and who can authorise the use of force against that enemy in the US system? This is a traditional political battle in the United States, directly linked to the relationship between the presidency and Congress. In the US constitutional framework, the president is the commander-in-chief of the armed forces, while Congress has the right to declare war. The constitutional problem lies in the definition of war itself. As Kenneth Moss writes, '[T]he absence of any [constitutional] definition or elaboration on war has been a factor in arguments on congressional and presidential authority'.[126] While Congress has the power to authorise wars and raise taxes to pay for the armed forces, the president, as commander-in-chief, has effective control over the organisations that

50 *American targeted killings*

ultimately use violence in service of political objectives. Complicating matters, the president reserves the right to take action independent of Congress. The 1973 War Powers Resolution (WPR) limited the president's ability to unilaterally use military force; however, as John Yoo notes, '[E]very President since [Nixon] has refused to acknowledge the WPR's constitutionality, and several have undertaken action in violation of its terms'.[127] However, there are also examples of federal agencies defining persons as enemies outside of this loop, both internally and externally. Between 1975 and 1976 the Church Committee examined the actions of federal agencies unilaterally defining persons or groups as threats to national security. This included the FBI's COINTELPRO operations, aimed at disrupting and suppressing organisations deemed subversive, as well as the CIA's participation in assassination plots abroad. The ability of agencies, particularly the CIA, to take such action was severely restricted after the Church Committee hearings, in effect leaving the executive branch charged with defining enemies, as well as with controlling the use of force. Legitimacy for the use of that force also comes from Congress, which has to authorise the expenditures for such activities. Furthermore, a system of congressional oversight keeps Congress informed of the outcomes of such activities. Even so, whether this system has the ability to provide sufficient control over the use of targeted killings is an oft-raised question.[128]

Regardless of criticism, both the Bush and Obama administrations considered their uses of force to be bounded by law, as defined by the Constitution. The principle remains constant – the use of force is not condoned where illegal. The liminality lies in where an act is neither proscribed as illegal nor positively described as legal. US politics is a key determinant of this, as John Yoo argues in his history of the presidency branch.[129] Although terrorists can be defined as military targets under certain circumstances in IHL, the decision to view them as such is a political one. In a May 1998 speech, President Clinton's concept of US counterterrorism focused on the capture of terrorists and did not mention the possibility of killing them.[130] In this context, the determination by President Bush that the threat posed by al-Qaeda required a military response is consistent with the US system – al-Qaeda were already defined as enemies, but the scale of the 9/11 attacks, and the potential threat that they posed to the United States, altered the political calculus regarding the use of force against these persons. This determination was supported by Congress when it passed the 2001 AUMF.

The legitimate use of force in the United States is predicated on its legality. Under international law the current use of targeted killings is, in effect, liminal legality, because it does not conform with either IHL or IHRL. Targeted killing of persons is illegal under IHRL, but the nature of contemporary terrorist networks is such that states argue that they form a threat to states outside the, effectively peacetime, boundaries of IHRL. Similarly, even though the US government argues that IHL is held to apply in the conflict between the United States and al-Qaeda, many critics of the US government disagree with this assessment. The legal semantics are therefore open to interpretation and, without resolution, the liminal legality of these actions is preserved. In these areas of law, politics and

American targeted killings 51

social norms of expected behaviour play an important role in authorising the use of force.

The political nature of use-of-force decisions is clear in recent US history, as are changing norms for the use of lethal force against individuals. The Church Committee represents a landmark in the regulation of the United States' intelligence community. The Committee's reports had wide-ranging effects and instigated a period of normative behavioural change in the intelligence community. Most importantly, Gerald Ford issued EO 11905, prohibiting 'political assassination'. This represented a break from the past, in which the CIA had been found by the Committee of conspiring in the assassination of many world leaders. The Committee found that Patrice Lumbaba (the first democratically elected leader of the Congo) had been targeted, but that the CIA had not been involved in his death; however, it did find that ranking government officials 'discussed, and may have authorized, the establishment within the CIA of a generalized assassination capability'.[131] The EO embodied a new form of legitimacy for the CIA, one in which the agency was not supposed to use force without presidential authorisation. Although it did not result in the CIA dismantling its Special Activities Division, any action taken that would class as political assassination could be taken to be illegal and illegitimate. As the Committee interim report stated: 'we find that assassination violates moral precepts fundamental to our way of life'.[132]

Presidents Carter and Reagan both updated the EO prohibiting assassination. The primary problem with these presidential bars on assassination is that the concept is defined neither in law nor within the documents themselves. President Ford's EO 11905, Section 5(g) states: 'Prohibition of Assassination. No employee of the United States Government shall engage in, or conspire to engage in, political assassination'. The only other mention of the term in the document is Section 2(a)(2), defining foreign counter-intelligence as activities conducted to protect the United States and its citizens from assassination, among other activities. The precise definition is therefore moot. President Carter removed 'political' from the definition in EO 12036, but again, the order provided no clarity on the definition. This change was preserved in President Reagan's EO 12333, which covered the period including the attempts to kill Osama bin Laden in 1998. EO 12333 allows for 'special activities' but does not define them. These documents therefore made the concept of targeted killing a liminal activity, and therefore one governed by political decisions. The orders banned 'political assassination' but placed no such bar on 'non-political assassination' or on any other such killing that could not be determined as such. The CIA's attempts to create a paper chain in Memoranda of Notification in regards to activities that might involve the death of terrorists underlines its unease at committing such acts independent of the executive's direct approval.[133]

EOs are, however, prone to change. Congress voted war powers to President Bush in the aftermath of the 9/11 attacks.[134] The passage of this Act constituted both another rule of law and legitimacy transition. In awarding the powers, Congress specifically enabled the targeting of individuals. This was an important

52 *American targeted killings*

watershed and acts as the legal basis for the subsequent targeted killing operations, underpinning their legitimacy in official terms.

The important shift in the legality of killing is accompanied by a semantic shift in Presidential Orders. EO 12333 authorised the CIA to conduct 'special activities' defined as:

> [A]ctivities conducted in support of national foreign policy objectives abroad which are planned and executed so that the role of the United States Government is not apparent or acknowledged publicly, and functions in support of such activities, but which are not intended to influence United States political processes, public opinion, policies, or media and do not include diplomatic activities or the collection and production of intelligence or related support functions.[135]

The updating of this order under President Bush is semantically important. EO 13470 strikes 'special activities' and replaces them with 'covert action':

> [C]overt action means an activity or activities of the United States Government to influence political, economic, or military conditions abroad, where it is intended that the role of the United States Government will not be apparent or acknowledged publicly.[136]

The CIA is barred from conducting activities in support of traditional military activities[137] but not from conducting activities that explicitly influence military conditions abroad. This order, in effect, enables the CIA to conduct military-like operations, which it had been doing since the commencement of post-9/11 targeted killings. Both EO 12333 and EO 13470 enabled the military to conduct special activities and covert activities, respectively, during time of war. Therefore the combined effect of the declaration of war, and the shift in EO 13470, legitimised and legalised covert military activity by the CIA. What is important here is that the Office of the President retained its function in defining enemies and directing the use of force. The CIA may be able to direct the use of military force, particularly with 'double-hatted' military personnel integrated into the organisation, but the president retains the authority to define enemies and outline the measures to be used against them. A key *New York Times* article on the process of deciding targets notes that President Obama has taken personal responsibility for the use of targeted killings.[138] The legitimacy of him acting on that is, however, political, and depends on the relationship between the executive and Congress. The use of targeted killings involves three judgements: first, the defining of a person as an enemy; second, a judgement relating to the threat that they pose; and third, the authority to take action against that person as a result. In the US system, it is the executive that defines enemies, defines the persons that form a part of them and defines what state bureaucracies will be used against a given enemy. This does not, however, mean that the president is unchecked in the use of force.

The Bush and Obama administrations' use of targeted killings is important because they have the specific authority to target individuals, afforded them by Congress in 2001.[139] The Bush administration used the AUMF to justify many contentious practices, while the Obama administration uses it to justify one of these – targeted killings. The AUMF overrides the traditional controls that Congress has over the president's ability to use force. Congressional oversight of war limits the unilateral deployment of troops – although the president is able to deploy troops without notifying Congress, the president can only do so for 60 days.[140] Examining the use of targeted killings in the US context, it is clear that the AUMF affords the Obama administration the (internal) legal authority to conduct targeted killings, unlike cases such as Operation Damocles. One must, however, note that this legitimation creates a political externality, one that has been commented on since the Bush administration – the AUMF affords the executive a large amount of authority and leeway in the use of force. Curtis Bradley and Jack Goldsmith define the powers assigned as broad, but not unlimited. The key limitation that they identify is the nexus with the September 11 attacks. However, this nexus depends entirely on the executive determining that a person either is a part of al-Qaeda or is aiding al-Qaeda in some fashion. This definition is now used to define persons in Al-Qaeda in the Arabian Peninsula (AQAP) as legitimate targets for targeted killings.[141] This is significant in the debates surrounding the constitutionality of targeted killings, which I will return to in Chapter 5.

Drones, spies and signature strikes

The president's authority to define enemies is an integral component of the Obama administration's defence of targeted killings. That the means of conducting targeted killings are both lawful and legitimate is a second integral aspect of this defence. The question therefore turns to whether the methods used by the United States to target and kill persons it defines as enemies are somehow inherently wrong. The defining feature of the US targeted killing campaign is its reliance on UAVs and drones. There is, however, evidence that the United States uses a mix of operational methods for targeted killings (such as its use of conventional aircraft and cruise missiles in Yemen, where the Bureau of Investigative Journalism report that six confirmed conventional airstrikes occurred between 2002 and March 2012).[142] Some critics, however, define the use of 'remote killing' platforms as essentially immoral in and of themselves.[143] This line of criticism combines two strands: first, that remotely controlled craft are illegal or immoral in themselves; and second, that this form of warfare is somehow illegal. Although some critics start from the proposition that all violence is immoral and illegitimate (pacifism), the use of UAVs to kill people poses a challenge to existing frameworks of morality and law.[144] For some, however, the most disturbing aspect of targeted killings is the role of the CIA, an intelligence agency with paramilitary authority, in the use of targeted killings. Also associated with the CIA is a targeting method known as 'signature strikes',

54 *American targeted killings*

where the precise identity of targeted individuals is unknown. Signature strikes are so-called 'pattern of life' targeting methods. Rather than targeting a known individual, these strikes rely on deriving a pattern of behaviour that is taken to signify that a person or persons are either militants or terrorists. One *Wall Street Journal* article notes, 'CIA officials defended the signature strikes by saying they frequently netted top terrorists, not just foot soldiers. Twice as many wanted terrorists have been killed in signature strikes than in personality strikes, a U.S. counterterrorism official said'.[145] Each of these elements, in turn, is defensible in its own way. Amalgamated, the prospect of an intelligence agency ordering strikes launched from remote platforms on the basis of a pattern of life is perhaps the least defensible aspect of the US use of targeted killings.

Criticism of remote platforms as a way of killing tends to ignore the long-term development of ranged weapons. UAVs eliminate one of the key limiting factors of aerial warfare: human biology. Manned aircraft are subject to the tolerable limits of the human body. For instance, humans need to eat and drink, which is difficult to do in small aircraft. The human body also places a limit on the flight dynamics attainable, because G-forces place considerable stress on the human body.[146] Taking humans out of the cockpit of an aircraft is not illegal, especially when one considers that other long-range weapons also provide a risk-free means of killing. The battlefield UAVs used to conduct targeted killings are part of the third generation of UAVs. The first was the development of remotely piloted ordnance, now commonly termed 'cruise missiles'. The second was the Cold War-era development of remote surveillance vehicles. Surveillance aircraft formed a key part of nuclear deterrence during the Cold War. The use of human pilots could cause embarrassment, as happened when Gary Powers' U-2 spy plane was shot down in Soviet airspace in 1960. This incident heralded the modern era of UAVs, according to Kendra Cook.[147] The first major use of UAVs was as reconnaissance craft such as the 'Lightning Bug' and 'Buffalo Hunter'.[148] Third-generation UAVs derive from Israeli deployments against Hizbullah in Lebanon in the 1980s. The United States has used these third-generation 'battlefield UAVs' since the mid 1990s.[149] There is little difference between strikes delivered by cruise missiles and those delivered by UAVs, as Michael Lewis states:

> there is nothing inherently illegal about using drones to target specific individuals. Nor is there anything legally unique about the use of unmanned drones as a weapons delivery platform that requires the creation of new or different laws to govern their use.[150]

The difference, therefore, lies in the utility and cost of these systems as compared with manned aircraft and cruise missiles.

The cost and tactical utility of UAVs leads to a second criticism: that these craft somehow make the use of force too easy, and/or that risk-free warfare is morally wrong. The most common argument is that the lack of risk involved in the use of unmanned vehicles avoids the most important calculation of risk involved in war: the potential death of service personnel.[151] This is an extension of Ignatieff's argument in *Virtual War*, which noted the asymmetry of risk involved in the NATO bombing of Serbia in 1999.[152] This asymmetry is not new; air power was used in the colonial era, although indigenous peoples were able to adapt to it and lessen its effects.[153]

UAVs are in some ways less expensive than traditional air platforms: '[T]he top-of-the-line Predator or Reaper model costs approximately US$10.5 million each, compared to the US$150 million price tag of a single F-22 fighter jet'.[154] However, this does not take into account the running costs of these vehicles. UAVs require two pilots and therefore have similar manning requirements to many conventional airframes. Because UAVs can be used for extended periods, a UAV orbit requires three UAVs and sufficient pilots to keep the orbit aloft for 24 hours a day. However, UAVs do allow for the projection of force where manned aircraft could result in a political crisis. Furthermore, their characteristics enable them to achieve a persistent precision strike capability without a risk to human operators, a situation beyond that of previous examples of the revolution in military affairs. The capture of pilots is a serious concern. For example, the public exhibition and treatment of the bodies of the crew of a downed helicopter after the Battle of Mogadishu caused significant political backlash in the United States, tempered by the fact that another US pilot, Mike Durant, had been captured during the battle.[155]

These arguments ultimately relate to Edward Luttwak's concept of 'post-heroic warfare'.[156] In his 1996 article, he notes that casualty-aversion was absent in the analysis of war: '[M]issing from such calculations is any measure of the overall foreign policy value of acquiring a means of casualty-free warfare by unescorted bomber, a weapon of circumscribed value but global reach'.[157] Luttwak's post-heroic warfare came to fruition in the Kosovo War of 1999, which Michael Ignatieff considered a 'virtual' war. The use of UAVs – implying a casualty-free method of delivering precision ordnance (the use of long-range missile systems such as Tomahawks excepted) – appears to herald an era of post-heroic warfare. Ignatieff's book, *Virtual War*, provides us with an account of externalised war in which:

> citizens are not only divested of their power to give consent. They are also demobilized. We now wage wars and few notice or care. War no longer demands the type of physical involvement or moral attention it required over the past two centuries.[158]

After 9/11 (a scant two years after Kosovo), Ignatieff's words appear as if written from a bygone era – the US population very much cares about the wars it fights abroad, even if the public does not necessarily understand the particularities of US efforts. What Ignatieff captures is the concept of war as being entirely externalised from a given population. In Ignatieff's account, this is due to the revolution in military affairs, as well as the mediation of war. Both Luttwak and Ignatieff rely on the concept of war being externalised from a democratic

56   *American targeted killings*

population. Ignatieff's book is built on warfare being completely separated from the populations of the countries that conduct it.[159]

Are either of these arguments enough to prove the inherent illegality or immorality of the use of UAVs? In the legal and ethical frameworks discussed later in this book there are no laws or explicit codes outlawing such weapons platforms. Unless one would also ban precision munitions, there are no legal codes that would also ban UAVs. Such methods are, however, in violation of the 'fair fight', which is perhaps assumed in both just war theory and IHL, since both derive from a time when the only way of delivering force required endangering one's own forces. What one can see in the use of UAVs in this manner is a political externality – an essentially subjective matter that relies on political values and choices which are connected to the legal and ethical frameworks that justify the use of violence; but such externalities cannot ultimately be used to invalidate the Obama administration's defence of targeted killings. They are, however, very important – as a value set, the use of UAVs endorses risk-free warfare, and the potential political problems that Ignatieff identifies.

A second criticism of the US use of targeted killings is the CIA's role in conducting a number of strikes. The CIA's role in targeted killings is acknowledged in media leaks and widespread reporting.[160] The actual percentage of strikes conducted by the CIA is unknown, but for present purposes this does not matter. Whether targeted killings conducted by the CIA can be defended as ethical or legal in principle is the most pressing problem, and one that the Obama administration's defence of targeted killings needs to take into account. Critics of the US use of targeted killings highlight the fact that the CIA is essentially illegitimate in using force in this manner.[161] Sourced media reports from leading media organisations and publications state that the targeted killing programme is partly overseen by the CIA, although US Air Force pilots operate the UAVs.[162] Beyond this, details are incomplete. It does appear that other – contracted – civilians are part of the targeting chains involved in UAV operations.[163] Greg Miller and Julie Tate's article also quotes a US official who states that '[Y]ou couldn't tell the difference between CIA officers, Special Forces guys and contractors.... They're all three blended together. All under the command of the CIA'.[164] This sentiment is apparent throughout the literature and reportage on the CIA's role in US targeted killings.

Is the use of the CIA to conduct targeted killings wrong in itself? The CIA, after all, derives its authority to use lethal force from both the president and Congress, and has used lethal force since its early days. However, division of the use of force between civilian and military agencies is a key principle of the laws of war. To gain the protections afforded combatants under IHL, individuals are supposed to belong to a state's military, not their intelligence agency, and unless incorporated somehow, 'are civilian in nature for the purposes of humanitarian law'.[165] Yet this is circumvented by the concept of 'double-hatting' military and civilian personnel.[166] In this manner, a person can have two roles to perform, which he or she is expected to switch between in a routine fashion. Ostensibly, this allows switching fluidly in and out of command chains, but more

American targeted killings   57

importantly, when fulfilling roles that use force, a person is considered part of a military chain of command. Critics argue that this blurs chains of command and also weakens institutional restraints on the use of force.[167]

Is this practice essentially illegal or in contravention of just war ethics? On the one hand, secrecy in the use of force is worrying, but at the same time it is not illegal. Alston defines this practice as the 'intentional blurring of what were once generally considered to be legally mandated hard and fast distinctions'.[168] However, this 'blurring' is performed in line with the rule of law. P. W. Singer might prefer soldiers and intelligence operatives to stay separate, but since these acts are conducted within the legal framework of the Constitution, it is difficult to argue that they are in violation of the rule of law at face value. Furthermore, one only has to look at the widespread involvement of private contractors in Western militaries to note that the idea of an exclusive military force is out of step with reality – states now outsource and integrate their military forces with civilian government employees and private contractors.[169] Since it appears from available evidence that the actual operators of the military equipment are military, 'hatted' as such, civilian status cannot be used against the CIA's involvement as such. What can be stated is that while individual operators may have clear status under the law, the exact command chains are unknown, and this fact is key to the discussions of just war theory and responsibility discussed in Chapter 6.

But on what basis is it legitimate to identify someone as a permissible target? The US government has not released the criteria by which it targets suspected al-Qaeda members. As the CIA is not a military organisation, it is not known what baseline it uses to target individuals. Despite this, some sources have made available outline details of the process by which targeted killings are authorised.[170] Importantly, there appear to be two methods of targeting network members. There are 'known' (targeted) killings, and also an emerging form of strike known as a 'signature strike'. Signature strikes are so called because rather than knowing the precise identity of the target, they function by identifying a 'pattern of life'. This pattern is taken to indicate that the persons are either terrorists or militants, and thus legitimate targets. The questions that this raises are examined further in Chapter 6. The key problem is that the standards for identification are not publicly known. The existence of signature strikes is on record from an unnamed source in the CIA.[171] The 'invention' of this method has been attributed to 'Roger', current chief of the CIA's Counterterrorism Center.[172] The existence of this type of targeting is backed by considerable investigative reporting by the *Wall Street Journal* and the *Washington Post*, as is the unattributed defence of this mode of targeting. This appears to be ample evidence for its existence. Since this mode of targeting is arguably less defensible than 'normal' targeting methods, the reason to raise the possibility of its existence appears to be in order to defend and legitimise it. One source that confirmed the existence of these strikes also stated that they are extremely effective: '[T]wice as many wanted terrorists have been killed in signature strikes than personality strikes'.[173] It is empirically impossible to identify differences in the effects that targeted killings

58 *American targeted killings*

and signature strikes have on networked non-state actors, given the constraints identified in the previous chapter. Although one suspects that they could have the same effect, there exists no evidence to suggest that their effects are entirely similar. The difference between 'known' and 'signature' strikes is important; however, substantial components of both types of operation are similar. The differences between the two are important when considering the long-term legitimacy of targeted killings, and will be discussed in Chapter 6.

Regardless of their efficacy, signature strikes have a legitimacy problem. Critics of US targeted killings argue that signature strikes are in many ways worse than 'normal' targeted killings, and the practice of targeting by 'pattern of life' criteria is widely reviled by critics. Jeremy Scahill compared them to walking into a shopping mall and opening fire onto a crowd of people, labelling it murder.[174] In a similar fashion, Jefferson Morley labelled David Petraeus' request to expand the use of signature strikes in Yemen a 'homicidal escalation'.[175] This method of targeting recently led to members of Congress writing to President Obama to question the use of methods that axiomatically do not use 100 per cent target identification.[176] The problem with this criticism is that it makes a key assumption about targeting knowledge that is not available – the standards by which persons are identified as legitimate targets. Key to this critique of targeted killings is the concept of objective positive target identification – that a target can be positively identified as a 100 per cent legitimate target in an objective manner. The normal military practice of targeting, however, is at odds with this concept. Both just war theory and IHL allow for subjective target identification. Legitimate targets must be positively identified, but the actual criteria on which this is done are contained in neither treaty law nor ethics. The function of knowledge in both frameworks creates a bivalent logical distinction between targets, but in practice such distinction is not possible without positive self-identification from the target itself.

To explain this difference, it is worth considering the function of these categories in conventional warfare. There are two important elements to this. First, the convention of pitched battle (a necessity for wars of the Napoleonic era and prior) allows for a bivalent distinction between 'us' and 'them': in effect, by removing violence from areas that civilians inhabit, a person's physical presence on a Napoleonic-era battlefield allows for bivalent distinctions to be drawn about their identity. The second method of self-identification is via uniform: by wearing a military uniform a person self-identifies as belonging to a structured military organisation, and thus as a belligerent. Therefore when targeting a non-conventional enemy, which is customarily a legitimate practice, the type of knowledge assumed possible by the critics of signature strikes is not necessarily available. Therefore the practice of targeting persons on less than complete knowledge is not, in standards of practice, essentially illegitimate. There are, however, considerable problems with conducting such strikes and remaining within the boundaries of IHL and just war ethics. These problems are examined in Chapters 5 and 6.

Conclusion

The targeting of individuals by states is predicated on the internal legitimacy of doing so, and also on the legitimacy conferred by the sovereign authority of the state. In the case of the United States, this is the public. An important internal legitimating factor in US culture is that the targeting itself takes place within the rule of law. Furthermore, the Obama administration derives its authority to target al-Qaeda from the 2001 AUMF, thus deriving legitimation for its actions from Congress. The character of the law itself is not eternal, and is subject to domestic political factors. Where rule of law norm transitions occur, the ability and inclination of the state to conduct these policies can change, as happened after 9/11.

Targeted killings are not inherently wrong as an activity; however, the way in which they are legitimised relies on the defining features of the Obama administration's defence – that they are lawful and morally acceptable acts of war. Criticisms of drones tend to ignore the role played by, and development of, long-range munitions in war, and exaggerate the novelty of UAVs. However, the CIA's operational command of these methods and its use of signature strikes, although not illegitimate in themselves, are a challenge for the Obama administration's overall defence of targeted killings. This entire basis for legitimising targeted killings is, however, predicated on them being acts of war. In the next chapter, we will look at the question of whether the president has the authority to resort to the use of force, rather than relying on law enforcement methods.

Notes

1　Greg Miller and Julie Tate, 'CIA Shifts Focus to Killing Targets', *Washington Post*, 2 September 2011.
2　Church Committee, 'United States Senate'.
3　The congressional approval awarded the President the specific power to target individuals, see Authorization for Use of Military Force.
4　Samuel Issacharoff and Richard H. Pildes, 'Targeted Warfare: Individuating Enemy Responsibility', *New York University Law Review* 88(5) (2013): 12–40.
5　John Yoo, *Crisis and Command: The History of Executive Power from George Washington to George W. Bush* (New York, NY: Kaplan, 2010).
6　Anderson, 'Targeted Killing'.
7　Mary Ellen O'Connell, 'When Is a War Not a War: The Myth of the Global War on Terror', *ILSA Journal of International and Comparative Law* 12 (2005).
8　Jens D. Ohlin, 'Targeted Killings Symposium: Jens David Ohlin Responds to Craig Martin', *Opinio Juris*, 4 June 2012. For a discussion of the principle of transnational conflict see Geoffrey Corn and Eric Jensen, 'Transnational Armed Conflict: A "Principled" Approach to the Regulation of Counter-Terror Combat Operations', *Israel Law Review* 42(1) (2010).
9　Peter Finn and Anne E. Kornblut, 'Guantanamo Bay: Why Obama Hasn't Fulfilled His Promise to Close the Facility', *Washington Post*, 24 April 2011.
10　National Commission on Terrorist Attacks upon the United States (NCTAUS), *The 9/11 Commission Report: Final Report of the National Commission on Terrorist Attacks Upon the United States* (New York, NY and London: W. W. Norton, 2004): 108.
11　NCTAUS, *9/11 Commission Report*: 116–33.

60 *American targeted killings*

12 George W. Bush, 'Address to a Joint Session of Congress' (Speech, US Capitol Building, Washington, DC, 21 September 2001).
13 Barry Buzan, 'Will the "Global War on Terrorism" be the New Cold War?', *International Affairs* 82(6) (2006): 1115.
14 Lawrence Freedman, 'The Coming War on Terrorism', in *Superterrorism: Policy Responses*, edited by Lawrence Freedman (Oxford: Blackwell, 2002): 40–1.
15 Stuart Croft, 'British Jihadis and the British War on Terror', *Defence Studies* 7(3) (2007).
16 John Gearson, 'The Nature of Modern Terrorism', *Political Quarterly* 73 (2002): 20.
17 George W. Bush, 'Address to the Nation' (2001).
18 Charles Tilly, ed., *The Formation of National States in Western Europe* (Princeton University Press, 1975).
19 Francis Fukuyama, *The End of History and the Last Man* (London: Hamilton, 1992).
20 Nils Petter Gleditsch *et al.*, 'Armed Conflict 1946–2001: A New Dataset', *Journal of Peace Research* 39 (2002): 616.
21 Mary Kaldor, *New and Old Wars: Organized Violence in a Global Era* (Stanford University Press, 1999).
22 Meredith R. Sarkees and Franck W. Wayman, *Resort to War: A Data Guide to Inter-State, Extra-State, Intra-State, and Non-State Wars, 1816–2007* (Washington, DC: CQ Press, 2010).
23 See, for example, Adam Edwards and Peter Gill, *Transnational Organised Crime: Perspectives on Global Security* (New York: Routledge, 2003).
24 Michael Kenney, *From Pablo to Osama: Trafficking and Terrorist Networks, Government Bureaucracies, and Competitive Adaptation* (Pennsylvania State University Press, 2007).
25 George W. Bush, 'Address to the Nation on 9/11' (Speech, The White House, Washington, DC, 11 September 2001).
26 Paul Hoffman, 'Human Rights and Terrorism', *Human Rights Quarterly* 26(4) (2004): 939–40; David H. Dunn, 'Bush, 11 September and the Conflicting Strategies of the "War on Terrorism"', *Irish Studies in International Affairs* 16 (2005): 14; Thomas J. Badey, 'US Counter-Terrorism: Change in Approach, Continuity in Policy', *Contemporary Security Policy* 27(2) (2006).
27 Plaw, *Targeting Terrorists*: 111–13.
28 Bush, 'Address to a Joint Session of Congress'.
29 Barry Buzan, 'Rethinking Security after the Cold War', *Cooperation and Conflict* 32(1) (1997).
30 Ole Wæver, 'Securitization and Desecuritization', *On Security* 66 (1995): 55.
31 Michael C. Williams, 'Words, Images, Enemies: Securitization and International Politics', *International Studies Quarterly* 47(4) (2003): 513.
32 Lawrence Freedman, *Deterrence* (Cambridge: Polity Press, 2004): 2.
33 Michael Howard, *War and the Liberal Conscience* (London: Hurst, 2008): 249.
34 Richard H. Ullman, 'Redefining Security', *International Security* 8(1) (1983); Neville Brown, 'Climate, Ecology and International Security', *Survival* 31(6) (1989); Ole Wæver and David Carlton, *Identity, Migration and the New Security Agenda in Europe* (London: Pinter, 1993).
35 Buzan, 'Rethinking Security'.
36 See, for example, theorists of biopolitics – Michael Dillon and Julian Reid, *The Liberal Way of War: Killing to Make Life Live* (London: Taylor & Francis, 2009).
37 Obama, 'Remarks by the President on National Security'.
38 Gallie, 'Essentially Contested Concepts'.
39 Sofia Näsström, 'The Legitimacy of the People', *Political Theory* 35(5) (2007).
40 Edward S. Herman and Noam Chomsky, *Manufacturing Consent: The Political Economy of the Mass Media* (New York, NY: Pantheon Books, 1988).
41 Walter Lippmann, *Public Opinion* (New York, NY: Harcourt, 1922).

American targeted killings   61

42 Habermas, *Legitimation Crisis*.
43 Authorization for Use of Military Force, 107–40.
44 This involved developing new inter-agency models of intelligence sharing and organisation; see William W. Newmann, 'Reorganizing for National Security and Homeland Security', *Public Administration Review* 62 (2002): 120–9.
45 The Uniting and Strengthening America by Providing Appropriate Tools Required to Intercept and Obstruct Terrorism Act of 2001 USA PATRIOT Act, 115 Stat. 272 (2001), henceforth the 'Patriot Act'.
46 Obama, 'Remarks by the President on National Security'.
47 Panetta, 'Director's Remarks'.
48 Holder, 'Northwestern University Speech'.
49 Jeh Johnson, 'Speech to the Heritage Foundation'; Jeh Johnson, 'National Security Law'.
50 Stephen Preston, 'Remarks on the Rule of Law' (Speech, Harvard Law School, Harvard, MA, 10 April 2012).
51 Koh, 'Obama Administration'.
52 Brennan, 'Strengthening Our Security'; Brennan, 'Ethics and Efficacy'.
53 Google, 'Your Interview with the President, 2012', *Google* (2012).
54 Obama, 'Remarks by the President on National Security'.
55 Obama, 'Remarks by the President in Address to the Nation'.
56 Barack Obama, 'Nobel Peace Prize Acceptance Speech' (Speech, Oslo, Norway, 10 December 2009).
57 Koh, 'Obama Administration'.
58 Harold Hongju Koh, 'The Lawfulness of the U.S. Operation Against Osama bin Laden', *Opinio Juris*, 19 May 2011.
59 Brennan, 'Strengthening Our Security'.
60 Jeh Johnson, 'National Security Law'.
61 Holder, 'Northwestern University Speech'.
62 Preston, 'Remarks on the Rule of Law'.
63 Audrey Kurth Cronin, *How Terrorism Ends: Understanding the Decline and Demise of Terrorist Campaigns* (Princeton University Press, 2009): 8.
64 The precise amount of change is up for debate: Marc Sageman and Bruce Hoffman, see Sageman, *Leaderless Jihad*; Bruce Hoffman, 'The Myth of Grass-Roots Terrorism: Why Osama Bin Laden Still Matters', *Foreign Affairs* 87 (2008); Marc Sageman and Bruce Hoffman, 'Does Osama Still Call the Shots?: Debating the Containment of Al Qaeda's Leadership', *Foreign Affairs* 87(4) (2008); Bruce Hoffman, 'The Leaderless Jihad's Leader: Why Osama Bin Laden Mattered', *Foreign Affairs* 90 (2011).
65 Cronin, *How Terrorism Ends*: 191–2.
66 Audrey Cronin, *Ending Terrorism: Lessons for Policymakers from the Decline and Demise of Terrorist Groups* (London: IISS, Adelphi Papers vol. 394, 2008): 95–8.
67 Peter R. Neumann, *Old and New Terrorism* (London: Polity Press, 2009): 57–62.
68 See, for example, Alston, 'CIA and Targeted Killings'; Proulx, 'If the Hat Fits, Wear It'; O'Connell, 'Unlawful Killing'.
69 *Al-Aulaqi* v. *Obama*.
70 Ibrahim Mothana, 'How Drones Help Al Qaeda', *New York Times*, 13 June 2012; Peter W. Singer, 'Do Drones Undermine Democracy?', *New York Times*, 21 January 2012; Vicki Divoll, 'Targeted Killings: Who's Checking the Executive Branch?', *Los Angeles Times*, 25 March 2012; Charles Krauthammer, 'Barack Obama: Drone Warrior', *Washington Post*, 1 June 2012.
71 Alston, 'CIA and Targeted Killings'; O'Connell, 'Unlawful Killing'.
72 David Kilcullen and Andrew Exum, 'Death from Above, Outrage Down Below', *New York Times*, 17 May 2009.

62 *American targeted killings*

73 Howard A. Wachtel, 'Targeting Osama Bin Laden: Examining the Legality of Assassination as a Tool of US Foreign Policy', *Duke Law Journal* 55(3) (2005); Raines, 'Osama, Augustine, and Assassination'; John Tinetti, *Lawful Targeted Killing or Assassination: A Roadmap for Operators in the Global War on Terror* (Newport, RI: Naval War College, 2004); Thomas Byron Hunter, 'Targeted Killing: Self-Defense, Preemption, and the War on Terrorism', *Journal of Strategic Security* 2(2) (2009); Byman, 'Do Targeted Killings Work?'; Ulrich, 'Gloves Were Never On'; Daniel Kretzmer, 'Targeted Killing of Suspected Terrorists: Extra-Judicial Executions or Legitimate Means of Defence?', *European Journal of International Law* 16(2) (2005); Kramer, 'Legality of Targeted Drone Attacks'; Abraham U. Kannof, 'Dueling Nationalities: Dual Citizenship, Dominant & Effective Nationality, and the Case of Anwar Al-Aulaqi', *Emory International Law Review* 25(3) (2011); Radsan and Murphy, 'Evolution of Law and Policy'.

74 Eric Posner and Adrian Vermeule, 'Accommodating Emergencies', *Stanford Law Review* 56 (2003); Eric Posner and Adrian Vermeule, *Terror in the Balance: Security, Liberty, and the Courts* (Oxford University Press, 2007); Yoo, *Crisis and Command*.

75 Ira S. Rubinstein, Ronald D. Lee and Paul M. Schwartz, 'Data Mining and Internet Profiling: Emerging Regulatory and Technological Approaches', *The University of Chicago Law Review* 75 (2008): 262–3.

76 Christopher Dandeker, *Surveillance, Power and Modernity: Bureaucracy and Discipline from 1700 to the Present Day* (Cambridge: Polity, 1990).

77 Tom R. Tyler, *Legitimacy and Criminal Justice: International Perspectives* (New York, NY: Russell Sage Foundation, 2007).

78 Kenneth Roth, 'The Law of War in the War on Terror: Washington's Abuse of Enemy Combatants', *Foreign Affairs* 83 (2004); Margaret L. Satterthwaite, 'Rendered Meaningless: Extraordinary Rendition and the Rule of Law', *The George Washington Law Review* 75 (2006).

79 It is the opinion of this author that waterboarding and associated/similar activities constitute torture. However, this book uses the term 'enhanced interrogation' due to the difference of opinion between the Bush and Obama administrations over this issue.

80 Obama, 'Remarks by the President on National Security'.

81 See 18 USC § 2340(1):

> 'torture' means an act committed by a person acting under the colour of law specifically intended to inflict severe physical or mental pain or suffering (other than pain or suffering incidental to lawful sanctions) upon another person within his custody or physical control.

82 Jay S. Bybee, Standards of Conduct for Interrogation under 18 USC [Sections] 2340–2340a: Memorandum for Alberto R. Gonzales, Counsel to the President (Washington, DC: Office of the Assistant Attorney General, 2002); Jay S. Bybee, Memorandum for John Rizzo, Acting General Counsel of the Central Intelligence Agency: Interrogation of Al Qaeda Operative (Washington, DC: US Department of Justice, Office of Legal Counsel, 1 August 2002); John Yoo, Memo to Alberto Gonzales (2002).

83 David Luban, 'Liberalism, Torture, and the Ticking Bomb', in *Intervention, Terrorism, and Torture: Contemporary Challenges to Just War Theory*, edited by Steven P. Lee (Dordrecht: Springer, 2007); Philippe Sands, *Torture Team: Uncovering War Crimes in the Land of the Free* (London: Penguin, 2009).

84 James D. Boys, 'What's So Extraordinary About Rendition?', *International Journal of Human Rights* 15(4) (2011).

85 Boys, 'What's So Extraordinary?': 592.

86 George W. Bush, 'President Discusses Creation of Military Commissions to Try Suspected Terrorists' (Speech, White House, Washington, DC, 6 September 2006).

American targeted killings   63

87 Giovanni Claudio Fava, 'Report on the Alleged Use of European Countries by the CIA for the Transportation and Illegal Detention of Prisoners' (European Parliament, 2007).

88 Fiona De Londras, 'Guantánamo Bay: Towards Legality?', *The Modern Law Review* 71(1) (2008).

89 Bush, 'President Discusses Creation of Military Commissions'. See also defences of practices such as enhanced interrogation by John Yoo – see John Yoo, *War by Other Means: An Insider's Account of the War on Terror* (New York: Atlantic Monthly Press, 2006).

90 ACLU, 'Key OLC Memoranda Relating to Interrogation, Detention, Rendition and/ or Surveillance' (Washington, DC: American Civil Liberties Union, 2009). See also Albert R. Gonzales, 'Remarks at the University of Chicago Law School', *Chicago Journal of International Law* 7 (2006).

91 Obama, 'Remarks by the President on National Security'; Obama, 'Remarks by the President in Address to the Nation'.

92 Charles Dunlap Jr., 'Does Lawfare Need an Apologia?', *Case Western Reserve Journal of International Law* 43 (2010).

93 David Luban, 'Lawfare and Legal Ethics in Guantanamo', *Stanford Law Review* 60 (2007): 1984.

94 Charles Dunlap Jr, 'Law and Military Interventions: Preserving Humanitarian Values in 21st Conflicts' (Presentation, Humanitarian Challenges in Military Intervention Conference, Harvard University, 29 November 2001): 1.

95 Tung Yin, 'Boumediene and Lawfare', *University of Richmond Law Review* 43 (2008): 879.

96 David Scheffer, 'Lawfare and War Crimes Tribunal: Whose Lawfare Is It, Anyway?', *Case Western Reserve Journal of International Law* 43 (2010): 216.

97 Mary Ellen O'Connell, 'The Choice of Law against Terrorism', *Journal of National Security Law and Policy* 4 (2010); Alston, 'Report of the Special Rapporteur'.

98 George W. Bush, 'Military Order of November 13, 2001 Detention, Treatment, and Trial of Certain Non-Citizens in the War against Terrorism', *Federal Register* (Washington, DC: Executive Office of the President, 2001): 57833.

99 *Johnson* v. *Eisentrager*, 339 US 763 (1950).

100 Allison M. Danner, 'Defining Unlawful Enemy Combatants: A Centripetal Story', *Texas International Law Journal* 43 (2007).

101 See *Hamdi* v. *Rumsfeld*, 542 US 507 (2004); *Rasul* v. *Bush*, 542 US 466 (2004). *Rasul* v. *Bush* established the right for detainees to challenge their detention under the habeas corpus statute, 28 U.S.3.§ 2241. Their ability to petition for habeas corpus was restricted by the Detainee Treatment Act (2005), which was subsequently rejected by the Supreme Court in *Hamdan* v. *Rumsfeld*, 548 US 557 (2006). This in turn led to the Military Commissions Act (2006), again restricting detainee access to federal courts. The Supreme Court reaffirmed the detainees' right to seek habeas corpus in *Boumediene* v. *Bush*, 128 S. Ct. 2229 (2008). This ruling left the process by which these detainees are interned intact. See Jennifer K. Elsea and Michael John Garcia, 'Enemy Combatant Detainees: *Habeas Corpus* Challenges in Federal Court', *Congressional Research Service*, 3 February 2010.

102 Johan Steyn, 'Guantanamo Bay: The Legal Black Hole', *International and Comparative Law Quarterly* 53 (2004); Diane M. Amann, 'Guantanamo', *Columbia Journal of Transnational Law* 42 (2003).

103 Diane Priest, 'CIA Holds Terror Suspects in Secret Prisons', *Washington Post*, 2 November 2005; Leila N. Sadat, 'Ghost Prisoners and Black Sites: Extraordinary Rendition under International Law', *Case Western Reserve Journal of International Law* 37 (2005); Mark Danner, 'US Torture: Voices from the Black Sites', *The New York Review of Books* 56(6) (2009).

64 American targeted killings

104 *Hamdi* v. *Rumsfeld*. established that US citizens (including dual-citizens) had the right to seek review of their status and detention in the civilian courts.
105 Neil A. Lewis, 'Red Cross Finds Detainee Abuse in Guantánamo', *Washington Post*, 29 November 2004. For reports of abuse in CIA detention facilities, see Geoff Loane, *ICRC Report on the Treatment of Fourteen 'High Value Detainees' in CIA Custody* (Washington, DC: International Committee of the Red Cross, 2007).
106 Scott Michaelsen and Scott C. Shershow, 'Beyond and Before the Law at Guantánamo', *Peace Review* 16(3) (2004): 293.
107 Barack Obama, 'Executive Order 13492: Review and Disposition of Individuals Detained at the Guantánamo Bay Naval Base and Closure of Detention Facilities', *Federal Register* (Washington, DC: Executive Office of the President, 2009).
108 Obama, 'Executive Order 13492'.
109 Stephen Grey, *Ghost Plane: The Inside Story of the CIA's Secret Rendition Programme* (London: Hurst, 2006).
110 Human Rights Watch, 'Black Hole: The Fate of Islamists Rendered to Egypt' (Report, Human Rights Watch, 2005).
111 Scott Shane, David Johnston and James Risen, 'Secret US Endorsement of Severe Interrogations', *New York Times*, 4 October 2007; Mark Danner, 'US Torture'; Jessica Wolfendale, 'The Myth of "Torture Lite"', *Ethics and International Affairs* 23(1) (2009).
112 George W. Bush, *Decision Points* (London: Virgin, 2010); Richard B. Cheney and Liz Cheney, *In My Time: A Personal and Political Memoir* (London: Threshold, 2011); Yoo, *War by Other Means*.
113 Richard Cheney, 'Speech to the American Enterprise Institute' (Speech, Washington, DC, 21 March 2009).
114 Obama, 'Remarks by the President on National Security'.
115 Carl Schmitt, *The Concept of the Political* (University of Chicago Press, 1996): 28.
116 Carl Schmitt, 'The Theory of the Partisan', *The New Centennial Review* 4(3) (1963): 63–4.
117 Carl Schmitt, tr. Jeffrey Seitzer, *Constitutional Theory* (Durham: Duke University Press, 2008): 166.
118 Liminality is a concept developed by Arnold van Gennep. See Arnold van Gennep, *Les Rites De Passage. Etitude Systematique Des Rites* (1909).
119 Arthur Saniotis, 'Re-Enchanting Terrorism: Jihadists as "Liminal Beings"', *Studies in Conflict and Terrorism* 28(6) (2005).
120 Cecilia Menjívar, 'Liminal Legality: Salvadoran and Guatemalan Immigrants' Lives in the United States', *American Journal of Sociology* 111(4) (2006).
121 Carlton F. W. Larson, 'The Forgotten Constitutional Law of Treason and the Enemy Combatant Problem, *University of Pennsylvania Law Review* 154 (2005).
122 Yoo, *Crisis and Command*.
123 See *Hamdi* v. *Rumsfeld*. The Bush administration relied on preventing these persons from gaining access to the US court system.
124 National Security Act Sec. 503 (e).
125 Human Rights Watch, 'Letter to President Obama: Targeted Killings by the US Government' (Letter, Human Rights Watch, 2011).
126 Kenneth B. Moss, *Undeclared War and the Future of U.S. Foreign Policy* (Baltimore, MD: Johns Hopkins University Press, 2008): 23.
127 Yoo, *Crisis and Command*: 353.
128 David Kucinich, 'Letter to President Obama' (Letter, Washington, DC: Congress of the United States, 12 June 2012).
129 Yoo, *Crisis and Command*.
130 NCTAUS, *9/11 Commission Report*: 101.
131 Church Committee, 'United States Senate': 5.
132 Church Committee, 'United States Senate': 257.

133 NCTAUS, *9/11 Commission Report.*
134 Authorization for Use of Military Force.
135 White House, 'Executive Order 12333', *Federal Register* (Washington, DC: White House, 1981): Sec. 3.5(h).
136 White House 'Executive Order 13470 Further Amendments to Executive Order 12333, United States Intelligence Activities', *Federal Register* (Washington, DC: White House, 2008): Sec. 4(g).
137 White House, 'Executive Order 13470': Sec. 4(g).
138 Jo Becker and Scott Shane, 'Secret "Kill List" Proves a Test of Obama's Principles and Will', *New York Times*, 29 May 2012.
139 Authorization for Use of Military Force.
140 Joint Resolution Concerning the War Powers of Congress and the President, Pub.L. 93–148.
141 Curtis A. Bradley and Jack L. Goldsmith, 'Congressional Authorization and the War on Terrorism', *Harvard Law Review* 118(7) (2005): 2133.
142 Jack Serle, 'Yemen Strikes Visualised', *Bureau of Investigative Journalism*, 29 March 2012.
143 See, for example, Benjamin, *Drone Warfare.*
144 John Kaag and Sarah Kreps, *Drone Warfare* (Cambridge, UK and Malden, MA: Polity, 2014): 143.
145 Adam Entous, Siobhan Gorman and Matthew Rosenberg, 'Drone Attacks Split US Officials', *The Wall Street Journal*, 4 June 2011.
146 David G. Newman, *Flying Fast Jets: Human Factors and Performance Limitations* (Farnham: Ashgate Publishing, 2014): 33.
147 Kendra Cook, 'The Silent Force Multiplier: The History and Role of UAVs in Warfare', *Aerospace Conference, 2007 IEEE* (2006): 2.
148 Cook, 'The Silent Force Multiplier': 3.
149 Thomas B. Lukaszewicz, *Joint Doctrine and UAV Employment* (Newport, RI: Naval War College, 1996); Daniel L. Haulman, *US Unmanned Aerial Vehicles in Combat, 1991–2003* (Air Force Historical Research Agency, 2003).
150 Michael W. Lewis, *Submission to Subcommittee Hearing: 'Drones II'* (Washington, DC: U.S. House of Representatives Committee on Oversight and Government Reform Subcommittee on National Security and Foreign Affairs, 2010).
151 Peter Singer, *Wired for War: The Robotics Revolution and Conflict in the Twenty-First Century* (2009); O'Connell, 'Seductive Drones'.
152 Michael Ignatieff, *Virtual War: Kosovo and Beyond* (London: Chatto & Windus, 2000).
153 David E. Omissi, *Air Power and Colonial Control: The Royal Air Force, 1919–1939* (Manchester University Press, 1990): 132.
154 Michael J. Boyle, 'The Costs and Consequences of Drone Warfare', *International Affairs* 89(1) (2013): 22.
155 Mark Bowden, *Black Hawk Down: A Story of Modern War* (London: Bantam Press, 1999).
156 Luttwak, 'Post-Heroic Military Policy'.
157 Luttwak, 'Post-Heroic Military Policy': 122.
158 Ignatieff, *Virtual War*: 184.
159 Ignatieff, *Virtual War*: 184.
160 Greg Miller, 'CIA Seeks New Authority to Expand Yemen Drone Campaign', *Washington Post*, 19 April 2012.
161 Alston, 'CIA and Targeted Killings'.
162 Greg Miller and Tate, 'CIA Shifts Focus'.
163 David S. Cloud, 'Civilian Contractors Playing Key Roles in U.S. Drone Operations', *Los Angeles Times*, 29 December 2011.
164 Greg Miller and Tate, 'CIA Shifts Focus'.

66 *American targeted killings*

165 Michael N. Schmitt, 'Humanitarian Law and Direct Participation in Hostilities by Private Contractors or Civilian Employees War', *Chicago Journal of International Law* 5 (2005): 525.
166 Peter W. Singer, 'Double-Hatting Around the Law: The Problem with Morphing Warrior, Spy and Civilian Roles', *Armed Forces Journal* 1 (2010).
167 Alston, 'CIA and Targeted Killings': 353.
168 Alston, 'CIA and Targeted Killings': 353.
169 Peter W. Singer, 'Outsourcing War', *Foreign Affairs* 84 (2005).
170 Daniel Klaidman, *Kill or Capture: The War on Terror and the Soul of the Obama Presidency* (New York, NY: Houghton Mifflin Harcourt, 2012).
171 Greg Miller and Tate, 'CIA Shifts Focus'; Adam Entous, Siobhan Gorman, and Julian E. Barnes, 'U.S. Relaxes Drone Rules', *The Wall Street Journal*, 26 April 2012.
172 Greg Miller, 'At CIA, a Convert to Islam Leads the Terrorism Hunt', *Washington Post*, 25 March 2012.
173 Entous, Gorman and Barnes, 'U.S. Relaxes Drone Rules'.
174 Jeremy Scahill, 'Interview on MSNBC' (Interview, MSBNC, 2 June 2012).
175 Jefferson Morley, 'Petraeus and the Signature of U.S. Terror', *Salon*, 19 April 2012.
176 Kucinich, 'Letter to President Obama'.

3 War and law enforcement

> the President is authorized to use all necessary and appropriate force against those nations, organizations, or persons he determines planned, authorized, committed, or aided the terrorist attacks that occurred on September 11, 2001.
>
> Authorization for Use of Military Force, 2001[1]

> To say that force is sometimes necessary is not a call to cynicism – it is a recognition of history; the imperfections of man and the limits of reason.
>
> Barack Obama[2]

Introduction

The Obama administration's defence of targeted killings hinges on the idea that the United States is at war with al-Qaeda, and that targeted killings represent a necessary act in the context of this conflict. It stands to reason that to define people as military targets, using the language of war, war of some form has to exist. Some argue that this kind of language, and way of thinking, is inappropriate. For example, Christopher Greenwood cautions against using the term 'war' in this context, because 'the concept of war in international law is confined to conflicts between states'; but this definition of war is derived from international law, not wider cultural or political understandings of what war is or represents.[3]

The problem with taking international law as a starting point for inquiry is that war is both a social and political concept, as well as a legal term of art. Taking the definition of war as defined in international law to be a starting point limits analysis, in part because what strategists (and states) might term war often falls well outside the stricter boundaries of international law. Nonetheless, the international law concept of war (and armed conflict) is important and will be examined in the following chapter. The real issue for some is whether a de facto state of war, or armed conflict, exists between the United States and al-Qaeda, regardless of whether this conflict, or actions taken within it, are legal or illegal under international law. The existence of war and its legality are often confused, particularly in the international law literature, which – for quite obvious reasons – is primarily concerned with the legal analysis of instances of political violence and conflict. Arguments of some lawyers, such as Mary Ellen O'Connell,

68   *War and law enforcement*

regarding the illegality of using military means against al-Qaeda ignore the fact that wars outside the strict definitions of international law exist, and that the non-applicability of IHL does not end a conflict.[4] Similarly, legal arguments in support of targeted killings sometimes presuppose that the discursive act of proclaiming war creates one.[5]

For present purposes, legal definitions are less important than the political and strategic choices that govern the recourse to the use of force and violence. The 2001 AUMF expanded the options available to the president to use against al-Qaeda to include military force.[6] Yet even if a state of armed conflict can be held to exist between the United States and al-Qaeda, this act does not answer the question of whether targeted killings are a necessary use of force within that armed conflict. Defining terrorists as enemies enables the use of military force against them, but the US use of military force is constrained by necessity, or is at least legitimised by a justification that the resort to violence is a necessary act.

The use of military force against security threats is contingent on the president's decision to use such means. For instance, in the 1990s a number of peace-keeping missions posed international security threats involving violent non-state actors, yet the Clinton administration refrained from using military means to contribute to their resolution. While humanitarian interventions were perceived by some as vitally important, Wyn Bowen and David Dunn state that 'while such universal missions have a place in the United States' moral and rhetorical tradition in foreign relations they are not a prudent basis for policy'.[7] The role of politics and perceived necessity is, in this case, clear; as Robert DiPrizio states, the 'response [to future humanitarian crises] will depend chiefly on the administration's perception of relevant security interests'.[8] Therefore, the role of the executive branch in justifying the use of force is important.

The language of necessity is often used interchangeably in debate about targeted killings. For example, there is the concept of necessity, with regards to self-defence in international law (as a reason to use force), as well as the implicit concept of necessity within IHL (that violence is only legal when it is necessary to achieve a military objective). In the present context, it is the concept of necessity regarding the use of military force in lieu of law enforcement measures. Both the Bush administration and the Obama administration have argued that the use of military force against individuals is a necessary component of the conflict between the United States and al-Qaeda. In the Obama administration, key claims about the necessity of targeted killings have been made by Obama, Koh, Panetta, Holder and Brennan.[9]

One must recognise the presence of the realist argument: that war exists simply because the executive branch states that it does, and that the question of necessity is entirely irrelevant. Alternatively, some authors, such as Jeff McMahan, argue a need for novel legal regimes. McMahan himself argues for an in-between legal regime in which terrorists are recognised as part criminals, part combatants.[10] It is clear from the Obama administration's discourse that it does not predicate its defence on either position. Instead, senior Obama administration figures articulate a position that relies on the fact that war exists de facto and that targeted killings are a necessary act within that war. Even though it is argued that US actions have had a considerable effect on al-Qaeda's operational capacity, senior Obama administration figures such as John Brennan still argue that the use of force is necessary: '[T]he core of al-Qa'ida – its leadership based in Pakistan – though severely crippled, still retains the intent and capability to attack the United States and our allies'.[11]

To what extent are such claims true? If the Obama administration's position that the use of targeted killings is a necessary act is shown to be demonstrably false, then its claim to legitimacy will be undermined. Moreover, if its decision to favour lethal militarised means over law enforcement options is illegal, then this would prevent the president from defining terrorists as potential targets of military force.

The first area of criticism consists of persons who claim that war between the United States and al-Qaeda either does not exist or should not exist. These arguments are either a direct or indirect call for the application of the law enforcement paradigm. Philip Alston encapsulates the indirect approach. In his report to the UN Human Rights Council, he argues that war does not exist (in terms of international law) and therefore the law enforcement paradigm (Alston is concerned with the application of IHRL) applies.[12] The second, more forceful, argument is that war *should* not exist between the United States and al-Qaeda.[13] This second argument is part of a wider criticism of US targeted killings – that rather than kill people, the US government should be treating terrorists as criminals. Among the key proponents of this argument is Mary Ellen O'Connell, who argues forcefully for the application of law enforcement measures, not military means.[14] Contained within this arena of criticism is the implicit idea that the law enforcement paradigm can be applied, a point that is contested by those who favour, or defend, military approaches.[15] Here, the Obama administration argues that the choice favoured by O'Connell and others does not exist, and that there exist certain places where military means such as targeted killings are required to effectively fight al-Qaeda. As John Brennan argues:

> The reality, however, is that since 2001 such unilateral captures by U.S. forces outside of 'hot' battlefields, like Afghanistan, have been exceedingly rare…. These terrorists are skilled at seeking remote, inhospitable terrain – places where the United State and our partners simply do not have the ability to arrest or capture them.[16]

Another alternative is state-building, which some argue is an alternative to militarised counterterrorism.[17] This is an important argument. The administration's claim that targeted killings are necessary rests in part on their necessity in areas beyond the reach of legitimate authorities. State-building, as encapsulated in counter-insurgency and capacity building, would give rise to the very choice that O'Connell and others argue prohibits the employment of targeted killings.

State-building is in essence a strategy – aiding allied states to increase pressure on al-Qaeda. Those who argue that the United States should focus on

70 *War and law enforcement*

state-building are in essence arguing that targeted killings are not necessary (or are counterproductive) to this effort. If the United States is at war with al-Qaeda, these critics argue, then targeted killings are the wrong method of conducting this war. As Dennis Blair, former Director of National Intelligence, states: 'the important question today is whether continued unilateral drone attacks will substantially reduce Al Qaeda's capabilities. They will not'.[18] In short, since targeted killings cannot end the conflict, they cannot be considered a military necessity. This argument suffers from the implicit assumption that all necessary military activity is somehow decisive. The Obama administration does make claims about the decisiveness of these strikes, but it also makes a concurrent claim – that these strikes have a disruptive effect. The use of force to disrupt an opponent is an integral part of warfare; arguing against this would render many uses of force illegitimate or illegal. The key problem is that utility is a subjective concept, as are many of the terms used to judge and describe acts of war. As Michael Walzer points out:

> [I]t would be difficult to condemn soldiers for anything they did in the course of a battle or a war that they honestly believed, and had good reason to believe was necessary, or important, or simply useful in determining the outcome.[19]

Nonetheless, the utility of targeted killings is an important aspect of arguing that they are necessary, as is considering the degree to which they may be counterproductive.

War and law enforcement

Does war exist between the United States and al-Qaeda? Can war exist between the United States and al-Qaeda? Should such a war exist? This set of three questions forms a key branch of criticism of US targeted killings, which argues that law enforcement measures should ultimately take precedence over military ones. The arguments offered by Philip Alston, Mary Ellen O'Connell and others seek to prove that the US use of targeted killings is illegal due to the inapplicability of IHL, or that it represents the wrong choice in the circumstances. This is important, because the Obama administration's defence of targeted killings relies on their purported status as a necessary act of war. If a state of war does not exist, then the grounds for necessity are drastically reduced. If the choice of using the law enforcement methods exists, then the argument that such methods represent a 'last resort' is also undermined.

There are two key problems with the assertion that war does not, or cannot, exist between the United States and al-Qaeda. The first is that many critics rely too heavily on *de jure* concepts of war, stemming from international law and IHL. The key fallacy here is that such laws do not determine the existence of war; they instead serve to classify which types of conflict are regulated by treaty, or customary, international law. The second issue in the critical account is the idea that the presence of war immediately rules out the application of law enforcement, or vice versa. This idea, implicit in the criticism offered by O'Connell, relies on war as representing a universal fact that excludes law enforcement, again deriving from the characterisation of the laws of war as a *lex specialis*.

Contrary to their critics, both the Bush and Obama administrations argued that a state of war existed between the United States and al-Qaeda, and acted accordingly. The language of war is integral to the Obama administration's justification for the use of targeted killings.[20] This particular debate focuses in no small part on the very definition of the phenomenon of war. What is required to prove the consistency of the Obama administration's defence of its targeted killing programme is the presence of a de facto state of war; conversely, a finding that a war does not exist between the two would undermine the administration's defence of targeted killings, which are predicated on war between the two.

The consistent use of military force by the United States and al-Qaeda against one another supports the contention that a de facto state of war exists between the two. This use of force is different from armed contestation, or combat. Al-Qaeda have conducted the 9/11 attacks and have played a role in a significant number of terrorist attacks since, and there is no evidence to suggest that they have unilaterally ceased planning to use force against the United States. Paradoxically, the targeted killings that O'Connell *et al.* argue are illegal support the contention that the United States considers itself to be at war with al-Qaeda (due in part to their sheer volume). Although US forces may not be engaged in perpetual armed combat, both parties are certainly in some sort of confrontation, and within that confrontation are willing to use, and do use, violence against one another where possible. At the very least, a state of 'peace' cannot be held to be present between the two. Furthermore, the arguments offered against this de facto state of war are flawed. Here, it is important to differentiate between the legal definitions of warfare and its conceptual definition. Clausewitz defined war as 'an act of violence intended to compel our opponent to fulfil our will'.[21] This basic principle is supported by dictionary definitions of the phenomenon: as an armed conflict between two or more parties. However, in legal terms war exists in a very circumscribed manner. The use of force (war) is prohibited by the UN Charter, except in self-defence (Article 51) and in support of UNSC resolutions. Therefore it is important to differentiate between a de facto state of war, which may or may not be illegal, and a *de jure* state of war or armed conflict according to international law. The problem for critics of the US use of targeted killings is that they use restrictive criteria to determine the existence of war and armed conflict. Alston's argument is that where the *lex specialis* of war is inapplicable, and armed conflict does not exist, war does not exist. From this, he further argues that human rights standards (inherent in Nils Melzer's idea of a law enforcement paradigm) bind states: '[T]he legality of a killing outside the context of armed conflict is governed by human rights standards, especially those concerning the use of lethal force'.[22] However, his and O'Connell's idea that there can ever be

72 *War and law enforcement*

objective criteria for defining the existence of a war is flawed. Drawing on legal forms of thinking about the existence of armed conflict, both Alston and O'Connell state that armed conflict can be determined by 'objective criteria'; as Alston states, '[W]hether an armed conflict exists is a question that must be answered with reference to objective criteria, which depend on the facts on the ground'.[23] O'Connell echoes this, although in fairness immediately derogates from this position by stating: '[T]his is not an entirely objective standard, however. The level of intensity is open to subjective assessment and situations of violence may wax and wane, leading to gray areas in which situations are not clearly armed conflict'.[24]

The problem here is that both the United States and al-Qaeda appear to be intent on launching armed attacks against one another, without contesting terrain in the manner required by Alston and O'Connell's objective standards. Simply put, the method by which both sides wage war on one another differs substantially from what an armed conflict 'should' appear to be according to Alston and O'Connell. Some, such as Jens Ohlin, argue that the material fact of drone strikes and targeted killings is enough to constitute armed conflict (in a legal sense) and therefore warrants the application of IHL.[25]

There are, however, two important arguments that arise from the recognition of a de facto state of war between the United States and al-Qaeda. A key problem that Philip Alston identifies is that allowing for military force to be used in this manner would massively expand the legal ability of states to use force against individuals outside criminal legal processes.[26] Statements by supporters of targeted killings give good reason for such fear. Commenting on hostilities, John Yoo writes: '[B]ecause the United States is at war with al-Qaeda, it can use force – especially targeted force – to conduct hostilities against the enemy's leaders'.[27] This simple logic, when considering the discursive aspect of declaring war, is what Alston apparently fears. There also exists the opposing argument: that war exists, and therefore automatically supersedes the use of law enforcement provisions. The Obama administration's argument is different in this respect, reserving the use of military force for areas where it is necessary to do so. In this context, the Obama administration's claim does not rely on the realist interpretation advanced by John Yoo. In short, the existence of a de facto war between the United States and al-Qaeda does not make military acts in that war necessary, nor does it preclude the use of law enforcement methods. John Brennan states that '[E]ven if we determine that it is lawful to pursue the terrorist in question with lethal force, it doesn't necessarily mean we should'.[28] Although both John Yoo and the Obama administration justify the use of military methods by citing self-defence, the Obama administration's position is clearly more limited than Yoo's. This differentiation is what separates the Obama administration's defence from pure realism, and key to this differentiation is the interaction between the war and law enforcement paradigms. In particular, the use of military means may be necessary where (if possible) the law enforcement paradigm stops being applicable. Far from overriding the law enforcement paradigm, the Obama administration's defence specifically relies on

War and law enforcement 73

its wider applicability, in effect recognising the duality of law and war in asymmetric warfare.

The liminal nature of terrorists makes them potentially subject to two paradigms – law and war. Nils Melzer separates the targeting of individuals with lethal force into paradigms of law enforcement and hostilities. Melzer's 'paradigm of law enforcement' 'includes the totality of rules, which balance the collective interest in enforcing public security, law and order against the conflicting interesting in protecting individual rights and liberties'.[29] Melzer accepts that this sometimes overlaps with the hostilities paradigm. Melzer's conception excludes operations that simultaneously occur as part of hostilities under *lex specialis*.[30] For his part, Alston notes that IHRL applies outside the context of armed conflict, and also takes issue with the term 'law enforcement', because these strictures apply to all.[31] On the other hand, Melzer's 'hostilities paradigm' is roughly in line with Alston's, in that it is a situation in which IHL applies.

Targeted killings foreground the liminal space between the two: '[M]ore than any other counterterrorism tactic, targeted killing operations display the tension between addressing terrorism as a crime and addressing it as war'.[32] This duality is in part due to the targets' definition as enemies. One of the key failings of Melzer's work on targeted killings is that it fails to recognise the presence of enemies within the law enforcement paradigm. Specifically, it fails to recognise the existence of a special type of crime – political crimes such as treason – in which criminals are characterised as political enemies. In Melzer's paradigm of law enforcement, all crimes are equal, but criminals are not enemies, whereas he explicitly recognises that the legal targeting of persons in wartime is predicated on them being 'enemies'.[33]

Due to the political nature of terrorism, persons defined as terrorists are almost always political enemies of states, and this is reflected in common pejorative labels for those found guilty of terrorist offences. Defining a person as an enemy does not, however, necessarily legitimise unrestricted violence against them, nor does it immediately legitimise the use of military means against them. The debates during the Bush administration over labelling captured persons as 'unlawful enemy combatants' centred primarily around the manner in which such definitions altered a person's legal access to the US court system, or were perceived to enable the use of enhanced interrogation techniques. This obfuscates a more important process – defining persons as enemies by labelling them terrorists. This differs from criminal or judicial processes. The concept of the terrorist suspect implies the due process afforded persons accused of terrorism or political crime within a judicial system, a challenge afforded to such definitions in judicial systems. Such a challenge does not exist within the hostilities paradigm; persons identified as enemies simply are enemies on the basis of definition and identification. IHL differentiates between legitimate and illegitimate targets, as well as circumstances for legal targeting with lethal force, but it does not allow combatants to challenge their identification as such.

Defining persons as terrorists places them in a liminal state, whereby they are potentially subject to two bodies of law. They exist outside the bounds of

74 *War and law enforcement*

'normal' crime by the fact that their actions and intentions are political; yet they do not constitute a traditional military force. In this sense, terrorists are between both spheres (war and law enforcement), but state responses to them place them in one or the other. The restrictions sought by O'Connell and Alston are not the definition of persons as terrorists, or political criminals, but the restriction on state activities that can be undertaken against people defined as such. Typically, territorially or politically internal enemies are dealt with via law enforcement measures, and states are limited as to what they are legally able to do against external enemies by international law.

Viewed from this perspective, it is possible to discern central flaws in the arguments of both O'Connell and Alston, as well as in those of John Yoo. O'Connell and Alston's arguments rely on treating external enemies in exactly the same manner as internal enemies, which defies state practice. On the other hand, John Yoo's argument considers that states should be near unbound in their treatment of external enemies, which stands in contrast to almost two centuries of instrumental legal development of IHL, as well as custom and treaty that preceded it. Even so, it is possible to construct from Alston and O'Connell's arguments a more sympathetic, and defensible, position: that states should not use force against external enemies where there is the possibility of using law enforcement. This accommodates the practice of war – because legal interactions between hostile states are governed by international law – and also the transnational asymmetric conflict that the United States is engaged in with al-Qaeda. This 'sympathetic' position restricts the use of force to areas where the law enforcement paradigm is in operation. In O'Connell's view, this is anywhere outside the *lex specialis* of war. The Obama administration's position, however, is that there exist areas where the law enforcement paradigm is inoperable. In such spaces, the use of military methods, including targeted killings, against al-Qaeda constitutes, according to the Obama administration, a necessary act of war.

The existence of a de facto state of war between the United States and al-Qaeda does not preclude the United States' use of law enforcement measures against al-Qaeda. In this regard, O'Connell's second argument – that law enforcement is a choice, and the correct one – forms an important critique of the position taken by the Obama administration.[34] In order for the Obama administration's position to be valid, it has to demonstrate that there are places in which the dual application of law enforcement and military measures is not possible, and that military means are the only available option.

John Yoo's argument relies on utility as a measurement for selection between the two paradigms. This is echoed by many similar writers; Michael Chertoff writes, '[T]he rationale is that the circumstances – and not abstract categories – should determine the tools and authorities that come into play' prior to advocating occasional use of military interrogations in the United States due to their utility.[35] In many senses, Yoo understands the liminal nature of terrorists and political enemies, but his criterion for choosing methods used to deal with them is rooted in the effectiveness of the method itself. This is in direct contrast to

O'Connell's idea of the primacy of law enforcement. There are two aspects of the Obama administration's defence of its targeted killing programme that stand in contrast to both of these. The first is that law enforcement takes precedence; the second, that there exist areas where this paradigm is inapplicable.

Of the two world views that compete with the Obama administration's defence, John Yoo's poses less problems. In some respects, Yoo is critical of the Obama administration, mainly for not going far enough: '[H]e [Obama] may have opened the door to further terrorist acts on U.S. soil by shattering some of the nation's most critical defences'.[36] The Obama administration's defence of its use of targeted killings relies fundamentally on its legal nature – this aspect of its legitimacy is woven into the key speeches by Brennan and Koh.[37] Although the use of targeted killings is proclaimed as an expansion of state authority by its critics, the defence offered by the Obama administration is careful both in limiting this expansion to areas where the law enforcement paradigm is inapplicable, and also in tying its legitimacy to its legality. In contrast, Yoo openly attacks restraints on the use of force by the executive branch.[38] If the Obama administration did not choose to defend its use of targeted killings in this manner, Yoo's utilitarian outlook would be of greater consequence.

To defend itself against the arguments advanced by O'Connell, the Obama administration's position requires proof that there exist areas where the law enforcement paradigm is inapplicable. In effect, this relates to the Obama administration's insistence that there exist areas where capture is not possible. Strictly speaking, capture operations by military forces also lie outside the law enforcement paradigm. Capture and detention by military forces can, however, be challenged by due process and petitions for writs of habeas corpus, whereas targeted killings cannot be undone.

Arguing that the areas where law enforcement is impossible is a two-step process: it must be shown, first, that such areas exist; and second, that methods for imposing the law enforcement paradigm are prohibitively costly or ineffective. The relative efficiency of the two methods is a realist interpretation and antithetical to the position of the Obama administration. Although the administration's defence of targeted killings calls on the principle of self-defence, this does not legitimise the use of military means over law enforcement. Ultimately this argument rests on there being areas outside state authority where the law enforcement paradigm fails, and therefore areas where the use of military means may be justified.

The edges of the state system

The presence of a de facto state of war does not mean that targeted killings are a necessary practice. O'Connell's argument is persuasive in one regard – that law enforcement measures should take precedence over military means. Tellingly, this is reflected in the Obama administration's discourse defending its use of targeted killings: Eric Holder stated that 'where capture is not feasible' is one of four key tests prior to authorising a targeted killing.[39] The Obama administration

76 *War and law enforcement*

argues that the use of military measures against al-Qaeda is predicated on the inapplicability of law enforcement means. Mary Ellen O'Connell's argument that terrorism is a matter of law enforcement excludes the legitimacy of military measures against terrorist networks.[40] Outside of battlefields, O'Connell argues that law enforcement measures should take precedence, and that terrorists killed with targeted killings could be arrested, and therefore should be.[41] Furthermore, precisely because law enforcement methods were used against terrorism, this differential treatment of terrorists in Afghanistan, the Philippines and Yemen disproved the George W. Bush thesis of 'global war'.[42] The problem with O'Connell's argument is that she offers no evidence for the practicability of employing law enforcement methods. The Obama administration's defence of targeted killings justifies their use where law enforcement measures – capture – are not possible. These two arguments effectively argue different points: whereas O'Connell argues that law enforcement should be used outside warzones and battlefields, the Obama administration holds that military methods such as targeted killings may be employed where law enforcement and detention are not possible.

This difference turns on a key point: the inapplicability of the law enforcement paradigm in areas beyond de facto state authority. *De jure* and de facto sovereignty are two different facets, and law enforcement approaches rely on the fact of state authority, as well as on a state's judicial obligations or territorial sovereignty in the system of states. This is because the law enforcement approach relies on a Western model of criminal justice, which itself relies on de facto state sovereignty. Low governance areas are typically characterised as abnormal, a condition implicit in the concept of failed states and ungoverned space, but they are a normal feature of statehood and the international system. Recent experiences of state-building demonstrate that the elimination of such regions is unlikely in the short or medium term. Therefore it is likely that areas beyond de facto state authority, where the law enforcement paradigm falters, are likely to persist in future, which undermines O'Connell and Alston's policy prescriptions.

O'Connell's argument requires that states are able to exercise authority uniformly over their territorial boundaries. State authority is not, however, uniform, nor is it ensured by *de jure* territorial sovereignty. The law enforcement paradigm relies on a particular type of state–society relations, which is encapsulated in de facto sovereignty. In this case, whatever political structures exist lack the legitimacy, monopoly on the use of legitimate force and bureaucracy necessary to discharge the functions of a state.[43] This Weberian definition is the most basic definition of statehood, although others exist.[44] Where states exert de facto authority, it is possible for them to successfully disrupt terrorist networks without military means. Fundamentally, when thinking of a law enforcement paradigm, states such as the United States are thinking in terms of effective application of criminal justice, not in terms of universal legal regimes such as IHRL. In this manner, Alston's universal application of IHRL is fundamentally different from the law enforcement paradigm at hand.[45] The argument that law enforcement should take precedence where criminal justice is effective makes sense; the argument that law enforcement should take precedence regardless of the effectiveness of criminal justice systems does not – it would lead to areas where non-state actors could act with impunity.

Western levels of law enforcement and criminal justice are a sign of de facto state authority, because the state generally has the power and ability to detain persons. To fully understand this concept, it is necessary to explore what the absence of de facto sovereignty is, and how the conceptualisation of this in the idea of failed states gives rise to the idea that such absences of de facto sovereignty are reversible. Sovereignty is a highly contested legal and philosophical concept. The most complete classical survey is Book 1, Chapter 8 of Jean Bodin's *République*.[46] Contemporaneously, it still refers in general to the supreme authority of the state over its subjects within a territorial dominion and the simultaneous freedom from interference by other states; yet '[N]o concept has raised so many conflicting issues and involved XIXth Century jurists and political theorists in so desperate a maze as the concept of Sovereignty'.[47] It is used here to denote the legal status of sovereign states in the international system of the UN, whereas issues of internal sovereignty are dealt with in the following chapter.

The international system is now constitutionally stable[48] – states can divide but do not often become subsumed by other states. *De jure* state failure is not an issue in this context, because illegitimate regimes retain sovereign borders, even if the protections of borders for regimes considered illegitimate by their neighbours or the international community are diminishing.[49] States such as Somalia, without functioning government for almost 20 years, still retain their legal protections under international law.[50] Somalia retained legal sovereignty over its territory and waters, even though 'the drafters [of the United Nations Convention on the Laws of the Sea] appear never to have conceived that a recognized state with recognized territorial waters would exist without the capacity to police those waters'.[51]

The discourses of failed states, weak states and ungoverned space conceptualise the absence of de facto state authority as an aberration. Weak and fragile state discourse originated in the 1980s, whereas the term 'failed state' appeared in the 1990s.[52] Gerald Helman and Steven Ratner coined the term 'failed state' in their article 'Saving Failed States'.[53] A failed state is a sovereign state that ceases to effectively function. Because analysts differ on the precise definition, the exact number of failed states differs from analyst to analyst.[54] The number is relatively low – Robert Rotberg states that there have been seven between 1993 and 2003.[55] Areas commonly termed 'ungoverned spaces', or variants thereof, are relatively new. The concept is introduced into major US strategy documents in 2006 US National Security Strategy.[56]

Critics point out that it is implicit in failed state discourse that states themselves are considered essential for the provision of public goods (stateless enclaves provide an important counterargument to this).[57] However, these same critics do not offer convincing alternatives to state authority that would provide

78 War and law enforcement

these same public goods – in particular the criminal justice institutions required to enforce the law enforcement standards of Western states – and hence allow for the applicability of the law enforcement paradigm in the context of targeted killings. For law enforcement to take precedence, and thereby render targeted killings potentially unnecessary, the police and security forces of the state in question would have to be able to disrupt or arrest terrorist networks. International criminal justice systems are diverse, and there is no standard model for policing.[58] Fundamentally, the law enforcement paradigm requires that states have the de facto ability to capture and arrest suspected terrorists within their territories.

The key question one must ask is whether the absence of de facto state authority required for criminal justice systems is an aberration. If the law enforcement paradigm relies on de facto state authority, the question of areas beyond de facto state authority becomes salient in the targeted killings debate. These areas form part of the rationale for the defence of targeted killings offered by the Obama administration. Furthermore, the presence of these areas would also amount to a significant hole in the arguments presented by O'Connell and Alston – if states could or should not use military means to combat terrorist groups operating in these areas, but law enforcement measures are unable to affect them, terrorist networks would be able to operate with impunity. This is a situation that neither author directly calls for, but that is still a possible consequence of the positions they take.

The failed state discourse relies on a Western conception of the state – particularly the relationship between government and population, where non-state governance structures tend to be viewed as poor alternatives for state-directed governance. After World War II, modernisation theory – social science applied to societies beyond the United States and Europe – emerged as its own field.[59] The comparison of 'modern and traditional political systems'[60] evolved into the study of these traditional systems to facilitate their development into modern ones. This comparison was challenged by revisionists of modernisation theory, who questioned the binary categorisation of 'modern' and 'traditional', and by dependency theorists, who questioned the necessity of such change and highlighted the colonial ideas inherent in modernisation theory.[61] Key here is that whereas in some places these traditional governance structures deliver the authority required of the law enforcement paradigm, in other places they do not.

In his analysis of state authority, Robert Jackson uses the analogy of a 'watermark of sovereignty' as a means of analysing the permeation of state authority in society.[62] In Western states, which are more or less free of independent governance structures, the watermark is low: there are not many activities that one can perform that the state does not, at some level or another, take an interest in. In postcolonial states, where a weak sovereign was built on extensive suzerain systems of governance, the watermark is high: there are considerable fields of action over which the state has no de facto or even, in some cases, *de jure* control. The weak/failed state discourse depicts these areas as aberrations, whereas in reality many areas outside de facto state control are not 'ungoverned' but simply governed in a manner outside state authority. The presence of such areas, normally outside the authority of states, where criminal justice systems required by the law enforcement paradigm are ineffective, supports the Obama administration's claim that targeted killings may be a necessary act for want of alternatives.

The argument that the present lack of sovereign authority in some areas makes targeted killings necessary does not, however, account for change over time. Although O'Connell and Alston do not make this argument themselves, it is easy to construe from their arguments that, should the possibility of using law enforcement techniques arise, these would be preferable to the use of targeted killings. Therefore, is it possible or plausible to alter the de facto sovereignty constraints that prohibit the use of law enforcement measures? If so, this could be offered as an alternative to the use of targeted killings, and therefore undermine the Obama administration's argument that these measures are necessary.

In the past decade, the United States has committed to large-scale counter-insurgency campaigns and state-building to create strong central authorities in Afghanistan and Iraq that could take charge of their territory, with mixed results. The practice of state-building – 'the creation of new government institutions and the strengthening of existing ones'[63] – would, in theory, offer an alternative to targeted killings by allowing for the use of law enforcement measures. David Kilcullen and Andrew Exum argue in favour of this approach in a 2009 article.[64] The United States and its allies did not intend to become heavily involved in the running of Iraq or Afghanistan, but did so to prevent the collapse of these states and the thriving of hostile non-state actors within them.[65] It is important to note that state-building strategies do not exclude targeted killing activities. In both Afghanistan and Iraq, the United States conducted military raids and targeted killings on insurgents, criminal networks and terrorists. Al-Qaeda's core remained in Pakistan, and it was there that the United States conducted the majority of its lethal targeted killings in non-warzones.

The US experiences in both Afghanistan and Iraq demonstrate the costs of attempting state-building, particularly where this process is opposed by armed groups. The areas in which the Obama administration is using targeted killings all feature armed groups opposed to the extension of authority by a centralised state. The prospects for state-building in Somalia and Yemen – locations of other targeted killings – is bleak.[66] For the law enforcement paradigm to apply, large-scale state-building campaigns must be successful, but the experience of the past decade tells us that this is not certain and, even where possible, comes at an incredibly high cost. Therefore, calls for the law enforcement paradigm to be applied to these areas are effectively predicated on the choice to conduct large-scale interventions in these areas – a choice that may be opposed even by host governments. For this reason, senior figures in the Obama administration such as John Brennan consider large interventions to be counterproductive.[67] It is therefore highly unlikely that state-building provides a means by which the law enforcement paradigm can be effectively implemented in these areas.

80 *War and law enforcement*

The necessary use of force

The Obama administration argues that targeted killings are a necessary act where law enforcement methods are inapplicable and where capture is not possible. A key question that critics raise is the utility of targeted killings. If targeted killings cannot comprehensively destroy al-Qaeda, what purpose do they serve? This question must be differentiated from the legal concept of necessity, which is discussed in the next chapter. As a precursor to necessity, the utility of targeted killings must be ascertained and, as a precursor to this, it is necessary to examine their purpose.

In recent years, a growing number of academics and policymakers have argued that containment is a viable strategy for dealing with al-Qaeda and other such groups. Barry Posen questioned the end-state of the War on Terror and outlined end-states similar to containment, but did not deal with containment explicitly.[68] Bruce Hoffman raises the spectre of containment, but does not connect the issue with al-Qaeda, except to note the lack of a similar grand strategy.[69] However, in order for containment to work, it must also function at the limits of the state system, where state authority is weakest.

The theory and practice of containment derives from interstate politics and the confrontation of the Cold War.[70] After 9/11, containment was explicitly rejected as a mode of dealing with terrorists.[71] It is here that there is a significant theoretical gap between Cold War conceptions of containment and its application to non-state actors in low governance regions. Patrick Porter argues that stealth power and targeted killings will play a role in any containment strategy, but does not directly address the problem of low and alternate governance areas.[72] Global counterterrorism efforts have since disrupted al-Qaeda's operations, but they have not ended the threat that they pose. Therefore, a form of containment is occurring as a side effect of the failure to eliminate threats. Matthew Elledge argues that this is intentional.[73]

The type of threat posed to Western states by al-Qaeda and non-state actors differs from that posed by the USSR. Therefore the containment policies for these threats must also differ. Audrey Cronin argues that al-Qaeda, like other terrorist organisations, will eventually end,[74] which formed a key component of Kennan's concept of containment. Prediction is a problem in this context. Kennan's correct assumption that the Soviet Union would end should be paired with the fact that Kennan believed German reunification would precede the end of the Cold War.[75] Therefore it is prudent to examine the use of force as part of a strategy for the long-term containment of terrorist networks such as al-Qaeda.

The most serious criticism of targeted killings is that they will not destroy targeted networks or groups outright: terrorism is political, and not stopped by violence alone. Furthermore, the Obama administration does not consider the use of targeted killings as its sole means of fighting al-Qaeda.[76] The use of military force is not restricted to the paradigm of interstate warfare. A different way of thinking of the use of military force is offered by Thomas Rid in his examination of Israeli military strategy: 'Israel's use of military force, increasingly, is not just one act of force to compel one actor to fulfil one specific political goal at one given time'.[77] Examining Israel's use of military force, Rid argues that its singular uses of force must be considered as part of a wider strategy of deterrence, where 'strategic planners have to assume that violence will never cease entirely. Success does not mean no violence; success means less violence'.[78] In the same manner, the US use of targeted killings appears aimed at reducing the number of successful violent acts and plots that al-Qaeda are able to plan in areas where the law enforcement paradigm does not function. The Obama administration's defence of these acts is that they are a necessary means to disrupt these plots. Its admission that these acts alone will not end the threat of al-Qaeda points to the use of targeted killings being an operational method of a strategy of containment; they should therefore be judged for their utility accordingly.

Containment formed the overarching strategy of the United States for 50 years and, as such, can be considered a legitimate policy. However, actions taken within the strategic framework of containment may not be considered legitimate. To what extent does containment work to legitimise targeted killings? There are problems applying the strategy to non-state actors. Cold War containment was a state-centric policy and concept, one that was predicated on the bilateral interactions of two states, the United States and the Soviet Union. In the early years of the War on Terror, the Bush administration rejected containment as a strategy, as a means of dealing with non-state actors such as al-Qaeda.[79] This was because al-Qaeda, and similar terrorists, were considered non-deterrable after 9/11, particularly in light of their perceived goal of acquiring a weapon of mass destruction.[80] As John Gearson argues, the reason for this is that deterrence by punishment, or the threat thereof, was taken to be the starting point for considering the applicability of deterrence. Since other forms of deterrence exist, the inapplicability of conventional deterrence theory does not invalidate the concept of deterrence itself.[81]

The state-centricity of containment relies on the decision-making processes of states, which are deemed to be rational. An oft-repeated criticism of containment and deterrence is that non-state actors do not behave in the same way that states do. Containment and deterrence both rely on a form of rational choice: unless another's course of action can be altered by threat or demonstration of force, that actor is essentially non-deterrable. John Stone argues that this criticism is false,[82] as do other authors, such as Alex Wilner.[83] It is important to consider that although individuals (such as suicidal terrorists) may be non-deterrable, terrorist groups are tactical – and the purpose of deterrence is to dissuade the group as a whole from following a course of action. John Stone argues that this is possible, because al-Qaeda are rational actors and may self-deter.[84] Furthermore, terrorist networks often rely on the support of states, against which traditional deterrence theory will apply. However, if deterrence does not work against al-Qaeda, then achieving the effect of deterrence may suffice. In this regard, the disruption of terrorist networks, rather than their deterrence, also functions as part of a policy of containment.

82   War and law enforcement

The US use of targeted killings has to be analysed alongside the overriding US goal of preventing al-Qaeda from conducting a spectacular coercive attack on the United States. The Obama administration's defence of targeted killings is predicated on their ability to aid this. The primary means by which al-Qaeda can produce coercion is by spectacular violence (also referred to as 'the propaganda of the deed' in reference to earlier anarchist theories)[85] and mass casualty attacks. Specifically, they can transfer the technical ability to carry out coercive acts of spectacular violence, as well as acquire the means to do so. To undertake these activities, terrorist networks require a structure that enables this transfer and acquisition, which also enables them to form executable decisions.[86] Terrorist networks are resistant to destruction, but their adaptability also makes them malleable in response to state policy. Certain network scales and typologies allow terrorist networks and non-state actors to coerce states. The ability of these networks to transmit information and knowledge across distances enables them to coerce states from areas of low state authority. Terrorist networks lack central knowledge repositories, such as libraries. In order to make members effective, they must learn to act. In al-Qaeda's case, this was done in training camps in Afghanistan. By restricting the ability of these networks to transfer key technical information and skills, their effectiveness can be reduced and their threat lessened. Bomb-making, although widely cited as possible from documents on the Internet, is a technical process. It requires training and preparation, which are best done with an instructor.[87] Where instruction is not available, or where preparation is not possible, the results can be amateurish. For example, Umar Farouk Abdulmutallab, the so-called 'Underwear Bomber', failed to detonate a bomb on Northwest Airlines Flight 253 on Christmas Day, 2009. Following the July 7 attacks in London (in 2005), a second group of would-be suicide bombers attempted to detonate explosives on the London Underground system, but only the detonators exploded. Another notable failure was the 2007 Glasgow International Airport attack. Lone-wolf terrorists such as Timothy McVeigh and Anders Breivik can cause significant damage, but networked terrorists present the state with a strategic challenge in that they enable repeated lethal attacks.

The key factor in the functioning of terrorist networks is trust. Carlo Morselli *et al.* argue that trust is related to security concerns, which in themselves are balanced with efficiency. In effect, the more open a group is, the easier it is to detect and disrupt.[88] Terrorist networks rely on trust to identify and integrate new members, as well as to select those with whom to acquire information from and transfer information to.[89] Furthermore, Marc Sageman argues that trust plays a key role in the formation of terrorist networks: '[T]he global Islamic terrorist social movement forms through the spontaneous self-organization of informal "bunches of guys", trusted friends, from the bottom up'.[90] By degrading the trust in a network, its cohesiveness is degraded. In a network that is leader-inspired, this can cause the network itself to fracture.[91] The continuation of al-Qaeda after the death of Osama bin Laden shows that this does not necessarily end a network. By increasing the uncertainty of the operating environment, state actions can degrade the amount of trust that network nodes have in forming

War and law enforcement 83

exterior connections. This trust degradation can be performed via revealed infiltration, sting operations or informants. The effect of the knowledge of informants on the IRA leadership during the 1980s was devastating to operational capacity.[92] Therefore there are a wide number of ways in which states can degrade trust in a terrorist network.

Daniel Byman tells us in no uncertain terms that targeted killings can work.[93] Targeted killings therefore have the potential to degrade and disrupt the network structure of al-Qaeda in places where the law enforcement paradigm provides no other alternative. If they are able to achieve this, then they would constitute a means of containing terrorist networks beyond the authority of states, and would therefore be defensible on the parameters set by the Obama administration. However, there are plenty of arguments against this. One is that targeted killings are counterproductive because they ultimately foster more grievances in the long run.

Counterproductivity and grievance

Do targeted killings create more problems than they solve? How do they help, or impede, the strategy of al-Qaeda? Core to both questions is the common criticism of targeted killings as counterproductive because they aid al-Qaeda more than they hinder them. At the epicentre of this criticism is the 'grievance critique', advanced by Kilcullen and Exum, among others.[94] The grievance critique is founded on a simple and logical premise: kill a member of someone's family, and they will bear a grudge. This is extrapolated to mean that these grudges directly translate into radical action, and therefore joining the terrorist networks that were targeted in the first place. As Ibrahim Mothana stated in a *New York Times* op-ed:

> A new generation of leaders is spontaneously emerging in furious retaliation to attacks on their territories and tribes' by targeted killings which 'is why A.Q.A.P. is much stronger in Yemen today than it was a few years ago. In 2009, A.Q.A.P. had only a few hundred members and controlled no territory; today it has, along with Ansar al-Sharia, at least 1,000 members and controls substantial amounts of territory.[95]

The key argument of this critique is that targeted killings produce more persons prone to committing violent acts of terrorism than they eliminate, and are therefore counterproductive in the long term. Targeted killings are highly unpopular with locals, who may die as a result, or lose friends and family. Despite administration assurances, and the flawed Jamestown figures, these strikes do kill civilians, and the scale of the US use of targeted killings produces a large number of civilian casualties. Even low (reliable) estimates of the civilian casualty count are significant, as even the lowest estimate of civilian casualties offered by the Bureau of Investigative Journalism is over 400, up to the end of 2015. In a state where public opinion directly influences government policy, such strikes would

84 *War and law enforcement*

create a sharp backlash. Pakistan and Yemen are not, however, Western democracies (not that public opinion directly translates to policy in the West, either). Public opposition to the targeted killing campaign in Pakistan is vocal and has recently translated into opposition within some branches of government.[96] This problem of grievance also feeds into the wider issue of regime stability in countries such as Pakistan.

The grievance critiques, and similar criticisms, suffer from a lack of evidence beyond casualty figures. In particular, there is no evidence of a direct causal link between the use of targeted killings and increased violence that threatens Americans. That is not to say that targeted killings do not anger people, but the causal links in the grievance critique miss key pieces of evidence and instead rely on assumptions. Targeted killings are very unpopular in areas where persons are targeted.[97] It is important, however, to identify two types of negative response that are sometimes conflated in the grievance critique. First, there is the argument that targeted killings radicalise families and communities in the areas where they strike – driving people to support al-Qaeda. Second, there is also the issue of negative legitimacy – that targeted killings reduce US legitimacy in the eyes of key global audiences.

The problem of tackling these questions is the same that is faced by counter-insurgency analysts – in hostile, relatively unknown environments, it is difficult to assess cause and effect. Metrics, or standards by which a conflict can be judged, are extremely difficult in unconventional wars. As a RAND survey states:

> In COIN, the intimate relationship of the political, social, economic, and military factors of the war makes metrics much harder to generate. If one subscribes to HAM theory, how does one measure the population's support for government or insurgent? If one subscribes to cost/benefit theory, how does one measure and optimise the effects of carrots and sticks? Conventional warfare metrics are of little use in this situation.[98]

The grievance critique therefore suffers from a self-selection bias – by focusing on one cause of anger, it neglects to consider other causes. Without such a holistic approach to assessing grievances and influences that would affect a person's behaviour, the evidence does not, therefore, support the link between the first assertion – that targeted killings anger people (almost certainly correct) – and the second – that this anger directly translates into recruitment for al-Qaeda. It is highly likely that targeted killings have directly translated into more individuals working with al-Qaeda, but it is impossible to determine whether this number is greater or lesser than other causes of local grievance. Without such a body of evidence, the grievance critique rests on an opinion – that the (unknown) number of persons joining al-Qaeda is worse for the United States than the disruption caused by targeted killings. Importantly, many critics who cite the grievance critique also examine targeted killings as a method of threat elimination rather than disruption. Therefore their opinion and analysis may be correct within their own framework, but do not, in the context of this thesis, disprove or undermine the defence for targeted killings offered by the Obama administration. This mirrors criticisms of the Israeli example of targeted killings, which does not end the long-term threat of terrorism, but is used by Israelis to conduct a form of deterrence. The transferability of the type of deterrence used by Israel is limited, however, because it relies on the ability to gauge retaliations to acts.[99]

If evidence does not exist that proves a causal link between targeted killings and violence against the United States, what of legitimacy? The question of legitimacy depends on audience. The targeted killing programme definitely undermines US authority in Pakistan and Yemen, and has been demonstrated to reinforce US authority in the United States itself. Neither of these, however, is crucial. Al-Qaeda's strategic goal is to alienate Muslims from their governments, and it is here that US targeted killings could be said to be aiding al-Qaeda's own strategy. In a 2011 Gallup poll of Americans that separated responses by faith, American Muslims clearly rejected violent military attacks on civilians, with 78 per cent stating that such attacks were never justified, and 21 per cent stating that they were sometimes justified. This divides the opinions of American Muslims from other faiths, all of whom considered attacks on civilians sometimes justified (between 52 per cent and 64 per cent); and opposition was roughly half that felt by Muslims (between 33 per cent and 43 per cent). Non-religious/atheist/agnostic respondents were marginally against attacks on civilians (56 per cent) but, even so, the 43 per cent who considered attacks on civilians to be sometimes justified was double that of the Muslim population.[100] Therefore there are clear divisions between the Muslim population and those of other faiths, as well as atheists, towards military targeting that may sometimes kill civilians. As reports demonstrate, targeted killings cause civilian casualties. American Muslims are probably predisposed to view targeted killings as wrong, and therefore the continued use of targeted killings is likely to alienate them from the government. This must, however, be balanced by the fact that approval for Obama has remained relatively steady (and high, at around 80 per cent) among the Muslim respondents. This statistic must be used cautiously – the polling contrasts with a 7 per cent approval rating among American Muslims for the final year of Bush's presidency, which means that Republican/Democrat partisanship must be taken into account, as must public antipathy towards Bush himself. Those that most approved of Bush's presidency (in 2008) least approved of Obama, and vice versa.[101]

American Muslims are not the only important group to al-Qaeda, which conceive of a global ummah. The United States has no official authority in Pakistan, where public opposition to US targeted killings is perhaps greatest. The New America Foundation's Pakistan Survey used a 1,200 sample size, examining opinions of UAV strikes in the FATA. Support for the strikes in North Waziristan was 10 per cent ('Strongly support' and 'Somewhat support') and 33 per cent in South Waziristan. There have been more strikes in the North than the South although, surprisingly, the support in South Waziristan was higher than in some other FATA agencies where there are relatively few strikes.[102] It is clear,

86 *War and law enforcement*

however, that targeted killings negatively affect the perception of the United States in most parts of the world. In this respect, targeted killings could be considered to be playing directly into the strategic interests of al-Qaeda. The degree to which this is significant cannot, however, be measured or tested.

This criticism of the US targeted killing programme must be balanced with the contrasting factors of Afghanistan and Iraq. US foreign policy programmes, actions and wars do not exist in a vacuum. The War on Terror has been characterised by many events that have divided world opinion and, in particular, have offended Muslims. US conduct after 9/11 was viewed negatively in the Middle East and wider Muslim world. Furthermore, actions such as extraordinary rendition and waterboarding, combined with places such as Abu Ghraib and Guantanamo Bay, are all visible events, processes and places that delegitimise the United States (further) in public opinion. But legitimacy is not a zero-sum game; it must be balanced with other concerns, such as security. The question, therefore, is the extent to which the US targeted killing campaigns delegitimise the United States in the context of these other processes. Is a relatively small-scale killing operation as bad, in the eyes of the global Muslim audience, as the occupation of Iraq or Afghanistan? The key problem is that there is insufficient evidence to decide this question.

Notably, a number of features ameliorate the delegitimising effects of the US use of targeted killings. Visual communications – images and videos – are key to legitimacy in the contemporary globalised world.[103] The physical occupation of a country such as Afghanistan is an activity that produces a constant stream of media footage via contemporary insurgent movements. In contrast, the US use of targeted killings produces relatively small amounts of imagery. This is not to say that such imagery does not exist.[104] The difference is that counter-insurgency operations, as practised by the United States, require large numbers of personnel active in urban centres and produce more images. To be clear – wars produce imagery of dead civilians, in particular powerful images of slain women and children, and even legitimate targets can be presented as slain civilians. US targeted killings, however, don't tend to produce visual evidence of these events in progress, nor do they allow for definitive visual attribution of these events, since Predators and Reapers can launch missiles and leave an area prior to journalists showing up. Furthermore, the Pakistani military has been active in preventing access to the areas in which these strikes occur.[105] Therefore targeted killings may be conflated with other US actions, but they are less visible.

The Obama administration's studious refusal to even acknowledge the use of targeted killings for a number of years reinforced this lack of visibility; hence the targeted killing programme has been popularly referenced as forming part of Obama's 'Shadow Wars'.[106] This has extended to the US media – journalists were initially given access to drone facilities, but as their use has become contentious, this access (and by extension, visibility) has been revoked.[107] It is therefore arguable that the methodology of the US targeted killing programme lessens its utility to al-Qaeda. In the context of a continued occupation in Afghanistan, this campaign produces far less imagery that delegitimises the United States.

The utility of targeted killings on al-Qaeda to 2015

The precise effect of US targeted killings on al-Qaeda is unknown. Given the discussions thus far in this chapter, to what degree is it true that they have some form of utility? The Obama administration patently perceives the use of targeted killings as a success. Key strikes, such as that which killed Anwar al-Awlaki, were celebrated, although not immediately avowed. In a speech on 30 September 2011, President Obama stated: '[T]he death of [Anwar] al-Awlaki marks another significant milestone in the broader effort to defeat al-Qaeda and their affiliates'.[108] Despite many press briefings stating that al-Awlaki had been killed by a CIA-commanded UAV, the administration did not go 'on record' regarding his death at the time. The Bush administration did not avow the use of targeted killings, and the Obama administration did not do so until 2012.[109] However, the conduct of the campaign, particularly during the escalation over the course of the Obama administration, meant that this public silence was not equal to the normal disavowal of covert operations. The use of highly advanced military technology that was observable from the ground – from airfields inside Pakistan – meant that the targeted killings were attributable to the United States. The persistence in using UAVs, as well as the escalation in strike numbers, meant that no other state, other than the United States, could have been responsible for the targeted killings in Pakistan.

The difference in the standards by which the utility of targeted killings is judged by the Obama administration and its critics is apparent in a critical op-ed by Dennis Blair, former Director of National Intelligence:

> Drones are no longer the most effective strategy for eliminating al-Qaeda's ability to attack us. Past American drone attacks did help reduce the Qaeda leadership to a fearful, hunted cadre that did not have the time or space to plan, train and coordinate major terrorist acts against the United States.[110]

Blair was concerned that drones as a strategy would not 'end' al-Qaeda. In his criticism of drone strikes on this point, he stated that they had had a disruptive effect on the network. Critics often cite this first point, and do not consider the disruptive effect to be useful enough to warrant the use of targeted killings. This is, however, a logical fallacy. Terrorism and war are political matters, and the use of force does not necessarily cause peace. The use of lethal force can have significant effects (such as the death of key leaders), but as Audrey Cronin states, 'the long-term effects of decapitation are inconsistent. While many campaigns end as a result, others barely falter and may even gain strength'.[111] In examining the utility of the use of targeted killings, it is important to differentiate between their utility in eliminating al-Qaeda outright, and their utility in disrupting these type of networks, an effect that Blair observes even as he criticises targeted killings. In order to be defensible under the terms set by the Obama administration's defence, these activities have to be able to at least disrupt a terrorist network, as pointed out earlier in this chapter.

88 *War and law enforcement*

Related to the utility criticism are accusations that US targeted killing strikes are indiscriminate. As Jefferson Morley states:

> It seems Petraeus and his allies in the current inter-agency debate do not want to be constrained by a list. They calculate if the U.S. slaughters a particular crowd of people at an al-Qaida funeral, they are sure to kill men plotting to attack the United States. The logic, if not the morality, is persuasive: If you kill the certainly innocent, you will also get some of the presumably guilty.[112]

This is an important component of utility – if the means to conduct strikes is such that they kill disproportionate numbers of civilians and non-combatants, then these methods are effectively useless, because they can be legitimated in neither IHL nor just war ethics.

Both those who argue for and those who argue against targeted killings cite the lack of reliable data to support their argument or to call the opposing argument into question.[113] Impartiality is therefore almost impossible. Instead, it is perhaps better to use the worst possible interpretations of available evidence to test the argument of a given side. For example, the TBIJ's dataset appears to support the conclusion that 39 per cent confirmed civilian casualties is the worst (in terms of civilian casualties) that occurred over the total 2004–15 period. Therefore testing the Obama administration's claims that this method is proportional will require using this statistic rather than more favourable interpretations of data. Similarly, by taking the maximum number of possible casualties and the minimum number of confirmed civilian casualties, TBIJ's data would point to 10.6 per cent confirmed civilian casualties, which is considerably more precise than 39 per cent. Nonetheless, the worst possible interpretation is important: can targeted killings be considered illegitimate, even if 39 per cent of deaths are civilians?

The problem that one encounters when thinking of targeted killings in this way is that there exists no 'normal' ratio of combatant-to-civilian deaths. Even at its worst, citing 39 per cent civilian casualties, the US use of targeted killings is less lethal for civilians than large-scale twentieth-century warfare or contemporary counter-insurgency operations.[114] The conflict appears to produce less civilian deaths than countries affected by land warfare in World War I, World War II, the Korean War and the Vietnam War. Richard Garfield and Alfred Neugut also note that Panama (1990) resulted in three civilian deaths for every two military deaths, and the 1991 Gulf War resulted in an almost 1:1 ratio (with post-war civilian deaths added).[115] For contemporary wars, low estimates of civilian deaths resulting from the 2003 Iraq War are around 100,000 people. Such comparisons cannot, however, be taken as 'positive' evidence, as some do, that such methods are justified. What the evidence does suggest is that targeted killings are not indiscriminate enough to warrant the criticism levelled at them, but neither are they the surgical tool that supporters portray them to be. Supporters of targeted killings might like to depict the type of warfare as a surgical scalpel, but the statistics suggest, as Michael Ignatieff puts it, that war remains a 'bloodstained sword'.[116] Thus the civilian casualty statistics do not invalidate the claims of the Obama administration, but they certainly demonstrate that the costs are higher than it is willing to publicly admit.

The open-source evidence does appear to support the central claim of the Obama administration – that targeted killings are useful for disrupting terrorist and militant networks. The list of 'high-value targets' killed by US targeted killings is long.[117] Furthermore, as Byman notes, skilled terrorists are limited in number.[118] Eliminating persons such as Anwar al-Awlaki is an important step, because each elimination of ranking members of al-Qaeda or Al-Qaeda in the Arabian Peninsula would, logically, require the network to reorganise or reconstitute itself. Here, the elimination of many ranking figures would constitute significant disruption (over 100 in Pakistan, according to the *Long War Journal*, including 72 al-Qaeda figures). The New American Foundation identifies a minimum of 1,748 militant deaths in Pakistan to the end of 2015. This is a considerable number and lends credence to the administration claims that the presence of these drones prevents these groups from stabilising in the region. Some criticise this claim; for example, Megan Smith and James Walsh argue that drone strikes have not impaired al-Qaeda's ability to produce propaganda. This criticism relies on their methodology, which holds the ability to produce propaganda to be correlated with the overall cohesiveness of the group as a whole.[119] This analysis relies on the authors' depiction of the necessary elements in the production of propaganda in the contemporary world,[120] whereas As-Sahab, the media wing of al-Qaeda, is an unknown entity in that its production methods are unclear. Because it uses internet delivery, it could also use decentralised production methods. As a New America Foundation report stated: '[T]he media strategy surveyed here provides no direct insight into the operational capabilities of a group that has plotted, and continues to plot, in secret'.[121]

Therefore, while the figures do not support the first claim (that targeted killings can eliminate al-Qaeda as a functional actor), they do appear to support the second, more limited claim (that these targeted killings significantly disrupt al-Qaeda). This is an important component in the legitimation of the practice of targeted killings, because it means that targeted killings can fulfil the utility requirement.

But are targeted killings indiscriminate? As far back as 2009, Andrew Exum and David Kilcullen argued that the targeted killing programme kills many militants, but that senior leadership appears to be a small number of these casualties.[122] This was used by Mary Ellen O'Connell, a leading critic of the targeted killing programme, to call the legality of the endeavour into question.[123] Neither analysis is a direct criticism of the programme's utility. Exum and Kilcullen are primarily interested in the effects of the programme on Pakistan – for good reason, because it borders Afghanistan and is a nuclear weapon state. They argue that it is an inefficient method of attacking al-Qaeda. But inefficiency is not the question. Inefficiency regards the tools available – the use of a cruise missile in place of a precision strike – would be inefficient. When Exum and Kilcullen were writing, the 'AfPak' concept/neologism was in vogue, which was thinking about the Afghan/Pakistan border and countries as interrelated.[124] This has since

90   *War and law enforcement*

fallen foul of the very messy conflict in Afghanistan. The state-building counter-insurgency operations that could, in principle, replace targeted killings are no longer an option. O'Connell, conversely, uses the data absent the key point that many of those killed were not strictly civilians – the New America Foundation report that she quotes includes statistics covering estimated militant deaths,[125] but she excludes these from her analysis, choosing instead to consider anyone not in al-Qaeda's leadership to be an innocent target. In one stated example, she details at length the death of Baitullah Mehsud.[126] The persons killed included civilians (Mehsud's wife and parents-in-law), Mehsud's bodyguards and a lieutenant, and Mehsud, from which O'Connell draws the conclusion that 'the strike killed twelve for one intended target'.[127] Here one can see the essential contradiction in interpretation – one could argue that the strike killed three non-combatants and nine legitimate targets (a 1:3 ratio), but in O'Connell's perception the ratio is 11 illegitimate targets to one possibly legitimate target (O'Connell later argues that these strikes are illegitimate anyway). If one is to consider Mehsud a legitimate target, it is difficult to see how O'Connell's rationale works when compared to other methods. Is there a method of killing a legitimate target – surrounded by seven bodyguards and a lieutenant, and co-located with civilians – that would likely not, at the very least, endanger the civilians, if not kill them? Absent such a method, it appears a logical fallacy to compare the possibility of killing Mehsud solo, to killing those with him. Breaking from the spectre of the solo kill, criticism of the targeted killing programme should be directed at the ratio between civilian deaths and those of militias. It should also be noted that O'Connell does not consider the use of military force to be legitimate in this instance; therefore her analysis does not include the legitimacy of the double-effect principle in both IHL and just war ethics. The principle of double effect allows for the incidental death of civilians, even if these deaths are likely, as long as they are not the target of the use of force, and as long as the number of civilians killed is proportionate to the military value of the target. The principle of double effect relates to subjective military judgements regarding the value of killing persons such as Mehsud, and how many civilian casualties are tolerable in relation to the value of the target. Double effect has no place within the law enforcement paradigm by which O'Connell judges this act, but it is an essential feature of IHL.

The defence of targeted killings offered by the Obama administration does not require these strikes to eliminate al-Qaeda – they are a means of disrupting networks in places where the law enforcement paradigm is inoperable. Therefore the fact that these strikes have not eliminated al-Qaeda, and that there is no evidence that they will do in the long run, does not undermine the specific claim of their utility. This utility is in turn integral to the claim of necessity made by the Obama administration. Whether these strikes are proportional is shown to be largely ontological – when militants and legitimate targets are defined in the way the Obama administration does, these strikes appear to be proportional, at a macro level, in terms of the general conduct of hostilities in the contemporary world. Manipulating the data to produce a worst-case scenario also produces a relatively benign civilian:combatant ratio, although not one that the United States would likely be proud of. Furthermore, analysis of the critical expectations about the status of persons, particularly the civilian assumption, demonstrates that these critical readings do not take account of the general conduct of hostilities. The definition of who is, and is not, entitled to the civilian protection rests in part on the classification process. Maxwell's criticism of recent International Committee of the Red Cross (ICRC) guidance on the notion of 'direct participation in hostilities' is that this examines the loss of protection for civilians on an individual level, not at the group level. As Maxwell writes: '[T]he acts of terrorists are not only acts of the individuals who directly do violence, but also the acts of the groups whose planning, command structure, and resources make the acts of violence possible'.[128] The question therefore turns to the degree to which membership of a terrorist or militant network in general makes a person liable for targeting, which will be discussed in Chapter 4.

Conclusion

Terrorists remain political 'enemies' regardless of whether law enforcement or militarised methods are used to counteract them. The defence of the use of targeted killings against al-Qaeda and associated groups is that they are active enemies (in a de facto state of war), that law enforcement is impossible and that the use of force against these networks can disrupt their otherwise lethal activities.

This chapter has demonstrated that a de facto state of war exists between al-Qaeda and the United States. This does not, however, preclude the use of law enforcement measures, nor does it give free rein to use military means. This chapter has, however, identified specific areas in which targeted killings are currently used (areas absent de facto state sovereignty) as places where law enforcement measures do not work. Lastly, this section identified two purposes for the use of targeted killings – deterrence and disruption, as part of a strategy of containment – a method of connecting political ends with means. The next chapter therefore examines US use of targeted killings to determine whether they are a useful means of achieving this.

The application of containment to a single non-state actor is unlikely; instead, if accepted, it would likely form the manner in which the United States, or other states, would seek to contain the non-state actors that they consider threatening, while using other means to attempt to draw the political conflicts that give rise to these adversarial relationships. This is an unhappy strategy. It is a far cry from the brave new world of Francis Fukuyama's *End of History*[129] and the United States' unipolar moment. Neither, however, is it the nightmare world envisaged by Robert Kaplan in *The Coming Anarchy*.[130] It is, however, a world in which states such as the United States use lethal force against networks of individuals, often in states with which they are not at war. Unless alternative methods of managing these networks or applying asymmetric containment can be found, these paramilitary methods will likely be one of the only ways that states can contain such actors.

Notes

1 Authorization for Use of Military Force.
2 Obama, 'Nobel Peace Prize'.
3 Christopher Greenwood, 'International Law and the "War against Terrorism"', *International Affairs* 78(2) (2002): 305.
4 O'Connell, 'Choice of Law against Terrorism'.
5 Yoo, 'Assassination'.
6 Yoo, *War by Other Means*.
7 Wyn Q. Bowen and David H. Dunn, *American Security Policy in the 1990s: Beyond Containment* (Aldershot, UK: Dartmouth, 1996): 100.
8 Robert DiPrizio, *US Humanitarian Interventions in the Post-Cold War Era* (Baltimore, MD: Johns Hopkins University Press, 2002): 166.
9 Obama, 'Remarks by the President on National Security'; Koh, 'Lawfulness of the U.S. Operation'; Panetta, 'Director's Remarks'; Holder, 'Northwestern University Speech'; Brennan, 'Ethics and Efficacy'.
10 Jeff McMahan, 'Targeted Killing: Murder, Combat or Law Enforcement?', in *Targeted Killings: Law and Morality in an Asymmetrical World*, edited by Claire Finkelstein, Jens D. Ohlin and Andrew Altman (Oxford University Press, 2012).
11 Brennan, 'Strengthening Our Security'.
12 Alston, 'Report of the Special Rapporteur'.
13 Mary Ellen O'Connell, 'The Legal Case against the Global War on Terror', *Case Western Reserve Journal of International Law* 36(2) (2004).
14 O'Connell, 'To Kill or Capture'; O'Connell, 'Choice of Law against Terrorism'.
15 Radsan and Murphy, 'Evolution of Law and Policy': 462.
16 Brennan, 'Ethics and Efficacy'.
17 Kilcullen and Exum, 'Death from Above'.
18 Dennis C. Blair, 'Drones Alone Are Not the Answer', *New York Times*, 14 August 2011.
19 Walzer, *Just and Unjust Wars*: 129.
20 Obama, 'Remarks by the President on National Security'; Brennan, 'Ethics and Efficacy'.
21 Carl von Clausewitz, tr. Michael Howard and Peter Paret, *On War* (London: Everyman's Library, 1993): 83.
22 Alston, 'Report of the Special Rapporteur': 10.
23 Alston, 'Report of the Special Rapporteur': 15.
24 O'Connell, 'Choice of Law against Terrorism': 345.
25 Jens D. Ohlin, *The Assault on International Law* (Oxford University Press, 2015): 175–6.
26 Alston, 'Report of the Special Rapporteur': 16.
27 Yoo, 'Assassination': 63.
28 Brennan, 'Ethics and Efficacy'.
29 Melzer, *Targeted Killing*: 85.
30 Melzer, *Targeted Killing*: 89.
31 Alston, 'CIA and Targeted Killings': 303. For his part, Alston notes that IHRL applies outside the context of armed conflict, and also takes issue with their use as 'law enforcement', because IHRL applies to all state agents using force.
32 Blum and Heymann, 'Law and Policy': 145.
33 Melzer, *Targeted Killing*: 243.
34 O'Connell, 'Choice of Law against Terrorism'.
35 Michael Chertoff, 'War v. Crime: Breaking the Chains of the Old Security Paradigm', in *Confronting Terror: 9/11 and the Future of American National Security*, edited by Dean Reuter and John Yoo (New York, NY: Encounter Books, 2011): 56.
36 Yoo, *Crisis and Command*: 444.

War and law enforcement   93

37 Koh, 'Obama Administration'; Brennan, 'Strengthening Our Security'.
38 Yoo, *Crisis and Command*: 442.
39 Holder, 'Northwestern University Speech'.
40 O'Connell, 'To Kill or Capture'; O'Connell, 'Unlawful Killing'; O'Connell, 'Choice of Law against Terrorism'.
41 O'Connell, 'To Kill or Capture': 326–7.
42 O'Connell, 'To Kill or Capture': 330.
43 Max Weber, *Politics as a Vocation* (Philadelphia, PA: Fortress Press, 1972).
44 Thomas D. Grant, 'Defining Statehood: The Montevideo Convention and Its Discontents', *Columbia Journal of Transnational Law* 37(2) (1998).
45 Alston, 'Report of the Special Rapporteur'.
46 Jean Bodin, tr. Julian H. Franklin, *On Sovereignty: Four Chapters from the Six Books of the Commonwealth* (Cambridge University Press, 1992).
47 Jacques Maritain, 'The Concept of Sovereignty', in *In Defence of Sovereignty*, edited by Wladyslav Stankiewicz (New York: Oxford University Press, 1969): 41.
48 Robert H. Jackson, *Quasi-States: Sovereignty, International Relations, and the Third World* (Cambridge University Press, 1990): 17.
49 Stuart Elden, 'Contingent Sovereignty, Territorial Integrity, and the Sanctity of Borders', *SAIS Review* 26(1) (2006).
50 For an outline of international interventions, see Nicholas J. Wheeler, *Saving Strangers: Humanitarian Intervention in International Society* (Oxford University Press, 2000): 178.
51 Martin N. Murphy, *Somalia: The New Barbary?: Piracy and Islam in the Horn of Africa* (London: Hurst, 2011): 125.
52 Robert Jackson and Carl Rosberg, 'Why Africa's Weak States Persist: The Empirical and the Juridical in Statehood', *World Politics* 35(1) (1982).
53 Gerald B. Helman and Steven R. Ratner, 'Saving Failed States', *Foreign Policy* 89 (Winter 1992/1993): 3–20.
54 Aidan Hehir, 'The Myth of the Failed State and the War on Terror: A Challenge to the Conventional Wisdom', *Journal of Intervention and Statebuilding* 1(3) (2007): 312.
55 Robert Rotberg, *State Failure and State Weakness in a Time of Terror* (Washington, DC: Brookings Institution Press, 2003): 10.
56 White House, *The National Security Strategy of the United States of America* (Washington, DC: White House, 2006). The most cited and thorough government assessment is that of Robert D. Lamb, *Ungoverned Areas and Threats from Safe Havens* (Washington, DC: Office of the Under Secretary of Defense for Policy, 2008). See also Angel Rabasa, *Ungoverned Territories: Understanding and Reducing Terrorism Risks* (Santa Monica, CA: RAND, 2007).
57 See, for example: Reece Jones, 'Sovereignty and Statelessness in the Border Enclaves of India and Bangladesh', *Political Geography* 28(6) (2009).
58 Alan Wright, *Policing: An Introduction to Concepts and Practice* (Devon, UK: Willan, 2002). For a comparative study of criminal justice systems, see Harry R. Dammer, Erika Fairchild and Jay S. Albanese, *Comparative Criminal Justice Systems*, 3rd edn (Belmont, CA: Wadsworth/Thomson Learning, 2006).
59 Walt W. Rostow, *The Process of Economic Growth*, 2nd edn (Oxford: Clarendon Press, 1960); Dean C. Tipps, 'Modernization Theory and the Comparative Study of National Societies: A Critical Perspective', *Comparative Studies in Society and History* 15(2) (1973).
60 Samuel P. Huntington, 'The Change to Change: Modernization, Development, and Politics', *Comparative Politics* 3(3) (1971): 285.
61 Alvin Y. So, *Social Change and Development: Modernization, Dependency, and World-Systems Theories* (Newbury Park, CA: Sage Publications, 1990): Chs 4–5.
62 Robert H. Jackson, *Quasi-States*.

94 *War and law enforcement*

63 Francis Fukuyama, *State-Building: Governance and World Order in the 21st Century* (Ithaca, NY: Cornell University Press, 2004): ix.
64 Kilcullen and Exum, 'Death from Above'.
65 Fatima Ayub and Sari Kouvo, 'Righting the Course? Humanitarian Intervention, the War on Terror and the Future of Afghanistan', *International Affairs* 84(4) (2008); Thomas E. Ricks, *Fiasco: The American Military Adventure in Iraq* (New York: Penguin Press, 2006).
66 Kenneth J. Menkhaus, 'Governance without Government in Somalia: Spoilers, State Building, and the Politics of Coping', *International Security* 31(3) (Winter 2006/07); Sarah Phillips, 'What Comes Next in Yemen? Al-Qaeda, the Tribes, and State-Building' (Report, Washington, DC: Carnegie Endowment for Peace, 2010).
67 Brennan, 'Ethics and Efficacy'.
68 Barry R. Posen, 'The Struggle against Terrorism: Grand Strategy, Strategy, and Tactics', *International Security* 26(3) (2002).
69 Hoffman, 'Changing Face of Al Qaeda'.
70 X (George F. Kennan), 'The Sources of Soviet Conduct', *Foreign Affairs* 25(4) (1947); John L. Gaddis, *Strategies of Containment: A Critical Appraisal of American National Security Policy During the Cold War* (New York, NY: Oxford University Press, 2005); Rupert Smith, *The Utility of Force: The Art of War in the Modern World* (London: Allen Lane, 2005): 181.
71 Dunn, 'Bush': 20.
72 Patrick Porter, 'Long Wars and Long Telegrams: Containing Al-Qaeda', *International Affairs* 85(2) (2009): 301.
73 Matthew Elledge, *The Global War on Terrorism: A Policy of Containment* (Fort Leavenworth, Kansas: United States Army Command and General Staff College, 2003).
74 Cronin, *How Terrorism Ends*.
75 John L. Gaddis, *George F. Kennan: An American Life* (New York, NY: Penguin Press, 2011): 534.
76 Brennan, 'Ethics and Efficacy'.
77 Thomas Rid, 'Deterrence Beyond the State: The Israeli Experience', *Contemporary Security Policy* 33(1) (2012): 141.
78 Rid, 'Deterrence Beyond the State': 142.
79 Ron Suskind, *The One Percent Doctrine: Deep inside America's Pursuit of Its Enemies since 9/11* (London: Simon & Schuster, 2006).
80 James R. Van De Velde, 'The Impossible Challenge of Deterring "Nuclear Terrorism" by Al Qaeda', *Studies in Conflict and Terrorism* 33(8) (2010).
81 John Gearson, 'Deterring Conventional Terrorism: From Punishment to Denial and Resilience', *Contemporary Security Policy* 33(1) (2012): 175.
82 John Stone, 'Al Qaeda, Deterrence, and Weapons of Mass Destruction', *Studies in Conflict and Terrorism* 32(9) (2009).
83 Alex S. Wilner, 'Deterring the Undeterrable: Coercion, Denial, and Delegitimization in Counterterrorism', *Journal of Strategic Studies* 34(1) (2011).
84 Stone, 'Al Qaeda': 765–8.
85 Neville Bolt, David Betz and Jaz Azari, *Propaganda of the Deed 2008: Understanding the Phenomenon* (London: Royal United Services Institute for Defence and Security Studies, 2008).
86 Kenney, *From Pablo to Osama*.
87 Kenney, *From Pablo to Osama*: 144–5.
88 Carlo Morselli, C. Giguère and K. Petit, 'The Efficiency/Security Trade-Off in Criminal Networks', *Social Networks* 29(1) (2007).
89 Rebecca Goolsby, 'Combating Terrorist Networks: An Evolutionary Approach', *Computational and Mathematical Organization Theory* 12(1) (2006): 15–17.

War and law enforcement 95

90 Marc Sageman, *Understanding Terror Networks* (Philadelphia: University of Pennsylvania Press, 2004): 69.

91 Cronin, *Ending Terrorism*: 394.

92 Mark Urban, *Big Boys' Rules: The Secret Struggle against the IRA* (London: Faber, 1992).

93 Byman, 'Do Targeted Killings Work?'; Byman, *A High Price*.

94 Kilcullen and Exum, 'Death from Above'.

95 Mothana, 'How Drones Help Al Qaeda'.

96 Declan Walsh, 'Pakistani Parliament Demands End to U.S. Drone Strikes', *New York Times*, 20 March 2012; Avery Plaw, Matthew Fricker and Brian Glyn Williams, 'Practice Makes Perfect?: The Changing Civilian Toll of CIA Drone Strikes in Pakistan', *Perspectives on Terrorism* 5(5–6) (2011): 53.

97 Sudarsan Raghavan, 'In Yemen, U.S. Airstrikes Breed Anger, and Sympathy for Al-Qaeda', *Washington Post*, 30 May 2012; Orla Guerin, 'Pakistani Civilian Victims Vent Anger over US Drones', *BBC News*, 3 November 2011.

98 Austin Long, *On 'Other War': Lessons from Five Decades of RAND Counterinsurgency Research* (Santa Monica, CA: RAND, 2006): 39.

99 Rid, 'Deterrence Beyond the State': 140.

100 Gallup, 'Muslim Americans: Faith, Freedom, and the Future', *Gallup* (Poll, 2011): 30.

101 Gallup, 'Muslim Americans': 18.

102 New America Foundation, 'Pakistan Survey', *New America Foundation* (2014).

103 Milena Michalski and James Gow, *War, Image and Legitimacy: Viewing Contemporary Conflict* (Abingdon, UK: Routledge, 2007); Bolt, Betz and Azari, *Propaganda of the Deed*.

104 Spencer Ackerman, 'Rare Photographs Show Ground Zero of the Drone War', *Wired*, 12 December 2011.

105 Reporters Without Borders, 'Call For Better Media Access To Tribal Areas', *Reporters Without Borders*, 10 November 2009.

106 Scott Shane, Mark Mazzetti and Robert F. Worth, 'Secret Assault on Terrorism Widens on Two Continents', *New York Times*, 14 August 2010; Spencer Ackerman, 'Obama's New Defense Plan: Drones, Spec Ops and Cyber War', *Wired*, 5 January 2012.

107 Dawn Lim and Noah Shachtman, 'Air Force Tells Reporters: You're Not Welcome at Our Drone Base Anymore', *Wired*, 29 November 2011.

108 Barack Obama, 'Remarks by the President at the "Change of Office" Chairman of the Joint Chiefs of Staff' (Speech, Ceremony Fort Myer, VA, 30 September 2011).

109 Google, 'Your Interview with the President'; Brennan, 'Ethics and Efficacy'.

110 Blair, 'Drones Alone'.

111 Cronin, *How Terrorism Ends*: 14.

112 Morley, 'Petraeus'.

113 McNeal, 'Are Targeted Killings Unlawful?'.

114 Richard M. Garfield and Alfred I. Neugut, 'The Human Consequences of War', in *War and Public Health*, edited by Barry S. Levy and Victor W. Sidel (New York, NY: Oxford University Press, 2008): 32.

115 Garfield and Neugut, 'Human Consequences of War': 33.

116 Ignatieff, *Virtual War*: 215.

117 Bill Roggio, 'Senior al Qaeda, Taliban, and Allied Jihadist Leaders Killed in US Airstrikes in Pakistan, 2004–2015', *Long War Journal*, 11 June 2015.

118 Byman, *A High Price*: 103.

119 Megan Smith and James I. Walsh, 'Do Drone Strikes Degrade Al Qaeda? Evidence from Propaganda Output', *Terrorism and Political Violence* 25(2) (2013).

120 Megan Smith and Walsh, 'Do Drone Strikes Degrade Al Qaeda?': 324–5.

121 Daniel Kimmage, 'Al-Qaeda Central and the Internet' (Washington, DC: New America Foundation, 2010): 16.

96 *War and law enforcement*

122 Kilcullen and Exum, 'Death from Above'.
123 O'Connell, 'Unlawful Killing': 57.
124 This neologism originates in the January 2009 appointment of Richard Holbrooke as Special Representative for Afghanistan and Pakistan by Barack Obama.
125 Peter Bergen and Katherine Tiedemann, 'The Year of the Drone: An Analysis of U.S. Drone Strikes in Pakistan, 2004–2010' (Washington, DC: New America Foundation, 2010): Appendix A.
126 O'Connell, 'Unlawful Killing': 10.
127 O'Connell, 'Unlawful Killing': 10.
128 Mark Maxwell, 'Rebutting the Civilian Presumption: Playing Whack-a-Mole without a Mallet?', in *Targeted Killings: Law and Morality in an Asymmetrical World*, edited by Claire Finkelstein, Jens D. Ohlin and Andrew Altman (Oxford University Press, 2012): 53–4.
129 Fukuyama, *End of History*.
130 Robert Kaplan, 'The Coming Anarchy: How Scarcity, Overpopulation, Tribalism and Disease Are Rapidly Destroying the Social Fabric of the World', *Atlantic Monthly*, February 1994.

4 International law

Islamist terror appears to be fragmenting into loose networks of shared ideology and aspiration rather than tightly vertical organizations linked by command and control. It will take successive feats of intellectual jujitsu to cast all of the targets such developments will reasonably put in the cross hairs as, legally speaking, combatants.

Kenneth Anderson[1]

The almost universal rule in remote times was, and continues to be with barbarous armies, that the private individual of the hostile country is destined to suffer every privation of liberty and protection, and every disruption of family ties. Protection was, and still is with uncivilized people, the exception.

The Lieber Code, article 24, 1863[2]

Introduction

The Obama administration argues that the use of targeted killings is consistent with US obligations in international law[3]; however, many international law scholars disagree.[4] Furthermore, questions of international law are often central to debates about targeted killings. Academic writing on international law relevant to targeted killings is one of the richest areas of present debate, but the deeper legal reasoning of the US government has been made public, in fragmentary form, through leaks, memos and speeches.[5]

The Obama administration's defence of targeted killings is predicated on a number of premises relevant to international law – that a state of war exists between the United States and al-Qaeda, that targeting individuals with lethal force is legitimate in the context of this war, that the use of force is necessary and that the means used are legitimate. Whereas the previous chapter addressed war in its conceptual and strategic sense, it is now necessary to reconcile this with the definitions of war and armed conflict found in international law. The US government legitimises targeted killings by articulating and maintaining their non-illegality. In order to do this, the Obama administration's defence relies on the liminal space between positively authorised activities in law and positively prohibited activities. Importantly, there are areas of international law governing

98 *International law*

the use of force for which there is an intentional lack of *opinio juris*.[6] Also, as previously noted (see p. 50), treaty law does not provide an immediate fit for classifying the type of conflict that the United States is in. Some commentators referred to the Bush administration's use of these gaps as creating legal 'black holes'.[7] However, unlike the Bush administration, which sought to limit the application of law and challenged the applicability of basic standards such as the Geneva Conventions, the Obama administration argues that it abides by the 'principles of the laws of war where the law is unclear'.[8]

In legal terms, the Obama administration's defence turns on the argument that the United States has the right to use force in self-defence, and that its use of force does not breach the sovereignty of other states. A second cluster of claims are that IHL applies in the context of targeted killings and that targeted killings do not contravene the *jus in bello* prohibitions of IHL. There are significant consequences to these arguments. The legitimation of the practice of targeted killing expands grey areas of international law, and the adoption of these positions by other states will serve to widen the scope for the use of force under existing interpretations of law. There are political externalities created by these wider interpretations that, although not positively undermining the Obama administration's defence, form an integral component of the defence that it offers.

The United States and international law

International law is inextricably linked to international politics.[9] Therefore before making an assessment of the legality of targeted killings in international law, it is first necessary to examine the particular way in which international law binds the United States. As previously noted, the United States is a permanent member of the UNSC; therefore it is effectively immune – via veto – from legitimate UNSC-sanctioned international intervention. It is also a nuclear weapon state and has a defence budget in excess of the next ten comparable states combined. The 2012 Military Balance states that the United States' planned defence expenditure in 2011 was 45.7 per cent of global expenditures.[10] These elements of power in international politics are a defining feature of the United States' foreign policy and role in global politics.

Key to the Obama administration's defence is that its actions are in accordance with international law; therefore in order for this defence to function, it cannot directly contravene the principles of international law. This claim is best explored in Eric Holder's speech. It is notable that Holder's claims for legitimacy and legality are founded in the *non-illegality* of the act of targeted killing. Working from the premise that it is 'entirely legal' under US law and 'applicable law of war principles' (note, not under IHL) to target al-Qaeda's leadership, Holder develops an argument that does not construct a case, so much as rebut specific claims of illegality. He states that targeted killings are not assassinations and are therefore not illegal under EO 12333 *et al.* He then balances 'due process' under the Fifth Amendment by arguing that it 'takes into account the realities of combat'. Holder's argument rests that it would be lawful to target a

US citizen after 'thorough and careful review' of the imminent threat posed, where capture is not feasible and where the targeting was conducted in accordance with law of war principles. Holder expands the concept of imminence outside that considered by IHL, in line with the same expansion that allows for liminal targeting. Holder's case is therefore not so much about proving targeted killings as a distinctly legal act, as about disproving the ability of legal principles and laws to classify them as illegal from first principles.[11]

Critics of the United States' targeted killing programme argue that the programme is illegal under international law. The primary argument of Alston, and others, is that targeted killings can be determined as illegal according to international treaties and their standard interpretation. Alston argues from the position of strict adherence to international law as defined in close readings of treaties.[12] Overenthusiastic supporters of the targeted killing programme are also its worst critics. Russell Christopher makes the argument that imminence, a key concept of international law, should be abandoned. While doing so, he notes that without such abandonment, targeted killings cannot be justified in self-defence under international law.[13] The Obama administration seeks to define itself as different from the Bush administration by claiming that *jus in bello* constraints defined in the Geneva Conventions apply. It does, however, claim its actions as legitimate without extension of existing law, in contrast to persons who advocate novel legal regimes.[14] In the unclear areas of law, the Obama administration argues that it acts in accordance with 'the principles of the laws of war'.[15] This caveat is important. What the Obama administration's defence of the practice implies is that where the law is unclear, it acts within the spirit of these laws.

Before examining the legal debates surrounding the practice of targeted killings, it is important to examine the United States' relationship to the international legal regimes that are central to this debate. The US government does not consider itself bound by international law in the same manner as many other states. The US court system interprets customary international law as federal law, but statutes take precedence over customary international law.[16] The US political system holds that the Constitution is the highest source of legal authority, a position that many international lawyers dismiss but that is at the same time highly relevant. Critics of US targeted killings state that they are illegal and that the United States' conduct undermines international law.[17]

The Obama administration's defence of targeted killings includes the caveat that it acts in accordance with the principles of international law. The United States displays its acceptance of key principles of international law in its internalisation of those laws. In particular, the United States' domestic military code, governing the use of armed force in wartime, is closely aligned with its duties as a party to the Geneva Conventions. Therefore the problem is not necessarily the Obama administration's rejection of international law, as its critics hold, but its particular interpretation of that law. In this, the Obama administration seeks to define a standard of conduct that is not illegal under international law. Here, it is important to note the many caveats contained in treaty law that define the US interpretation of these treaties. For example, the United States' declaration

100 *International law*

(1) on signing the International Covenant on Civil and Political Rights (ICCPR) declared that it considered the bulk of its articles are non-self-executing, meaning that they must be formulated in national law to be binding in the US legal system. Non-acceptance of the United States' position on the matter is evident in the assumption that the rights afforded persons exist independent of its treaty interpretation, but does not change the matter from the perspective of the United States.[18] Critics of the United States point to the fact that international law, as well as world order, serve US interests. Nico Krisch argues that in times of hegemony, dominant states either instrumentalise or withdraw from international law. His argument is correct in saying that these two poles do not wholly characterise the relationships between dominant states and international law.[19] As noted in this chapter, the United States seeks neither to refashion IHL to its use (although critics assert this), nor to withdraw from its constraints; instead, it seeks to redefine terms within IHL and increase the uncertainty of interpretation of these treaties. What is more important to consider is that if the use of targeted killings can be reconciled with international legal restrictions on the use of force, this sets a precedent in customary law, and the United States' international stature is such that other states may follow suit.

There are three primary fields of law that interact: law regarding the resort to the use of force (commonly referred to as *jus ad bellum*), law governing the use of force within a conflict (*jus in bello*) and IHRL. *Jus ad bellum* is international law independent of IHL; *jus in bello* is IHL. Alston argues that IHRL applies at all times, even within war; however, the laws of war represent a *lex specialis*, thus superseding them where they apply. The relationship between IHL and IHRL is complex. Some consider them to be complementary; however, this is a relatively novel interpretation.[20] Key to understanding the difference is whether human rights standards apply outside the context of targeting decisions, or whether IHL, as *lex specialis*, supersedes IHRL during a conflict. The complementary approach effectively 'okays' derogations from IHRL standards where IHL applies; the latter interpretation, in many ways considered the standard outside academic circles, is that IHRL considerations do not apply in wars. The key point of contention is that Alston considers the laws of war to only apply where they are defined in treaty law, whereas the United States and others consider the laws of war to apply where a war exists in fact, or as a matter of state definition. As Alston states: '[T]o the extent that IHL does not provide a rule, or the rule is unclear and its meaning cannot be ascertained from the guidance offered by IHL principles it is appropriate to draw guidance from IHRL'.[21]

However, as Schabas notes, there are stricter interpretations advanced by the Human Rights Council.[22] A wider approach, noted by W. H. Parks, is that IHL applies in general during a conflict, and that IHRL is entirely subsumed during a conflict.[23] As argued in the previous chapter, this is a matter of interpretation, given the United States' status and known positions on the issue. What is key is whether the United States' actions directly violate the principles of the laws of war, as well as whether they are reconcilable with the treaty law.

International law 101

The two key questions of international law pertinent here are whether the United States can legally use force against al-Qaeda, and whether its conduct within that conflict is legal. In answering these two key questions, the debate centres on three key areas: international law and the use of force (primarily focused on the question of self-defence),[24] the type of conflict that exists between al-Qaeda and the United States, and the relevant status of persons that the United States defines as enemies within that conflict. Following a resort to force, the second area refers to the question of whether the armed conflict can be classified in international law as an IAC or an NIAC, both of which have different criteria for assessing belligerency and combatant status.[25] The third area is the question of combatant status, linked to the type of conflict that the United States is in. Within an IAC, there are privileged and unprivileged combatants, whereas the law governing participation in an NIAC is far less clear. Of particular importance is the concept of 'direct participation in hostilities', which is discussed later in this chapter (see p. 105).[26]

In the previous chapter I argued that the United States is in a de facto state of war with al-Qaeda. Whether the United States has a legal justification or not for waging war on al-Qaeda is the first major area of contention. Strict interpretations of the use of force constrain the ability of states to use force, and would thus render the use of targeted killings illegal. A strict reading of the *Caroline* doctrine would negate the applicability of self-defence versus terrorist networks. Similarly, strict readings of IHL argue that the United States cannot be in either an IAC or an NIAC with a non-contiguous extraterritorial non-state actor (any use of force in such a conflict would also be illegal). However, a significant number of analysts and scholars argue that the United States is legitimately allowed to use force in self-defence. Wachtel argues that the persistence of threat allows for targeting under self-defence.[27] Guiora argues that the Israeli experience proves the need for active self-defence to be enshrined in law.[28] Anderson points out that, fundamentally, the United States has long reserved the right to use force in self-defence against any use of force.[29]

The question of self-defence centres on the question of whether states are legally allowed to use preventative measures against hostile entities, and the temporal constraints on doing so. Key to this is the *Caroline* doctrine. This relates to an attack by British forces in Canada on the *Caroline*, a ship in US territory. The British argued that they did so out of self-defence; the US reply stated that necessity depended on a threat being 'instant, overwhelming, leaving no choice of means, and no moment for deliberation'. Examining the concept of self-defence, Murphy differentiates between persons who adhere to the 'imminent threat' doctrine and those who concur but consider that groups or states can pose a qualitative threat that can provoke the use of force in self-defence.[30] For its part, the Obama administration claims both that it is at war with al-Qaeda – as well as being engaged in an armed conflict with al-Qaeda – and that it is legally justified to resort to the use of force due to the principle of self-defence. This covers two areas: the type of conflict and the *jus ad bellum*. The use of force in self-defence is a contentious issue, because nuclear weapon

102   *International law*

states reserve the right to use nuclear weapons in self-defence, which violates the principles of discrimination and proportionality. In 1996 the ICJ gave an advisory opinion on the threat and use of nuclear weapons, stating that their use had to be strictly in accordance with UN Charter principles; but the court was evenly split and could not 'conclude definitively whether the threat or use of nuclear weapons would be lawful or unlawful in an extreme circumstance of self-defence, in which the very survival of a State would be at stake'.[31] This decision is taken to signal that the maximum level of force permitted for a state acting in self-defence is uncertain. However, the Obama administration considers itself bound by the Geneva Conventions, even in self-defence, while not referring to the use of nuclear weapons.

The Obama administration's defence of targeted killings includes adherence to *jus in bello* principles, while using self-defence as a basis for legitimacy. In effect, the Obama administration is arguing for one type of *jus ad bellum* while stating that it considers itself bound by IHL regardless. This does appear to conform with the principles of the laws of war, as espoused by Holder.

The type of conflict is, however, important, because two types of armed conflict exist in IHL: IAC and NIAC. This difference is defined in the 1949 Geneva Conventions; Article 3, common to all conventions, sets out a standard of minimum conduct '[I]n the case of armed conflict not of an international character occurring in the territory of one of the High Contracting Parties'. Fundamentally, war does not legally exist between a state and a non-state actor across borders in international law. The SCI applied IAC to the conduct of targeted killings, but did so in order that the use of force be held to a higher standard.[32] The Court held that a standard higher than that found in IHL should apply to the conduct of targeted killings, since it stated that these acts could only occur where capture was not possible. This rationale is similar to that used by the Obama administration to defend targeted killings, but it is not bound to do so.[33] The result is essentially an impasse, and one likely to be solved by evolving custom rather than treaty. One can, however, see a key problem in allowing states to use legal regimes that are easier to interpret in their favour, such as NIAC, but in this instance the Obama administration does not appear to depend on this regime's extended flexibility. It seems prudent, therefore, to examine the legality of the more inflexible and higher standard of the two in examining whether the use of targeted killings violates the laws of *jus in bello*.

The legal classification of war is important because it affects the privileges and protections afforded state combatants, non-state militants and civilians alike. Of particular relevance to the US use of targeted killings is the notion of direct participation in hostilities. Direct participation is especially salient because it determines if and when a civilian becomes a legitimate military target, by committing acts that cause them to lose their protected status in IHL. There are two competing modes of thought regarding participation. The first is that a person is liable to attack only when directly participating and posing a physical threat (the 'revolving door'). The second is that a person is liable for attack if they participate in a belligerent group in a manner that can be called a 'continuous combatant function'. This is central to the way in which Israel and the United States justify targeting individuals who are members of terrorist networks, even if they do not pose an immediate threat at the point of conducting a targeted killing. Both states claim to target individuals identified as parts of terrorist networks to disrupt plots; however, this cannot be judged with publicly available information.[34] Here, one can see that the Obama administration's defence relies on persons identified as being members of al-Qaeda, or associated groups, who are involved in planning violent attacks, being legitimate targets. This is, in effect, a membership model with an indistinct boundary between membership and continuous combat function. This is substantially different from the 'revolving door' of direct participation advocated by Alston, Melzer and the ICRC.

Rather than take a realist position, antithetical to the rule of law in international relations, the Obama administration argues that it is supporting the overall framework and spirit, seeking to apply the principles where precise law is inapplicable. Therefore, the Obama administration's defence of targeted killings promotes a particular understanding and interpretation of international law, not a complete derogation.

As previously argued (see p. 73), guerrillas and terrorists represent a liminal category of conflict participant. Discourse legitimises or prohibits the use of force against these actors, and this discourse emanates from the state party to conflict (and its detractors). One of the key criticisms of the United States' use of targeted killings is that they are illegal under international law because terrorists should be treated as civilians. However, these acts cannot be proven strictly illegal under international law due to the liminal nature of terrorist networks and concepts such as military necessity. Proponents of tightly defined, instrumental international law are at a disadvantage, in that such constraints are not interpreted in the same way by the executive branch, and international legal structures do not hold sufficient importance to significantly constrain US actions.

Critics tend to rely on a strict interpretation of treaty law, ignoring custom and practice, as well as the liminal nature of many of these categories. Their criticisms cannot define these acts as illegal except by fundamentally departing from the US government's interpretation of relevant law. Alston's criticism of the US use of targeted killings is comprehensive in sweep, as befits a former UN Special Rapporteur who has produced a report on the subject for the UN Human Rights Council. Alston is critical of targeted killings and considers them illegal under international law. In later work, Alston criticises the oversight mechanisms of the targeted killing programme, stating that these do not provide sufficient ability to demonstrate that the United States constrains its use of force.[35] Although this argument is persuasive, it neglects the 'double-hatting' of personnel. The dual-integration of these programmes simultaneously confuses chains of command, but also allows the United States to claim that its military is conducting the operations.[36] Alston's analysis is important, because his work on the subject is of the highest standard and is widely cited.

There are three primary arguments that Alston makes about targeted killings: they are illegal outside of the context of armed conflict, they violate the laws of

104 *International law*

armed conflict and they violate international law governing the use of force. Alston considers that targeted killings of the scale, nature and intention of the US use are, fundamentally, human rights violations. Melzer notes that targeted killings also occur within the law enforcement paradigm, but in order to be legal they must be the extreme choice rather than the intention. Alston clearly believes in the primacy of international law and therefore considers that, regardless of domestic legality, these acts are illegal on all three fronts.[37] This interpretation entirely ignores, or rather dismisses, the political dimension of international law. This is a problem, because the two cannot be separated, given the nature of international law and the nature of law itself. Nonetheless, the argument is still worth considering, even if the United States will never face judgment or sanction by the UNSC.

Targeted killings clearly contravene IHRL, if IHRL is the applicable framework. Common clauses of the ICCPR, as well as the International Covenant on Economic, Social and Cultural Rights, define humans as having the innate right to prevent states from unilaterally harming them or depriving them of life. Article 6 of the ICCPR states that '[E]very human being has the inherent right to life.... No one shall be arbitrarily deprived of his life'. Article 4 expressly states that states cannot derogate from this even in time of emergency. The United States did not reserve or interpret this differently at the time of ratification, although it did declare these articles 'not self-executing', meaning that US legislation would be required to enact and enforce them in the United States. The United States is nonetheless party to these treaties, meaning that it is bound by their constraints subject to its interpretation, and cannot derogate from them except by necessity. The United States is not, however, inclined to do so; instead, the government, by defining itself as being in an armed conflict with al-Qaeda, is asserting that IHL applies to its use of targeted killings. Thus any reconciliation with international legal regimes would rely on the interpretation of the relationship between IHL and IHRL, which relies on exclusivity, not complementarity.

Several commentators consider that IHL does not apply to the conflict between the United States and al-Qaeda. In the strict interpretation of the terms, al-Qaeda is not a nation state, therefore IHL regarding IAC does not apply to the conflict. Since the campaign is extraterritorial, Ramsden expressly states that a state of NIAC does not apply to 'the United States versus al-Qaeda'.[38] Alston argues that it is 'problematic for the US to show that – outside the context of armed conflicts in Afghanistan or Iraq – it is in a transnational non-international armed conflict against al Qaeda, the Taliban and other associated forces'.[39] The fallback position is that the United States is bound to respect IHL despite its noncompliance, as per the *Tadic* decision, which holds IHL restrictions on the use of force as customary law absent the presence of conflict as defined in IHL.[40] Arguments that rely on the fact that there exists no law to define the conflict between the United States and al-Qaeda are flawed. If both the United States and al-Qaeda consider themselves to be at war with one another, then a de facto state of war exists in a political and conceptual sense; the absence of legal regulation for such conflict does not change this fact. This is expressly against Alston's conditions for determining the existence of armed conflict. Alston argues that:

> Whether an armed conflict exists is a question that must be answered with reference to objective criteria, which depend on facts on the ground, and not only on the subjective declarations either of States ... or, if applicable, of non-state actors, including alleged terrorists.[41]

Alston's argument here is highly problematic, because there exists no 'objective criteria' for defining war. Here, Alston most likely refers to the positivist notion of close reading of treaty law, but even so this is problematic. Theoretically, al-Qaeda could plan and prepare for September 11-style attacks that occur once a year, which would fall outside such 'objective' considerations for 364 days per year, because members would not be actively engaged in posing a physical threat for this period. Yet it is patently absurd that such a prolonged, intended campaign of violence not be considered a war. Therefore the question is which set of laws best describes this conflict, rather than its non-existence.

In a close reading of treaty law, the United States is not in an armed conflict, because an armed conflict cannot be deemed to exist.[42] Furthermore, even if IHL did apply, the United States' targeting of individuals is likely to be found illegal; but this illegality is predicated on the 'revolving door' protection and ignores the fact that a person can be simultaneously part of a plot to cause massive harm, yet not a direct threat in the manner outlined in international law. Thus one could argue that finding the targeted killings outright illegal relies on an interpretation of international law that ignores not only state practice but also the inherent interpretability and intentional lack of *opinio juris* in some regards. This approach relies on negating many of the interpretative and purposefully non-delineated spaces of law, and therefore cannot be held to determine targeted killings illegal a priori. However, the question therefore turns to what the application of the Obama administration's interpretation of international law would mean for international legal regimes. Specifically, can it be held to be in accordance with the rule of law?

Network membership and direct participation

The primary legal prohibition relevant to targeted killings in IHL is the legal status of those targeted by the United States. The principle of distinction means that it is fundamentally illegal to target civilians; the principle is 'the most significant battlefield concept a combatant must observe'.[43] We have already seen how the United States defines members of al-Qaeda as a militant group that poses a threat that warrants the use of military force (see p. 34–5); however, beyond this, at a legal level, this means determining whether individuals are participants in an armed conflict, and whether this means that they lose the protections that are afforded civilians.

The targeting of individuals, rather than an anonymous group, is important in targeted killings. John Yoo argues that the targeting of individuals has always been legitimate.[44] Notably, Yoo also relies on the example of airstrikes directed against Libya in 1986, stating that they were targeted at Libya's leader,

106   *International law*

Muammar Gaddafi, which is explicitly denied by William Hays Parks (who was part of that decision process).[45] Yoo conflates the tactical targeting of individuals on battlefields with the strategic practice of targeted killing policies conducted against groups and terrorist networks. Here, the key differentiation is between the battlefield targeting of anonymous but self-identified enemies, and known, unilaterally identified enemies. This process may appear tautological at first, but it is important because the manner in which persons are identified as enemies by placement with an opposing force, and the identification of individuals as enemies by process of individuation and network targeting, produce two different identities of enemy: the anonymous soldier, and the personally identified individual (terrorist). The key differential is the process of identifying individuals as legitimate targets of attack. States such as Israel and the United States argue that they must target individuals identified as belonging to terrorist networks with lethal force, because otherwise they are unable to target these groups.

The Obama administration's defence of targeted killings therefore relies on two elements: first, an interpretation of IHL that permits persons to be targeted as if they were no different to, say, an armed guerrilla in a firefight; and second, the targeting process involved allows for the United States to unilaterally make such judgements. One key differentiating factor is the role of knowledge in the practice of targeted killings, which is different than that of conventional warfare. Key to this are the sets of knowledge that identify a person as a legitimate target in conventional warfare and targeted killings. The logic contained within treaty IHL reflects its origins in the eighteenth-century battlefield. Arguments about IHL are rooted in informal logic, which is described by Anthony Blair and Ralph Johnson as being 'the normative study of argument. It is the area of logic which seeks to develop standards, criteria and procedures for the interpretation, evaluation and construction of arguments and argumentation used in natural language'.[46] Within the frameworks of IHL, there are a number of points that are mutually agreed on. One is that the categories of permissible and impermissible targets are mutually exclusive (whereas who or what belongs in each category, and why, is very much open to debate). The importance of this is that the Obama administration's defence relies on a particular way of thinking about the definition of a category in IHL – direct participation in hostilities – as well as ways of identifying people as belonging to that category.

The United States justifies its targeting of al-Qaeda in ways similar to the membership model found in the SCI judgment on targeted killings.[47] Jens Ohlin outlines five modes of membership: direct participation, co-belligerency, military membership, control, and complicity and conspiracy. Of these, the membership model favoured by the Israelis is a hybrid of direct participation and complicity/conspiracy, which Ohlin argues is a hybrid of IHL and criminal law.[48] However, the United States differs from the Israeli case because, unlike Israel, US courts have by and large refrained from exercising authority over the substantive issues involved in targeted killings. Since the rebuttal of the American Civil Liberties Union's (ACLU) *Al-Aulaqi* case, the United States' judicial system has

International law 107

challenged the use of targeted killings, and a post-fact legal challenge to the killing of Anwar al-Awlaki, plus his son, Abdulrahman, and another US citizen, Saamir Khan, was rejected in 2014.[49] Therefore, the US expansion of membership targeting differs from Israel's because it does not include integral judicial oversight.

Many commentators have criticised the extension of legitimated targeting to membership of a terrorist network. The membership model in effect posits that membership of a terrorist network constitutes direct participation in hostilities. The ICRC interpretive guidelines for this note that the concept is not defined in treaty IHL.[50] The membership model treats members of a terrorist network as being members of an organised armed group; thus, they cease to be afforded the protection against physical attack that civilians are. ICRC guidance advocates that 'functional membership' of organised armed groups makes a person liable to direct attack.[51] The ICRC considers that persons have to undertake a 'continuous combat function' to remain liable to direct attack.[52] This function is structured so as to legitimate direct attack on tactical threats rather than strategic ones. Both US and Israeli targeting widens this concept, arguing that terrorist networks, by virtue of their nature and methods of attack, cannot be targeted solely on the criterion of posing an immediate tactical threat. Therefore the US interpretations consider that membership of a terrorist network in an organisational capacity constitutes a continuous combat function. This differs from the ICRC guidance, which considers persons in political or administrative activities to be an 'exclusively non-combat function'.[53] The crux of this model is that an active participant in a terrorist network can be considered a direct participant in hostilities. As Jens Ohlin states: 'one might describe the functional version of membership as a hybrid concept that straddles the distinction between status and conduct – an appropriate result for the context of terrorist organisations'.[54] This is substantially different from the ICRC's interpretation of direct participation in hostilities, even if the ICRC guidance is not a source of law.[55] Even though the validity of the ICRC's interpretation is questioned by William H. Parks as having no basis in customary or treaty law, it is included here because it represents an opinion that tightly constrains state action.[56]

By using the word 'suspect' to define terrorists, critics of targeted killings turn attention not only to the key role of knowledge in the practice, but also to the standards used to judge individuals as legitimate targets or prohibited ones.[57] As noted previously, critics tend to define terrorists as terrorist suspects, which not only places them in the law enforcement paradigm but also, more importantly, implies a lack of perfect knowledge about the person. Remember that in Western criminal justice systems, guilt – a form of socially accepted knowledge – is assigned by courts. In conventional warfare, however, the status of a soldier is a given – traditionally through self-identification. Framing these persons in military terms includes an assumption that this 'perfect' knowledge about their status is a given. There are issues with mixing this framework. For example, Daniel Kretzmer argues for the use of a 'mixed model' of humanitarian and human rights law. Here a 'suspected terrorist' could be an enemy combatant.

108 *International law*

This is technically impossible; a terrorist could be a combatant or a direct participant in hostilities, but a 'suspected terrorist' is equivalent to a 'suspected enemy combatant' – a term that is absent from IHL because these categories involve a different way of thinking about identity. Kretzmer's use of the term 'suspected combatant' is, in this sense, mixing not only bodies of law, but also logics of identification.[58] Instead of questioning whether a person is, or is not, an enemy, examination tends to begin one step forward, with the question of legitimate targeting of persons in IHL. The framing role of knowledge in defining a person as an enemy is critical to legitimating them as a potential target for a targeted killing operation. The difference between law enforcement and non-military targeted killings is, in this regard, a difference in both ontology and epistemology. This characterisation of the 'enemy' is critically important, because it plays a considerable role in the method by which persons can be identified as such.

A key criticism of targeted killings is the process by which persons are targeted. As Jeremy Scahill states: 'I'm not saying that those people were not al-Qaida operatives or that they weren't militants, but what I'm saying is we have no way of independently verifying who these people are that were killed'.[59] Scahill's concern is, like Alston's, verification and accountability. But his concern relates to the wider question of the identity of persons targeted by targeted killings and how this legitimates their targeting. The work of Curtis Bradley and Jack Goldsmith is instructive here, as they questioned (in the context of detention) the definitions of al-Qaeda and how a person might be construed to be a part of that group. They examined these categories for the purposes of examining presidential authority, not to examine the processes by which a person could be defined as belonging to one of these categories; however, these two issues are related, but the question of presidential authority is considered in the next chapter.[60]

Some arguments that support the use of targeting killings in limited circumstances also raise the problem of identity. Gabriella Blum and Philip Heymann do not, however, go into detail about the process by which a person should be identified; they say only that such identification must be accurate.[61] On the one hand, the United States knows enough to target these persons; on the other, it chooses to kill them (while arguing that it has no other choice). One of the key shifts here is the manner in which an enemy is defined in military terms and the manner in which a person is identified as an enemy. Conventional warfare relies on a process of self-identification, which also means that a person's identity is unimportant – by identifying themselves as belonging to an opposing force, they legitimise themselves as a target. Conversely, the identification of persons belonging to terrorist networks relies on defining that network and thereby identifying persons who belong to it. The difference between the two forms of knowledge is personal identity and public identity. Furthermore, it is possible to discern two sets of criteria that legitimise a person as a target – their membership of a belligerent group, and a specific set of criteria in IHL relating to the conduct of hostilities.

Personal identity is neither known nor sought in conventional warfare. Soldiers publicly identify themselves either by their wearing of uniforms or by their physical presence at arms alongside a conventional force. In *Intelligence in War*, John Keegan outlines a specific form of knowledge – military intelligence – that in his book is predicated on the pre-existing set of knowledge whereby the enemy is already known at the group level.[62] The focus on conventional warfare ignores the fact that contained within conventional bounds, knowledge of the public identity of an individual is near-axiomatic – uniforms and physical location provide for public self-identification. These are, however, public self-identifications of membership and combatant respectively, and this difference is important. While the strategic and operational intelligence operations examined in Keegan's book defined important knowledge about an enemy force, the identity of the enemy group was already known, and the general structure and character of their forces, while not known, are the focus of knowledge generation via intelligence collection. The effectiveness of this process is the focus of Keegan's work, but it is reflective of the wider field – the focus is clearly on the knowledge required to identify and delineate targets. Whether or not an individual is a legitimate target relies on their public identity and the manner in which it links to the definition of the group. For example, persons either identifying themselves as members or combatants, or both, form legitimate targets, subject to criteria within IHL. However, medical personnel publicly identify themselves as belonging to a group, but also publicly identify themselves as medical personnel, thus rendering them ineligible for attack under IHL. Knowledge regarding personal identity is not required, because conventional warfare in IHL is an anonymous affair. Protection is afforded officers, but they are only classified as such within their own rank system, which is itself a recognition of the prevailing method of organising military units in mass conventional armies.[63] The enemy are defined by their uniform mass (and uniforms), not their individual persons and capabilities. In conventional warfare one can identify three classes of knowledge: knowledge of the enemy at a group level (nation, army, military unit), an individual's public identity and an individual's personal identity. Personal identity is irrelevant, but an individual's public identity renders them liable to attack by linking them to a known (and predefined) enemy at the group level.

Here one can see a clear distinction in the role of identity and anonymity between conventional warfare and non-conventional warfare – the 'group' level of knowledge cannot be assumed. In particular, the knowledge that is assumed in conventional warfare (the identity of the group) is unknown, and therefore knowledge that is not needed in conventional warfare (personal identity) is key to defining whether an individual is a belligerent. Analysts such as Michael Kenney depict terrorist and non-state actor networks as simple networks, or chains of networks.[64] The boundaries of a terrorist network are, however, indistinct – at what point does a facilitator become part of the network? It is important to recognise that these 'simple' networks are embedded within the larger complex network of a given population. The methods by which one analyses simple and complex networks differ, in part due to questions asked of simple

110   *International law*

networks, which make no sense with larger scale, complex networks.[65] Identifying a terrorist network is equivalent to separating or individuating it from the complex network within which it operates. This leads us to the question of definition: how does one define a non-conventional opponent?

The manner in which a simple network is defined from the context of a complex social network is important – this is the process by which the 'enemy' is formed in both targeted killings and non-conventional warfare. The key feature of this is that the standards used to define this enemy are qualitative – beliefs, actions and perceived intentions – and therefore lack the bivalent distinctions found in IHL. One can never perfectly know whether an individual is a member of this group or network, because non-conventional opponents do not self-identify. This is the function of two processes. First, terrorist networks and other non-state actors tend not to identify themselves to their opponents at the individual level. Therefore the 'uniform' standard of public self-identification by a belligerent is absent. Second, non-conventional wars lack the physically contested battlefields and standing armies by which persons would physically identify themselves as members of a belligerent group. Thus the only method by which persons can publicly self-identify themselves is by fulfilling targeting criteria in IHL, which occurs in a fleeting manner. Therefore the only way of knowing if persons are members of a belligerent group, and thus enemies, is to personally identify them as such via intelligence collection. This uncertainty militates against the bivalent distinctions of IHL, which are in theory predicated on perfect knowledge. In effect, identifying a member of a terrorist network or non-conventional opponent has to use fuzzy logic. Functional identification differs from perfect identification. The subjective nature of proof required to legitimate and legalise violence in IHL means that perfect identification is not required; it is only required to a given level, above which a target is given as 'identified' as legitimate. Fuzzy logic performs this with fuzzy sets and class membership functions. Once sufficient qualitative information is acquired about a subject to place them above a given threshold, they are defined as a legitimate target. Furthermore, the implicit disregard for self-identification by non-conventional forces means that the only way to determine whether a person is, or is not, a member is to acquire knowledge about personal identity.

The discursive definition used by the United States to target non-conventional opponents has a significant drawback. In Afghanistan, NATO forces have merged insurgents, terrorists and, importantly, drug traffickers into its 'joint integrated prioritized target list'.[66] This list provides a NATO-wide targeting structure that allows NATO forces to target enemy combatants in their area. However, the inclusion of drug traffickers and criminals on this list leaves them open to lethal targeting by NATO forces. IHL specifically prohibits the targeting of civilians. However, the line between civilian and combatant has been blurred – some say intentionally – by the presence of criminals that support combatant non-state actors. The evolution of 'narco-guerillas' and 'narco-terrorism' discourses conflates the threat posed by such actors to states with their populations, but does not change their status under IHL. Novel terms such as 'narco-terrorism' are often the

International law 111

subject of disagreement; both terms were called a 'myth' by Abraham Miller and Nicholas Damask.[67]They have, however, seen a resurgence of late.[68] Some terms, such as Tamara Makarenko's 'crime-terror continuum', effectively abolish distinctions between categories based on their activities and interoperability.[69] The degree of support that they offer combatants (lawful and unlawful) could give rise to their targeting as unlawful combatants, but data that would differentiate the two, or provide clarity as to what activity warrants placement on joint priority targeting lists, are not publicly available. Fundamentally, the practice of targeting such persons with imperfect information raises questions as to the levels of accuracy required to define them as functional members of such organisations.

If personal identity can connect persons to a terrorist network, and enough is known about them to classify them as taking direct part in hostilities, what about those whose identity is unknown? For some, the most problematic aspect of the United States' use of targeted killings is the nature of the targeting method defined as 'signature strikes'.[70] IHL relies on categories and epistemology of theoretically perfectly known targets, which are required for its constraints of positive identification – the onus being on the state to know that it is targeting combatants. Knowledge of the existence of a combatant is based on observation, and on that observation providing enough information so that a decision can be formed that categorises the individual as a combatant. Conversely, signature strikes work by identifying patterns of behaviour. These patterns are outlined in the articles on signature strikes, but not detailed. Therefore although the process is known, details such as the arbitrary threshold at which a person is identified as being a legitimate target are not. We do not know the level at which enough information is accrued about persons to define them as legitimate targets.[71] This pattern is taken to form knowledge of their likely status. It should be noted that signature strikes can only be verified as accurate *after* the conduct of the strike itself, even if the belief formed by observed patterns is a precondition for targeting a person. This uncertainty is at the heart of signature strike targeting. Attacks that cannot determine whether a target is legitimate are illegal in IHL thanks to the ban on indiscriminate attacks in Article 51 of Additional Protocol I (1977). While the United States is not party to this treaty, it accepts certain elements of it as customary international law, as well as the inherent requirement for distinction.[72]

The importance of signature strikes is that they highlight the myth of bivalent discrimination contained within the laws of war. This is not that discrimination should not exist – far from it. Instead, the information required to perfectly identify a target is often unavailable, and the rules governing conduct in war allow for imperfect information and judgement. In essence, the argument that delineates signature strikes illegal on theoretical grounds is predicated on a false dichotomy – one between a standard of perfect identification and a standard where identification is made above a given threshold of information. Once it is understood that the only way to attain bivalent identification of legitimate targets is via public self-identification by an opponent, it is possible to discern that every other method of identifying a person as a legitimate target requires some form of

112   *International law*

judgement and, furthermore, is predicated on subjective interpretations of information. State practice on targeting combines target identification elements, the principle of self-defence and subjective interpretation of events to provide a membership function to persons, as well as a (shifting) standard of minimum membership to the class of legitimate targets as identified by persons or networks involved in targeting lethal force. Particularly in regard to non-uniformed/willingly identified combatants, bivalent identification is impossible. Within IHL, there exists a commonly agreed framework of standards, which includes interpretable elements and military necessity. Thus imperfect knowledge and inference can work within these parameters and still provide an approximation of bivalence required by treaty law, and have done so for as long as modern armies have fought non-conventional opponents. One can discern clear 'patterns of life' within IHL – for instance, persons belonging to a military organisation are identified by a shared set of identifying markers, such as uniform and movement in units and other such formations. The question of signature strikes is therefore not about the problem of 'patterns of life', but about the standards to which a particular set of characteristics legitimises targeting. This highlights the issue of membership: if persons are assigned membership of an organisation, then the degree to which they belong is predicated on the definition of that organisation itself.

This examination of targeted killings demonstrates the flexibility of the practice and highlights the important feature of subjectivity in the practice – bounded by social limits, as well as by international law. The flexibility of treaty interpretation means that the act of defining an enemy is important, because it axiomatically determines persons who are then classed as an enemy, as is the process – individuation – by which they are personally identified as enemies. Given the expansive nature of these concepts, it is therefore important to examine the limitations of the use of force in the United States – who can define persons as enemies, and who has the legitimacy to act on that definition.

Self-defence, battlefields and sovereignty

Targeted killings are characterised by the targeting of individuals (enemies) in third-party states, something that is not provided for in strict interpretations of treaty law. The territoriality of IHL is founded on the bordered system of sovereign states, whereas targeted killing programmes treat the individual target's person as the battlefield. In particular, Israel's 'Operation Wrath of God' and the US use of targeted killings did not restrict themselves to a particular territory. In defining the target as the individual, and that target as subject to lethal force at any time due to the latent threat that they pose, the 'battlefield' is theoretically composed of the terrorists' bodies, wherever they may be. Whether or not this conception of warfare is legal forms an important question, because it feeds into Alston's critique of expansive definitions.

The Obama administration's defence of targeted killings is that it is legitimate to target persons identified as enemies in areas where the law enforcement

International law 113

paradigm is inoperable. Axiomatic to this is the lack of contested physical territory or space, which leads to a criticism of targeted killings – that they occur away from a defined 'battlefield'. Mary Ellen O'Connell, for example, states that '[T] hese treaties [IHL] provide little or no right to use military force against individuals far from battlefields'.[73] O'Connell does not, however, define 'battlefield' at any point in the article. This is a key assumption, and a key flaw, because O'Connell's use of the term heavily implies a physically contested, territorial zone, and her analysis is predicated on this idea. Critics commonly allude to the fact that states such as Pakistan and Yemen are not 'battlefields'. IHL positively recognises conflict between states (IAC) and conflict within states (NIAC). The missing category of law would cover conflict between a state and a non-state actor external to the territory of the state. As Michael Ramsden argues, 'it would be absurd to suggest that there is some form of global NIAC between the USA and Al-Qaeda'.[74] Yet the conflict between the two is not perceived by the United States in these terms; these are merely the most applicable set of laws extant. Absent a treaty that allows for war between states against non-state actors in other states, commentators have selectively held both that the US use of targeted killings should be restricted by provisions in NIAC (due to the *Prosecutor* v. *Tadic* test),[75] and that conflict does not apply (because it cannot be characterised as such under the Geneva Conventions). The Geneva Conventions are rooted in a now-dated conception of sovereignty, territoriality and the concept of the battlefield itself.

The Obama administration's defence of targeted killings forces us to think of war and conflict in terms that do not include physically contested territories. International lawyers argue that without territorial constraints, war becomes unlimited, or global. There is key overlap here with the practice of renditions, whereby persons considered members of al-Qaeda were targeted for capture regardless of physical location, although state complicity was sometimes in evidence. This, however, reduces the argument to whether law should constrain state action, or whether the law of armed conflict inherits physical restraints from the past. By Alston's own account, conflicts that cross territorial boundaries do not automatically become IACs under IHL;[76] but to state that war therefore cannot occur extraterritorially is patently absurd. Laurie Blank offers a middle path, where conflict can be determined as happening where a state takes such measures as to make it a conflict (use of armed force, etc.), but this sidesteps the essential question: the nature of the battlefield in conflicts between terrorist networks and states.[77]

Critics citing the battlefield criteria rely on a close reading of international law, one that is rooted in sovereign territoriality. The tiered approach is rooted in the nature of mass warfare, not terrorism. To be considered a war, physical damage must occur; as Thomas Rid states: '[A] real act of war is always potentially or actually lethal'.[78] This physicality is essential to war, but lethal force does not axiomatically have to control, or contest, physical territory. IHL is rooted in the concept of war as a physical contest in a particular territorial space, and this is reflected in its development. Pre-1949 Geneva IHL reflects the nature of mass land warfare. Articles 41–49 of the Laws of War on Land (1880) denote

114 *International law*

the treatment of territory and invasion. Escape from enemy or invaded territory also had notable effects, such as freeing spies from responsibility for their actions (Article 26). The Hague Convention IV (1907) expands this concern; Articles 42–56 govern conduct towards occupied territories. The legal constraints on war reflected the increased size of armies and the fact that modern mass warfare resulted in the occupation of territories by military forces, rather than smaller armies moving from battlefield to battlefield. By 1907, Article 47 ('Pillage is formally forbidden') replaced a string of lengthy adjudications over the forcible requisition of private property in 1880. Both the 1949 Geneva Conventions and Additional Protocol II reflect the idea that conflict occurs within the territory of belligerent states. Importantly, precision air warfare either with UAVs or missile strikes effectively reverses this extension of conflict from a field of battle to a territory; in many ways, it reduces it further than was physically possible prior to the advent of mass warfare. Pitting a drone against an individual strikes many as patently unfair, but it also reduces the zone of conflict to a single person rather than to a 'battlefield'. Even supposedly critical deconstructions of the 'battlefield' retain the idea of war occurring in a physically contested space that war moves beyond.[79] The concept of the battlefield is nonetheless rooted in the idea of a contestable physical geographical zone. Western armies can contest physical spaces, but state practice and attitudes to the conduct of war are no longer fundamentally tied to physical battlefields. This is reflected in both state practice and thought. The concept of the battlefield has given way to 'battlespace', in which physical geography plays a part but is not dominant.[80] The revolution in military affairs and network-centric warfare,[81] combined with contemporary operational concepts, means that state practice is now to deliver effect on targets rather than to contest or control a particular geographical zone. The critical focus on UAVs neglects the fact that they are, in military terms, merely a more efficient method of delivering lethal force than a cruise missile. The 1998 Operation Infinite Reach used Tomahawk Land Attack Missiles fired from the Red Sea against targets in Afghanistan and Sudan.[82] A conventional understanding of battlefield territoriality would expand the 'battlefield' in this instance to span half the globe, over the thin span of the cruise missiles' flight paths. Additionally, this battlefield disappeared as soon as the missile strikes ceased.

The US conception of its war on al-Qaeda is that the battlefield is co-located with the persons that it cannot target by means of law enforcement. In effect, the physical bodies of the network's members are the battlefield. This is a redefinition of the battlefield, which takes into account the de facto method of waging war on terrorists. Transnational terrorism is a deterritorialised activity. Critics of the targeted killing programme often raise the spectre of worldwide warfare. This misunderstands the underlying premise – that persons are targetable where they pose a threat (subject to targeting principles such as proportionality, etc.). Instead, the contemporary battlefield is best thought of as being the bodies of the terrorists themselves. This prevents the use of force where these persons are not active, but also allows states to continually target them outside of 'direct pursuit' across state boundaries. It also removes the need for a country to declare war on

International law 115

a non-participating government in order to wage war on a terrorist network. This expands the zone of operations, because the physical persons may move across the world, but it also constrains it. The personal and individual nature of the battlefield means that there can be no use of force for secondary targets, or expansive collateral damage. This is reflected in the operational intention of targeted killings, although critics allege not in practice. This is a reinterpretation of international law, one that semantically redefines the understanding of the battlefield in a manner that is likely to upset many international lawyers. However, this is not simply US unilateralism – it is the outgrowth of targeting non-conventional opponents and network-centric warfare. Furthermore, it is, theoretically at least, in line with traditional derogations from codes of conduct governing warfare where one party refuses to fight in a conventional manner. In many senses, this returns to the underlying principles of just war theory. As Walzer outlines, where armies refused to fight in pitched battle by taking refuge in walled cities, their continued refusal to surrender would expand the legitimacy of acts that would otherwise be considered unjust (the sacking of a city), because there would be no other way for an army to deal with its opponent. In effect, targeted killings against terrorist networks resurrects this principle in an age where sacking a city would be grossly illegal.[83]

The fact that the United States uses targeted killings in the territory of other states is, however, an issue. The conduct of operations across territorial borders is prima facie a violation of state sovereignty, one of the key legal principles that constitutes the international system of states. Article 1 of the UN Charter states that '[T]he organization is based on the principle of the sovereign equality of all its Members'. Furthermore, Article 7 states that outside of Chapter VII ('Peace enforcement') measures, '[N]othing contained in the present Charter shall authorize the United Nations to intervene in matters which are essentially within the domestic jurisdiction of any state'. However, international law, and the UN Charter, recognise the right to self-defence. Article 51 of the UN Charter states that '[N]othing in the present Charter shall impair the inherent right of individual or collective self-defence if an armed attack occurs against a member of the United Nations'. The US use of targeted killings is framed as an act of war, justified in terms of self-defence. Although the normative use of such force is technically expansive, in principle and practice it is applied where the United States, or another state, is unwilling or unable to act. In practice, this is not so much widening the scope of self-defence in international affairs, as it is widening the scope of states to use pre-emptive force against non-state actors.

The use of force constitutes an act of war when conducted against another state. However, the use of force against non-state actors is not necessarily targeted at the 'host' state. These individuals remain citizens of states. It is important to note that the majority of people targeted by drone strikes are not Americans. If the United States were to continue using UAV strikes as part of a strategy of asymmetric containment, it would be creating a norm of behaviour where states can legitimately, and legally, kill the citizens of other states across state borders outside of a war, basing such an action on an extended concept of

116 *International law*

self-defence. This is not peace, but neither is it war as commonly understood. Such actions have precedent, but the standard set is open to interpretation by states with purportedly baser motives. The normalisation of the unilateral use of force across borders would contravene close readings of Chapter 1, Article 2, Section 4 of the UN Charter. The section reads: '[A]ll Members shall refrain in their international relations from the threat or use of force against the territorial integrity or political independence of any state'; however, an expanded reading of this Article could interpret the US targeted killing programme differently. Because the United States is not directing its attacks against the state of Pakistan (and this programme has the de facto consent of the government of Pakistan), the programme is not intended to threaten the territorial integrity of the state, and respects the government's sovereignty in the matter. Given the United States' position as a permanent member of the UNSC, this is unlikely to cause immediate legal problems. As a permanent member, it has a veto on any action the UNSC may take, and the UNSC is the only international body that can legally authorise the use of force to restore peace and security. The normalisation of non-absolute sovereignty in this manner by the United States does undermine the principle of territorial sovereignty, and would also risk creating a norm that other permanent members, such as Russia or China, could copy. The norm of states violating territorial integrity with the use of lethal force risks undermining one of the core principles of the UN.

Challenges and political externalities

The Obama administration's justification for, and practice of, targeted killings will affect the United States' relationship to an emerging body of international law – international criminal law. International criminal law makes individuals prosecutable under international laws defined in the Rome Statute. Unlike IHL and human rights law, it does not rely on states to prosecute individuals, this function being provided by the ICC. The Court is, however, subordinate to national courts. It can only exercise jurisdiction where national courts are unable or unwilling to prosecute an indicted offence. The United States has not ratified the treaty, and has withdrawn its signature, because it found itself opposed to the ICC at the time of the statute's signing.[84] The United States declared its intention not to become a party to the Rome Statute in 2002, thus indicating that it has no intention of ratifying the treaty, and denying the ICC's jurisdiction. The United States is not, therefore, subject to the jurisdiction of the ICC, nor are its personnel. However, it is important to examine the ICC's jurisdiction, because Article 12 of the Rome Statute gives the ICC jurisdiction where a crime has occurred on the territory of a state party to the treaty:

> Article 12.2: 'the Court may exercise its jurisdiction if one or more of the following States are Parties to this Statute or have accepted the jurisdiction of the Court in accordance with paragraph 3: (a) The State on the territory of which the conduct in question occurred.'

International law 117

The Rome Statute has now been ratified by 120 states; therefore US operations on the territory of those states would subject the operators to the jurisdiction of the court. Afghanistan has acceded to the treaty, although it has also signed an Article 98 agreement with the United States, which prohibits it from transferring US personnel to the custody of the ICC.[85] This exploits a legal loophole in the Rome Statute, which pits the treaty against bilateral treaties between states. Article 98 treaties are bilateral in nature and tied to domestic US legislation such as the 2003 Protection of Service Personnel Act. An American Society of International Law report states that the United States no longer actively seeks these treaties; however, they have been concluded where necessary, meaning this statement cannot be considered evidence to sustain a claim that the United States has renounced the process.[86] It is conceivable, however, that the United States may take action against a non-state actor on the territory of a state that is party to the Rome Statute and that has not signed an Article 98 treaty. Doing so would place the participants of such an operation under the jurisdiction of the ICC. Examining the degree to which the case study operations are considered crimes under the Rome Statute is therefore important.

Article 8.1 of the treaty states that '[T]he Court shall have jurisdiction in respect of war crimes in particular when committed as part of a plan or policy or as part of a large-scale commission of such crimes'. This is important, because a policy of asymmetric containment which included means that the Rome Statute defines as criminal would give the court jurisdiction so long as the operations took place on the territory of a state party to the ICC. With capture/kill raids, such as the Abottabad raid, this would place US personnel under the jurisdiction of the Court, if the case were referred by the state party itself or by the Court's prosecutor. With targeted killings, the jurisdiction is less clear; however, it is likely that UAV operators and their chain of command could be held responsible for the operations. Since the Court has no power of compulsion and relies on state parties transferring custody of persons to it, given the stated US opposition to it, these personnel are unlikely to find themselves before the Court.[87] Crimes prosecutable by the ICC include those common to Article 3 of the 1949 Geneva Conventions.[88] This includes armed conflict not of an international character, which covers actions against non-state actors. Therefore, serious Article 3 violations would constitute a prosecutable crime under the Rome Statute. The most likely to commit such serious violations as to warrant prosecution by the ICC are UAV operators. If targeted killings are defined as war crimes (in violation of IHL), those acting in their commission are subject to ICC indictments. Because targeted killings do not have the possibility of capture, it is relatively easier to discern the intent to kill than it is in capture/kill raids.

Perhaps more important than theoretical prosecutions is the policy predicament that the normalisation of targeted killings would place the US government in. President Obama signalled a willingness to change approach from President Bush's adamant opposition to the Court from the outset of his presidency.[89] The United States is still unlikely to become party to the treaty in the near future, however. Maintaining a programme of targeted killing would place the United

118 *International law*

States in a tough predicament if it were to ratify or accede to the Rome Statute. It would likely be impossible to enable the legislation necessary to ratify the Rome Statute while continuing a policy of targeted killing. If the United States was to ratify the Rome Statute, any state on whose territory a targeted killing took place could refer the case to the ICC, or the ICC's prosecutor could be authorised by the statute to refer cases to the Court independently.[90] Furthermore, the Article 98 treaties would either have to be rescinded on accession or ratification by the United States, because parties to treaties are not allowed to undermine them in such a manner. Article 98 treaties between parties to the Rome Statute would be in violation of the fundamental principle of *pacta sunt servanda* and contravene Article 18 of the 1969 Vienna Convention, which states that '[A] state is obliged to refrain from acts which would defeat the object and purpose of a treaty'. The result would be that in the event of a severe Article 3 violation, which could be caused by a significant number of civilian deaths as the by-product of targeted killings by UAVs, the operators of those drones would find themselves subject to the ICC, as could, theoretically, the President of the United States. Although it is highly unlikely that either would be turned over to the ICC's custody, in order to prevent this the United States would have to initiate investigations or proceedings against its own nationals under the provisions of Article 17.1 of the treaty.[91] Furthermore, the US government could not simply maintain a policy of deciding not to prosecute, because this provides no defence under Article 17.1.b of the treaty.[92] Therefore a policy of targeted killing that resulted in sustained civilian casualties would require the US government to either prosecute its own employees (or senior administration figures) or hand them over to ICC custody. Either option would be politically toxic. Therefore the US government would not be able to ratify the treaty while such a policy remained standard practice. This has important international implications. Continued US non-ratification of the Rome Statute places the United States outside mainstream opinion on international law – in many ways the Court represents the apex of the human rights movement since 1945.[93]

Conclusion

This chapter has outlined the process by which the United States maintains the non-illegality of its targeted killing programme. Targeted killings cannot be defined as illegal in international law without evidence to the contrary. The liminal nature of guerrillas and terrorists means that they cannot be considered civilians or non-combatants. US discourse, and recourse to the fundamental principle of self-defence and normal means of targeting in armed conflict, is a normative-forming interpretation of targeting that unfortunately excludes legal oversight.

If the United States uses targeted killings in containment, or otherwise makes such acts a normal activity, it will set a precedent for states to act in this way. The normalisation of the US use of targeted killings would mean that it is the normal state practice of the most powerful state to kill persons for involvement

International law   119

in a group that the state deems to be a terrorist organisation. Britain and France do not have the resources to attempt such a programme, but both Russia and China do. These states are important, because as permanent members of the UNSC they can effectively escape censure under international law. The normalisation of the US targeted killing programme would make the extraterritorial killing of persons involved in terrorist networks a normatively condoned act by both states. Jeremy Waldron argues that 'we should not make the case for such a norm based on the improbable supposition that only fine people like us will be involved in its administration'.[94] Legitimising these methods opens the door to the normatively legal use of targeted killings by other states. This is important, not only because other powerful states such as China and Russia are likely to acquire significant UAV capacity, but also because their use by the United States reinforces softened ideas of sovereignty.

Notes

1 Anderson, 'Targeted Killing': 4.
2 Francis Lieber, *General Orders No. 100* (Washington, DC: Government Printing Office, 1898).
3 Koh, 'Obama Administration'; Holder, 'Northwestern University Speech'; Brennan, 'Ethics and Efficacy'.
4 See O'Connell, 'Unlawful Killing'; Chris Jenks, 'Law from Above: Unmanned Aerial Systems, Use of Force, and the Law of Armed Conflict', *North Dakota Law Review* 85(3) (2010): 649–71; O'Connell, 'Seductive Drones'; Dore, 'Greenlighting American Citizens'; Downes, '"Targeted Killings"'; Proulx, 'If the Hat Fits, Wear It'.
5 Greg Miller, 'Legal Memo Backing Drone Strike That Killed American Anwar Al-Awlaki Is Released', *Washington Post*, 23 June 2014; Department of Justice Office of Legal Counsel, 'Memorandum for the Attorney General Re: Applicability of Federal Criminal Laws and the Constitution to the Contemplated Lethal Operations against Shaykh Anwar al-Aulaqi' (Memo, 16 July 2010).
6 William H. Parks, 'No Mandate, No Expertise and Legally Incorrect', *New York University Journal of International Law and Policy* 42(3) (2010).
7 Amnesty International, 'Guantánamo Detainees: The Legal Black Hole Deepens', *Amnesty* (Report, Amnesty International, London, 2003); Steyn, 'Guantanamo Bay'.
8 Holder, 'Northwestern University Speech'.
9 Anne-Marie Slaughter Burley, 'International Law and International Relations Theory: A Dual Agenda', *American Journal of International Law* 87(2) (1993); Anne-Marie Slaughter, Andrew S. Tulumello and Stepan Wood, 'International Law and International Relations Theory: A New Generation of Interdisciplinary Scholarship', *American Journal of International Law* 92(3) (1998): 367–97.
10 IISS, *The Military Balance: 2012* (London: The International Institute for Strategic Studies, 2012): 31.
11 Holder, 'Northwestern University Speech'.
12 Alston, 'Report of the Special Rapporteur'.
13 Russell Christopher, 'Imminence in Justified Targeted Killing', in *Targeted Killings: Law and Morality in an Asymmetrical World*, edited by Claire Finkelstein, Jens D. Ohlin and Andrew Altman (Oxford University Press, 2012): 284.
14 Roy S. Schondorf, 'Extra-State Armed Conflicts: Is There a Need for a New Legal Regime?', *New York University Journal of International Law and Policy* 37(1) (2004–2005).
15 Holder, 'Northwestern University Speech'.

120 *International law*

16 Malcolm N. Shaw, *International Law*: 144–5.
17 Alston, 'Report of the Special Rapporteur'.
18 International Covenant on Civil and Political Rights.
19 Nico Krisch, 'International Law in Times of Hegemony: Unequal Power and the Shaping of the International Legal Order', *European Journal of International Law* 16(3) (2005).
20 William A. Schabas, 'Lex Specialis? Belt and Suspenders? The Parallel Operation of Human Rights Law and the Law of Armed Conflict, and the Conundrum of Jus Ad Bellum', *Israel Law Review* 40(2) (2007).
21 Alston, 'CIA and Targeted Killings': 301.
22 Schabas, 'Lex Specialis?'.
23 Parks, 'No Mandate': 798–9.
24 Wachtel, 'Targeting Osama Bin Laden'; Downes, '"Targeted Killings"'; Amos Guiora, 'Targeted Killing as Active Self-Defense', *Case Western Reserve Journal of International Law* 36(2) (2004); Kenneth Anderson, 'Efficiency *in Bello* and *Ad Bellum*: Making the Use of Force Too Easy?', in *Targeted Killings: Law and Morality in an Asymmetrical World*, edited by Claire Finkelstein, Jens D. Ohlin and Andrew Altman (Oxford University Press, 2012); O'Connell, 'Unlawful Killing'; O'Connell, 'Law from Above'; Benjamin R. Farley, 'Targeting Anwar Al-Aulaqi: A Case Study in US Use of Force Justifications', *American University National Security Law Brief* 2(1) (2011).
25 Kretzmer, 'Targeted Killing of Suspected Terrorists'; Afsheen Radsan and Richard Murphy, 'Measure Twice, Shoot Once: Higher Care for CIA Targeted Killing', *University of Illinois Law Review* 4 (2011); Chesney, 'Who May Be Killed?'.
26 Nils Melzer, 'Interpretive Guidance on the Notion of Direct Participation in Hostilities under International Humanitarian Law', *ICRC* (Geneva: ICRC, 2009); Parks, 'No Mandate'.
27 Wachtel, 'Targeting Osama Bin Laden': 710.
28 Guiora, 'Targeted Killing': 334.
29 Anderson, 'Targeted Killing': 16.
30 Sean D. Murphy, 'The Doctrine of Preemptive Self-Defense', *Villanova Law Review* 50(3) (2005).
31 International Court of Justice, 'Advisory Opinion on the Legality of the Threat or Use of Nuclear Weapons', 1996 ICJ 226: Paragraph 105.
32 See *Public Committee against Torture in Israel* v. *Government of Israel*.
33 Parks, 'No Mandate': 792–3.
34 Kramer, 'Legality of Targeted Drone Attacks'; Parks, 'No Mandate'; Melzer, 'Interpretive Guidance'.
35 Alston, 'CIA and Targeted Killings'.
36 Singer, 'Double-Hatting Around the Law'.
37 Alston, 'CIA and Targeted Killings': 301–8.
38 Michael Ramsden, 'Targeted Killings and International Human Rights Law: The Case of Anwar Al-Awlaki', *Journal of Conflict and Security Law* 16(2) (2011): 390.
39 Alston, 'Report of the Special Rapporteur': 18.
40 Christopher Greenwood, 'International Humanitarian Law and the Tadic Case', *European Journal of International Law* 7 (1996): 238.
41 Alston, 'Report of the Special Rapporteur': 15.
42 Alston, 'Report of the Special Rapporteur'.
43 Gary D. Solis, *The Law of Armed Conflict: International Humanitarian Law in War* (New York, NY: Cambridge University Press, 2010): 251.
44 Yoo, 'Assassination': 64–5.
45 Parks, 'No Mandate': 789; William H. Parks, 'Lessons from the 1986 Libya Airstrike', *New England Law Review* 36(4) (2002).
46 J. Anthony Blair and Ralph H. Johnson, 'The Current State of Informal Logic', *Informal Logic* 9(2) (1987).

International law 121

47 Byman, 'Do Targeted Killings Work?'.
48 Jens D. Ohlin, 'Targeting Co-Belligerents', in *Targeted Killings: Law and Morality in an Asymmetrical World*, edited by Claire Finkelstein, Jens D. Ohlin and Andrew Altman (Oxford University Press, 2012).
49 *Al-Aulaqi* v. *Panetta.*
50 Melzer, 'Interpretive Guidance': 41.
51 Melzer, 'Interpretive Guidance': 72.
52 Melzer, 'Interpretive Guidance': 33.
53 Melzer, 'Interpretive Guidance'.
54 Ohlin, 'Targeting Co-Belligerents': 86–7.
55 Melzer, 'Interpretive Guidance': 6.
56 Parks, 'No Mandate'.
57 See, for example, Proulx, 'If the Hat Fits, Wear It': 877–8.
58 Kretzmer, 'Targeted Killing of Suspected Terrorists': 205.
59 Jeremy Scahill, 'Interview on National Public Radio', *NPR* (Interview, NPR Radio, 16 May 2012).
60 Bradley and Goldsmith, 'Congressional Authorization': 2107–17.
61 Blum and Heymann, 'Law and Policy': 169.
62 John Keegan, *Intelligence in War: Knowledge of the Enemy from Napoleon to Al-Qaeda* (London: Pimlico, 2004).
63 See, for example, the Lieber Code, which stipulates higher penalties for officers: '[O]ffenses to the contrary shall be severely punished, and especially so if committed by officers'. Lieber, *General Orders No. 100*: Art. 11.
64 Kenney, *From Pablo to Osama*: 29–36.
65 For a discussion of complex networks see Stefano Boccaletti *et al.*, 'Complex Networks: Structure and Dynamics', *Physics Reports* 424(4) (2006). Fernando Vega-Redondo explains their applicability in terms of complex social networks; see Fernando Vega-Redondo, *Complex Social Networks* (Cambridge University Press, 2007).
66 James Risen, 'U.S. to Hunt Down Afghan Drug Lords Tied to Taliban', *New York Times*, 9 August 2009.
67 Abraham H. Miller and Nicholas A. Damask, 'The Dual Myths of "Narco-Terrorism": How Myths Drive Policy', *Terrorism and Political Violence* 8(1) (1996).
68 Gretchen Peters, *Seeds of Terror: How Heroin Is Bankrolling the Taliban and Al Qaeda* (New York: Thomas Dunne, 2009).
69 Tamara Makarenko, 'The Crime-Terror Continuum: Tracing the Interplay between Transnational Organised Crime and Terrorism', *Global Crime* 6(1) (2004).
70 Entous, Gorman and Rosenberg, 'Drone Attacks'.
71 Entous, Gorman and Rosenberg, 'Drone Attacks'; Entous, Gorman and Barnes, 'U.S. Relaxes Drone Rules'.
72 Department of Defense General Counsel, *Department of Defense Law of War Manual* (Washington, DC: Department of Defense, 2015).
73 O'Connell, 'Choice of Law against Terrorism': 361.
74 Ramsden, 'Targeted Killings': 390.
75 Ramsden, 'Targeted Killings': 390.
76 Alston, 'Report of the Special Rapporteur': 18.
77 Laurie Blank, 'Targeted Strikes: The Consequences of Blurring the Armed Conflict and Self-Defense Justifications', *William Mitchell Law Review* 38(5) (2012).
78 Rid, 'Deterrence Beyond the State': 7.
79 David Grondin, 'The Other Spaces of War: War Beyond the Battlefield in the War on Terror', *Geopolitics* 16(2) (2011).
80 Stuart E. Johnson and Martin C. Libicki, eds, *Dominant Battlespace Knowledge* (Washington, DC: National Defense University, 1996).
81 Owens, 'Emerging U.S. System-of-Systems'.

122 *International law*

82 Micah Zenko, *Between Threats and War: U.S. Discrete Military Operations in the Post-Cold War World* (Stanford University Press, 2010): 63.

83 Walzer, *Just and Unjust Wars*: 163–4.

84 Ruth Wedgwood, 'The International Criminal Court: An American View', *European Journal of International Law* 10(1) (1999).

85 'International Criminal Court Article 98: Agreement between the United States of America and Afghanistan', *Department of State* (Treaty, Washington, DC, 20 September 2002).

86 William H. Taft, Patricia M. Wald and Sandra Day O'Connor, *US Policy toward the International Criminal Court* (Report, ASIL, 2009).

87 American opposition to the legal text of the treaty encompasses the 2004 notification not to become a State Party to the treaty, as well as the codification into national law of the American Service-Members' Protection Act 2003.

88 Rome Statute, Article 8.2.3.

89 Stephen J. Rapp, 'U.S. Statement to the Assembly of States Parties of the International Criminal Court' (New York, NY: US Department of State, 2011).

90 Rome Statute, Article 15.1.

91 the Court shall determine that a case is inadmissible where: (a) The case is being investigated or prosecuted by a State which has jurisdiction over it, unless the State is unwilling or unable genuinely to carry out the investigation or prosecution.

92 the Court shall determine that a case is inadmissible where: (b) The case has been investigated by a State which has jurisdiction over it and the State has decided not to prosecute the person concerned, unless the decision resulted from the unwillingness or inability of the State genuinely to prosecute.

93 William A. Schabas, *An Introduction to the International Criminal Court* (Cambridge University Press, 2001): 20.

94 Jeremy Waldron, 'Justifying Targeted Killing with a Neutral Principle', in *Targeted Killings: Law and Morality in an Asymmetrical World*, edited by Claire Finkelstein, Jens D. Ohlin and Andrew Altman (2012): 112–13.

5 Constitutional protections

A drone missile is not due process of law.

Jameel Jaffer[1]

'Due process' and 'judicial process' are not one and the same, particularly when it comes to national security.

Eric Holder[2]

Introduction

Does the president have the legitimate authority to define individual persons as enemies, even if they are US citizens? As we have seen so far, the US legitimation of targeted killings hinges on them being a lawful activity, and therefore the role of the president and the executive branch is a key issue. The US system of constitutional government distributes sovereign authority via a system of checks and balances. The basic structure of the system (a president, and Congress divided into the Senate and the House of Representatives, as well as the Supreme Court) prevents the complete allocation of power in any single branch of government; however, this idealised system does not necessarily represent the actual functioning of modern government.[3] Within this system, the president has a key executive role, as is demonstrated in the discursive ability to define individuals as members of al-Qaeda. However, the power of the president is meant to be limited by the system itself. Therefore, is the president's ability to define persons as enemies lawful and legitimate within the US political system? In other words, are such discursive acts constitutional? To answer this question, we need to examine the interaction between power, politics and law in the United States. The argument presented here is not, however, a legal argument, even though it uses considerable amounts of case law to trace the process by which the president can define US citizens as enemies. This study of bounded political authority raises questions of sovereignty and law. Instead, the major cases that enable the president to define citizens as enemies and act against them on the basis of this definition forms the focus of attention.

One of the significant features of the Bush administration is the authority that the executive apparently arrogated itself as a result of the War on Terror. Critics

124   *Constitutional protections*

commonly reference the AUMF and the Patriot Act as key bills that extended the power of the presidency. David Barron and Martin Lederman refer to Bush as pushing the 'preclusive' claims of power to their 'logical extremes'.[4] The executive and legislature's long-running battle with the judicial branch over Guantanamo Bay is also cited as weakening this important third-branch check on executive power. The legal challenges to presidential authority over the definition and detention of persons held at Guantanamo Bay are therefore important to understanding the limits placed on the executive by the US legal system and judicial branch of government.[5] Some argue that the Obama administration's conduct is evidence that the Bush-era power shifts have not reset. Richard Jackson argues that the US counterterrorism approach has become embedded in both the institutions and culture of the United States, and that the Obama administration accepts these narratives and the authority that accompanies them.[6] The Obama administration's defence of targeted killings is that its ability to define persons as enemies is part of its legitimate authority within the constitutional system. In particular, this references the discursive difference between the Bush administration and the Obama administration – the Obama administration seeks to define its powers as within traditional constitutional boundaries, yet the use of targeted killings requires that the ability to define persons as enemies (by means of defining them as belligerents) is held by the president. Taken together, the Obama administration therefore requires the ability to define persons as enemies as a normal function of presidential authority.

The ability claimed by the Obama administration (and the Bush administration that preceded it) is predicated on the fact that the United States is at war with al-Qaeda. The key fear is that the power this gives the president is expansive. This criticism comes from across the political spectrum; as the right-wing libertarian Ron Paul wrote, '[T]he precedent set by the killing of Awlaki established the frightening legal premise that any suspected enemy of the United States – even if they are a citizen – can be taken out on the President's say-so alone'.[7]

In contrast, the Obama administration argues that its power to use these methods is specific and limited. The clearest definition is offered by Eric Holder:

> Let me be clear: an operation using lethal force in a foreign country, targeted against a U.S. citizen who is a senior operational leader of al Qaeda or associated forces, and who is actively engaged in planning to kill Americans, would be lawful at least in the following circumstances: First, the U.S. government has determined, after a thorough and careful review, that the individual poses an imminent threat of violent attack against the United States; second, capture is not feasible; and third, the operation would be conducted in a manner consistent with applicable law of war principles.[8]

Even John Yoo acknowledges that '[T]his is not to say that American agents have a hunting license for anyone suspected of being an al-Qaeda operative', despite his well-known legal opinions in favour of strong presidential authority.[9]

Constitutional protections 125

Therefore, the specific question of defining enemies is connected to the wider debate surrounding the constitutional limits to presidential authority in times of emergency. Critics of the US targeted killings argue that the power shifts that the use of targeted killings engenders are novel and/or unconstitutional. Lindsay Kwoka writes that '[T]he targeted killing of a U.S. citizen presents a novel issue that cannot easily be resolved';[10] whereas Ben McKelvey questions the executive's basis for the use of force against US citizens and notes that '[C]urrently there is no independent enforcement of due process rights when the Executive targets Americans with lethal force on the basis of unsubstantiated accusations'.[11] In reaction to Holder's speech that parsed due and judicial process, David Cole asked: '[I]f we require such [due] process even for the search of a backpack, shouldn't we demand at least as much before the President orders the non-battlefield killing of a human being?'[12]

In reply, senior figures in the Obama administration such as Harold Koh and Eric Holder depict this method of war as being no different to other methods, and therefore the only legal expansion of executive power in response to threats is contained within the AUMF.[13] It should be noted that Harold Koh has come under criticism for his change in stance. Prior to serving in the Obama administration Koh was a long-time critic of the use of military commissions.[14] Koh also signed a letter in 2008 stating that the ICCPR and IHRL apply in times of war, a fact noted by Kenneth Anderson in a 2009 article on targeted killings.[15] Koh's subsequent defence of targeted killings in an official capacity caused consternation in the liberal commentariat, which had largely assumed he would take a different position on the matter. The Obama administration's defence has failed to persuade many, and critics of US targeted killings assert that, at the very least, the executive's killing of US citizens such as Anwar al-Awlaki is unconstitutional without due process.

Targeted killings in US law and politics

Critics of the targeted killing programme consider the use of targeted killings against a US citizen to be a breach of their constitutional rights.[16] As commander-in-chief, one of the key powers of the president within the US constitutional system is the ability to define persons external to that system as enemies. However, the ability to define persons internal to the constitutional system – citizens – as enemies is limited by Article 3 of the Constitution.[17] The key process at work is that by which persons internal to the constitutional system are defined as external enemies. This is criticised by critics such as the ACLU because it gives the president 'unreviewable power to kill any American whom he deems to present a threat to the country'.[18] The Obama administration's defence of targeted killings relies on its ability and legitimate authority to do this in specific circumstances – in particular, with reference to the killing of Anwar al-Awlaki.[19] Eric Holder's speech is commonly assumed to be the first explicit defence of this killing: he first defines al-Awlaki as the leader of AQAP, and subsequently outlines a defence of the theoretical targeting of a senior al-Qaeda leader.

126 *Constitutional protections*

The use of targeted killings is predicated on defining persons as enemies. Two ways of thinking about the way that persons can exist as enemies in relation to the Constitution are: as internal enemies – accused of treason and thus subject to the US legal system and protected by Article 3 of the Constitution – or as external enemies – and thus subject either to legal process (if captured and processed through the federal court system) or to military force (as regulated by IHL, or the Uniform Code of Military Justice [UCMJ] in the case of detentions). In the specific case of detentions, the Geneva Conventions provide the IHL framework for the conduct of these detentions, but the national-level legal framework is the UCMJ, designed to be in compliance with IHL.

The role of law in defining enemies dates almost to the birth of the United States; importantly, this traditionally established a separation between internal and external enemies, where a person subject to treason law (a citizen) could not be subjected to military law and thus externalised from the system. The Alien and Sedition Acts of 1798 defined Americans, as well as criminalising acts against the state beyond that allowed for in the Constitution. Treason is not, however, a wartime act. Carlton Larson contends that the treason clause limits the ability of the executive to apply military law: '[A] core principle of the forgotten constitutional law of treason is the distinction between civilian and military authority'.[20] Key to understanding treason is the concept of allegiance, which is owed by citizens and residents.[21] This division was enforced in 1806 legislation as well as in case law during the War of 1812 – 'New York's highest court rules that persons subject to the law of treason could not be subject to military authority'.[22] This principle, Larson argues, found its apex in *Carlisle* v. *United States* (1873), where all resident persons and those who hold allegiance are subject to treason law, but cannot, therefore, be subject to military law; concurrently, 'the military has authority over those who do not owe allegiance to the United States'.[23] This is the traditional separation of internal and external enemies – persons who could be defined as internal enemies (those who hold allegiance to the United States) could not be subjected to military law, and thus externalised. Furthermore, the decision in *Kawakita* v. *United States*[24] also holds US citizens subject to treason laws external to the United States.

The defence of targeted killings offered by the Obama administration externalises citizens and persons from the US legal system due to their membership of a belligerent force. This is possible due to specific US case law that altered the constitutional protections offered persons acting as part of an opposing force. The cases of *Ex parte Milligan*[25] and *Ex parte Quirin*[26] are separated by almost 80 years and reached entirely different conclusions.

In *Ex parte Milligan*, five persons were accused of actions relating to irregular warfare during the American Civil War. Union authorities detained Lambdin Milligan and four others because they were believed to be part of a pro-Confederate conspiracy in 1863, in the midst of the American Civil War. They were tried in a military court and sentenced to death, but were able to argue their case as the Civil War ended before their execution. The court held that the suspension of habeas corpus was lawful, but that citizens could not be tried before military courts while civilian courts were still functional. Furthermore, military courts only had the ability to try criminals for as long as necessary. In a majority opinion the chief justice stated:

> The Attorney-General conceives that all persons whom he and his associates choose to denounce for giving aid to the Rebellion, are to be treated as being themselves a part of the Rebellion,-they are public enemies, and therefore they may be punished without being found guilty by a competent court or a jury. This convenient rule would outlaw every citizen the moment he is charged with a political offence. But political offenders are precisely the class of persons who most need the protection of a court and jury, for the prosecutions against them are most likely to be unfounded both in fact and in law.[27]

The crux of the *Milligan* decision was that the Attorney General, and by extension the government, could not remove someone's constitutional rights due to their activities in support of a force opposed to the United States. Outside of martial law (emergency), the Constitution held. The two tests established were the presence of actual fighting, and the operation of open civil courts. According to these tests, the *Milligan* decision would apply to contemporary Americans due to the functioning of the court system during the time of war.

Ex parte Quirin involved eight saboteurs who landed in the continental United States operating on behalf of Germany. They were tried before a military commission and six (who were caught on the evidence of two) were executed, including Herbert Haupt, a US citizen. The decision awarded the president the ability to define persons as enemy combatants in wartime, hence its role in the Guantanamo Bay decisions. In contrast to *Ex parte Milligan*, *Ex parte Quirin* found that '[C]itizenship in the United States of an enemy belligerent does not relieve him from the consequences of a belligerency which is unlawful because in violation of the law of war'.[28] Whereas the *Milligan* decision established that the executive could not unilaterally declare a person to be a belligerent (and therefore subject to military jurisdiction and tribunal), *Quirin* found that a person's constitutional rights were no protection against their actions during wartime. The decision reached in *Quirin* blurred the traditional distinction between internal and external enemies. This judgment allowed the military to try US citizens accused of breaches of the laws of war, thus breaching the division between civilian and military authority. This introduces the double-applicability of treason and military law, as Larson notes:

> Quirin effectively holds that a person levying war against the United States or adhering to its enemies without a uniform is subject to military authority. Of course, it will almost always be the case that a person committing an act of treason – levying war against the United States or adhering to its enemies – will be doing so without a uniform and accordingly might be defined as an

128 *Constitutional protections*

unlawful combatant. As a result, any civilian accused of treason could simply be shunted into the military system and executed without any of the protections provided by Article III.[29]

Regardless of Larson's rebuke, the *Quirin* decision stands as an important source of law. The *Quirin* decision establishes a point of duality in which defined enemies participating in a belligerent force are potentially subject to both federal law and military law – therefore subject to dual authority. In effect, by subjecting a person to military law, they are externalised from the constitutional system, because their rights and privileges contained in the Constitution do not apply.

The effect of the *Quirin* decision is to make it so that US citizens are potentially subject to two sets of law at once, as long as they participate in a belligerent force against the United States. But the *Quirin* decision is essentially negative – it does not indicate who should make the decision between either set of law. The executive can make decisions in war; the question is whether the decision relies on the AUMF, or whether it is an axiomatic authority of the president. Curtis Bradley and Jack Goldsmith argue that the wording of the AUMF, as well as 'the standard view that wartime delegations to the President[,] should be broadly construed',[30] but cannot answer the question of how persons should be defined as belonging to an organisation. Therefore the ability to identify persons as belonging to an organisation is key to defining them as an enemy, and this is not contained within the AUMF.

The external nature of the United States' conflict with al-Qaeda is key to understanding its use of targeted killings. The Obama administration defines this conflict as external to the US constitutional system to generate legitimacy for its use of targeted killings. Citizens can be defined as belligerents while they are external to the United States – for instance, Gaetano Territo, who was detained as an Italian prisoner of war in World War II. Gaetano Territo was captured in Italy and subsequently transferred to California as a prisoner of war. He pursued a writ of habeas corpus in the Californian courts, but was denied because he was captured on the field of battle.[31] However, war cannot be waged on those internal to the system – the use of force internally is constrained by constitutional law. That said, US citizens are internal to the system, regardless of location – citizenship is not removed at the United States' sovereign borders. Furthermore, internal enemies are accorded due process rights in the Constitution – the executive branch cannot legally use force against them without court proceedings. Military force can only be used against enemies external to the system. In order for persons to be legitimate targets of targeted killing, they must be external enemies, which relies on their identification as belligerents.

The key difference between the case of Milligan and that of al-Awlaki is the standard by which they were judged to be belligerents. This standard is implicitly related to the definition of the organisation to which they were held to belong. Milligan referred to persons who had joined the German military and were working as saboteurs.[32] The cases of both Territo and Lindh referred to persons who had been fighting as part of military units, as both persons were

Constitutional protections 129

detained by military forces on or near territorially defined battlefields or war-zones. The definition for belligerency by becoming part of the al-Qaeda network is not apparent. As seen in Chapters 3 and 4, the definition for membership of al-Qaeda is essentially a product of the process by which persons are identified as such, which in turn relies on the definition of al-Qaeda as a group by the executive. Furthermore, belligerency is no longer a physical fact – persons can form a functional part of a belligerent organisation by participating in a decentralised terrorist network. Therefore the standard for defining participation, thus belligerency, and thus definition as an external enemy, is set by the executive branch. This point is seized on by critics as a reason to limit the executive's authority.

There is some confusion about who the executive judges to be an enemy, fuelled by a *New York Times* story, which stated that:

> Mr Obama embraced a disputed method for counting civilian casualties that did little to box him in. It in effect counts all military-age males in a strike zone as combatants, according to several administration officials, unless there is explicit intelligence posthumously proving them innocent.[33]

This is commonly used by critics to imply that the Obama administration considers all persons in a given territorial area to be legitimate targets. The caveat is that this is a method of assessing casualties, which occurs after a targeted killing. It is worrying, and no doubt a reason for the wide disparity between the casualty counts identified by the Obama administration and all publicly available sources.[34] However, it cannot be taken as evidence that the Obama administration uses this calculation for targeting purposes, or for defining persons as belonging to al-Qaeda. Ultimately, criticism is primarily directed at the actions taken as a result of the executive's designation, and the manner in which the executive judges those actions necessary.

So far we have differentiated between three related concepts, nested within one another. First, is the authority of the executive to define a person as an enemy; second, the ability of the executive to judge the threat that this defined enemy poses; and third, the authority of the executive to take action as it sees fit. It is this third category, or asserted right, that is highly contentious. President George W. Bush was heavily criticised for his use of authority to define persons as 'enemy combatants' and thus externalise them from the constitutional system. Of particular interest is that both the Bush administration and its critics conflated the executive's ability to define persons as enemies with its ability to act on that definition. The latter is predicated on the act of definition, but some critics restricted themselves to criticising the act rather than questioning the executive's ability to define a person as an enemy. Questions of due process and rights stem from the actions of the executive based on a definition, rather than the act of definition itself. The *Rumsfeld* v. *Padilla* case (discussed below) produces direct evidence of this definition coming from the president himself. On 9 June 2002, President George W. Bush sent an order to the Secretary of Defense stating:

130 *Constitutional protections*

> I, GEORGE W. BUSH, as President of the United States and Commander in Chief of the U.S. armed forces, hereby DETERMINE for the United States of America that:
> (1) Jose Padilla, who is under the control of the Department of Justice and who is a U.S. citizen, is, and at the time he entered the United States in May 2002 was, an enemy combatant.[35]

The Obama administration relies on precisely the same authority to define citizens such as Anwar al-Awlaki as enemies, and thus legitimise the use of targeted killings against them. Yet the Obama administration considers this authority to be in accordance with the rule of law and the Constitution. In particular, the Obama administration's defence considers it axiomatic that the persons designated as enemies and externalised are, in fact, enemies. This is key to the uproar regarding Eric Holder's speech that differentiated between 'due' and 'judicial' process.[36] Here it is important to differentiate between the authority to define persons as enemies and the use of means against those persons. The Bush administration used its authority to define persons as enemies, but also attempted to remove legal rights from them by arguing that the Geneva Conventions did not apply.[37] The Obama administration used the same authority to define persons as enemies, but also attempted to sharply define the legal systems to which persons were subject. Obama's 2009 speech determined that persons detained would be either reinternalised into the US system (prosecuted in federal courts), processed in military courts for violations of IHL or sent to another judicial system. Persons whom targeted killings are used against are externalised from the system but at the same time placed within the legal structures governing conduct in war.[38] Included in this is the use of military force, which the Obama administration considers subject to the laws of war, as well as the Constitution, therefore not usable in the domestic context as per *posse comitatus*.[39] Furthermore, it restricts its use, as detailed in Chapter 3, to areas where the law enforcement paradigm is inapplicable. The Obama administration does not, therefore, claim the expansive powers that critics argue that it arrogates itself; instead, it derives the authority to act on its definition from the AUMF. It does, however, argue that the executive should have the power, in times of emergency, to define enemies as it sees fit.

Detention and due process

The legal debates that frame the targeted killing campaign cannot be extricated from the legal battles regarding Guantanamo Bay. The legal challenges of the two are not directly comparable, due to the lethal nature of targeted killings. There are, however, similarities in the cases of José Padilla, Yaser Hamdi and Anwar al-Awlaki. All three are US citizens. Both Padilla and Hamdi brought cases that challenged their indefinite detention in Guantanamo Bay and sought the protection of the US court system. Both were eventually successful. *Hamdi* v. *Rumsfeld* ended in a mixed decision that held that the executive branch could

Constitutional protections 131

not hold a US citizen indefinitely without due process and judicial review. *Rumsfeld* v. *Padilla*, a petition for habeas corpus, was being reviewed by the Supreme Court when the executive decided to bring a criminal case against Padilla, which stopped the process. Both these cases revolved around the basic point of judicial oversight of the executive's actions towards a US citizen. This was the crux of *Al-Aulaqi* v. *Obama*, but the issue was not adjudicated on. Murphy and Radsan argue that the due process models developed in *Hamdi* v. *Rumsfeld*. (as well as *Boumediene* v. *Bush*) constitute the basis of an accountable system for the use of targeted killings.[40]

Defining enemies relies on two primary elements: the ability of the executive to define persons as enemy belligerents and thus externalise them from constitutional protections; and whether the judicial system has the authority and ability to review that definition and thus reinternalise them. The 2009 Military Commissions Act means that the jurisdiction for military commissions is restricted to 'alien unprivileged enemy belligerents' under Chapter 47A of title 10, U.S. Code.[41] This means that US citizens cannot be tried by military commissions. The 2012 National Defense Authorization Act gave the president the authority to permanently detain US citizens;[42] however, this authority was deemed unconstitutional by a district judge.[43] This means that any US citizens detained are automatically reinternalised to the US court system, because they cannot be tried by military commission, and they cannot be detained indefinitely.

The key element of judicial review is the concept of habeas corpus. If a court has the authority to issue a writ of habeas corpus, this signals that the court holds jurisdiction over the case. The question of habeas corpus is in many ways central to the five primary cases surrounding the detention of terrorist suspects in the War on Terror: *Rumsfeld* v. *Padilla*, *Rasul* v. *Bush*, *Hamdi* v. *Rumsfeld*, *Hamdan* v. *Rumsfeld* and *Boumediene* v. *Bush*. Of these, *Hamdi* v. *Rumsfeld* is particularly important because it concerns the detention of a US citizen. This case, along with those of John Walker Lindh[44] and Anwar al-Awlaki, is of particular interest when examining the constitutional limits to presidential authority.

Rumsfeld v. *Padilla* posed two questions: whether the president (as commander-in-chief) had the authority (with the AUMF) to capture and detain a US citizen based on the executive's unilateral determination of this fact, or whether 18 U.S.3. § 4001 (a) (which holds that 'no citizen shall be imprisoned or otherwise detained by the United States except pursuant to an Act of Congress') prevents this; and second, whether the district court had jurisdiction over the case and habeas petition. *Rasul* v. *Bush* determined whether foreign citizens had access to the US court system while detained at Guantanamo Bay (where the government argued that Cuba held ultimate sovereignty). In a 6–3 decision, the degree of control that the US government had over the base was held to trigger the right to habeas corpus. *Hamdi* v. *Rumsfeld* legitimised the government's ability to detain 'illegal enemy combatants', but ruled that US citizens had the right to challenge their detention in the US court system. The *Hamdan* v. *Rumsfeld* decision held that the military courts set up to try detainees could not

132   *Constitutional protections*

proceed because the structures and procedures violated the UCMJ and the Geneva Conventions. In *Boumediene* v. *Bush*, which took place after the 2006 Military Commissions Act, it was held that the constitutionally guaranteed right of habeas corpus review applied to persons classed as enemy combatants at Guantanamo Bay.

In contrast to the Guantanamo Bay jurisprudence, the United States' courts have thus far abdicated responsibility for overseeing US targeted killings.[45] This marks a key difference between the US and Israeli conduct of targeted killings. The Israeli model is predicated on the fact that Israel's expanded membership targeting requires judicial oversight. Conversely, the US model has explicitly avoided such oversight, and the US court system has so far declared targeted killings to be a purely political matter, under its 'political question doctrine'. The decision that dismissed the *Al-Aulaqi* case referred to the political question doctrine, which holds that the courts cannot adjudicate on political matters because determining whether 'drastic measures should be taken in matters of foreign policy and national security is not the stuff of adjudication, but of policymaking'.[46] Although this doctrine does not preclude oversight, the manner in which the US use of targeted killings has been justified makes legal oversight by the US judicial system extremely difficult. The United States is also unique because a series of case law decisions have made its citizens subject to both military and constitutional law at the discretion of the executive in times of war because of a breakdown in divisions between military and criminal law found in the *Quirin* decision, as well as the evolving nature of non-conventional forces. The Obama administration's ability to use targeted killings is predicated on its ability to define persons, including US citizens, as enemies, and therefore legitimate targets. However, its defence is predicated on this being constitutional, and not an overextension of presidential authority.

War, emergency and presidential authority

The power of the president to define persons (including US citizens) as enemies, and to furthermore take military action against them, is key to the conduct of targeted killings. The externalisation of a citizen in this manner is a legal and political act. For this reason, critics such as Philip Alston and the ACLU argue that the executive's ability to do so changes fundamental political relationships between the citizen and the state by removing an individual's protection afforded by legal rights against an arbitrary death. The complaint in the *Al-Aulaqi* v. *Obama* case states:

> The government's refusal to disclose the standard by which it determines to target U.S. citizens for death independently violates the Constitution: U.S. citizens have a right to know what conduct may subject them to execution at the hands of their own government. Due process requires, at a minimum, that citizens be put on notice of what may cause them to be put to death by the state.[47]

Critics of targeted killings cite the unconstitutionality of these attacks when used against US citizens. Eric Holder's 2012 speech sidestepped the question of due process by parsing due and judicial process, thus negating a common observation as put forth by McKelvey: '[T]argeted killing is a unilateral government execution that completely circumvents traditional notions of law enforcement and violates even minimum notions of established due process'.[48] Does the Office of the President have the legal authority to define US citizens as enemies within the legal boundaries of the US Constitution?

Some argue yes: Eric Posner and Adrian Vermeule posit a two-pronged thesis – that the extension of executive privilege in a time of emergency is constitutional, and that lawyers have little standing to claim otherwise.[49] These basic arguments are transposed by John Yoo to defend the use of targeted killings. Yoo uses the concept of emergency to outline the transition from criminal law to war 'concerns' in defence of targeted killing.[50] This should be read in light of his work on the executive's crisis powers, where he is generally in favour of the extension of executive authority.[51]

If these authors are correct, why is it important to differentiate the arguments of the Obama administration from these persons? The crux of Posner and Vermeule's argument is the security/liberty trade-off, which is attacked by critics. Posner and Vermeule knowingly enter one of the longest-running debates in US politics. Benjamin Franklin's famous 1775 quote, 'They who can give up liberty to obtain a little temporary safety, deserve neither liberty nor safety', encapsulates the opposing, libertarian position. Critics not only take issue with Posner and Vermeule's thesis, but many criticise conceptualising these ideas as trade-offs in the first place.[52] Obama's first major speech on national security explicitly rejects the trade-off thesis; in many senses, this is the capstone concept of the Obama administration's approach to national security.[53] Posner and Vermeule's argument is rooted in a theory of law that considers security and liberty as tradeable concepts, in a proportional fashion.[54] In *Crisis and Command*, Yoo constructs an argument that the executive is justified, and constitutionally sound, in seizing power in times of emergency. As Yoo states: '[E]mergencies and foreign affairs sit at the core of the purpose of the executive, and no President has successfully responded by passively following Congress' lead and forsaking his right to independent action'.[55]

The Obama administration's defence is therefore situated between those who consider the executive to have no power to define persons as enemies and those who consider this authority to be a constitutional expansion of executive authority. Arguing against both Yoo and the security/liberty trade-off, the Obama administration effectively argues that the power to define persons as enemies is a normal function of the executive that relies neither on emergency nor on the derogation of citizens' rights. Eric Holder's comments on due and judicial process are intended to separate the question of the use of targeted killings from the concepts of due process contained within the Constitution (and commonly thought to include a judicial element). Thus the rights of citizens are not, in this idea, impinged on by the use of targeted killings in circumstances where a citizen

134   *Constitutional protections*

is defined as a belligerent.[56] There is, however, one more component to this, which is that the Obama administration cannot be acting in a sovereign manner – to do so would be unconstitutional within the US system of government, because no single branch of government is sovereign. Therefore the Obama administration's authority to define persons as enemies must also be examined in relation to the works of Carl Schmitt and Giorgio Agamben, to determine whether it can be determined sovereign, or exceptional and thus destructive to the constitutional system of law. Schmitt considers the ability of the sovereign to define exceptions to the rule of law as the definition of sovereignty, and thereby included within a legal system, or an act that can create an entirely new one. Agamben considers that the ability to define exceptions leads to a 'state of exception' where government rules by necessity, not law, yet includes persons within the legal system regardless.[57]

The reason that it is important for the Obama administration's defence to differentiate its position from the arguments of Posner, Vermeule and Yoo is the role of emergency in the extension of presidential authority. The Obama administration claims the authority to define persons as enemies as a normal constitutional function of the executive. Conversely, the legal realism espoused by Posner, Vermeule and Yoo depicts this authority as the extension of normal powers, due to the nature of emergency threats – in this case, war.

Posner and Vermeule depict emergencies as lying:

> on a continuum, or sliding scale. At one end are routine domestic policies adopted in peacetime, where bureaucracies churn out incremental policy changes, judges repeatedly see similar issues and become familiar with the costs of blocking or permitting government action, and the stakes of particular judicial decisions are low. At the other end are policies adopted in times of full-blown crisis, when it might be reasonable to believe that serious harms threaten the nation.[58]

In subsequent references to Pearl Harbour and 9/11, it is clear that 'war' lies on the latter end of this scale. Furthermore, they consider many methods of dubious legality (indefinite detention and 'enhanced interrogation') as being legitimised by this crisis. War, for Posner and Vermeule, is to be contrasted with peace. Yet apart from these end-to-end definitions, this construct does not allow for its central feature – a sliding scale. In Yoo's examination of the executive, war plays a similar role – a defining issue for the presidents that he devotes chapters to: George Washington, Thomas Jefferson, Andrew Jackson, Abraham Lincoln and Franklin D. Roosevelt.[59] Both accounts derive the idea of emergency from this type of war.

There are a couple of features that can be generalised from the types of war and conflict from which both texts derive their concept of emergency. First, these wars were mostly external, being pitched against defined enemies and having a definitive commencement period, as well as a defined end. The clear exception to this is the American Civil War, which was not external; but

Constitutional protections   135

Abraham Lincoln effectively led one side of this war. Aside from this, it shares the same characteristics of the wars fought by the other presidents. Here one can find an immediate problem with Posner and Vermeule's depiction of emergencies as having a 'half life'.[60] Emergencies may indeed display these characteristics, but these are effectively frozen by the conduct of hostilities. The internment of Japanese-Americans did not cease until the end of World War II. Posner and Vermeule do not appear to join in with the 'post hoc revulsion' at the detention of Japanese-American citizens.[61] Yoo, for his part, is also mute on the right or wrong of this exertion of executive power. Instead, he appears to excuse Lincoln's detention of 12,600 people in the American Civil War by depicting the Japanese-American internments as worse.[62] Furthermore, his subsequent statement on the internments – that Japanese-Americans 'were interned because of their potential threat'[63] – serves in Yoo's construction of an argument that such uses of emergency power to detain are a legal use of power.

The emergency, as depicted in both the Posner/Vermeule thesis and Yoo's rationale, ends at some point. Actions taken during the emergency period are legitimated by crisis, and all three authors are loathe to pass judgement on it. Yet all three assume that these crises have a definitive ending. Posner and Vermeule's arguments against any restraint on executive authority by the courts must be seen in this light. An argument for 'judicial deference'[64] can only be made in a democratic state in light of the in-built assumption that at some point this deference will end. Without such an end point, persistent judicial deference is equal to the breakdown of the political system. Yoo attempts to tackle a long-term emergency by depicting the Cold War, in which 'the possibility of war was the gravest challenge to the United States in its history', as an emergency in total.[65] Here, Yoo stretches the concept of crisis and emergency past the point of analytical credibility, stating that victory 'would have been impossible without the exercise of presidential power from the Korean War, to the Cuban Missile Crisis, to the Reagan Doctrine'.[66] Presidential power may have been important, but it is problematic to attribute US victory in a 44-year confrontation between two superpowers – in a power struggle that spanned the globe – to the power invested in a single office, particularly since presidential authority is contextual. It is instructive that in both the Posner/Vermeule and Yoo accounts of emergency and US politics, the conflict between the federal government and the American Indians of the nineteenth century is entirely absent. The Cold War cannot be cohesively depicted as an emergency, and as this book has so far argued, the War on Terror does not have the precise ending of the other 'emergency' wars used by all three authors to justify the unbound authority of the executive within the constitutional framework.

The concept of emergency is clearly flexible, and the use of this concept in legal realism to argue for the extension of presidential authority worries many. The problem is that the extension of authority, or powers assumed by the president, in times of emergency is not differentiated in the accounts of emergency presidential authority from baseline powers. The power to identify a person or group as an enemy enables the use of emergency authority, but it axiomatically

136 *Constitutional protections*

forces neither the use of this authority nor its expansion. The ability to define a person as an enemy is an axiom of the president's role as commander-in-chief, but the ability to act on this authority – the president's war powers – is a constitutional issue traditionally settled between president and Congress, and a function of the emergency at hand. The Bush administration sought to expand its ability to act against enemies by derogating from congressionally approved treaties; the Obama administration uses targeted killings against enemies in line with the expansive authority afforded it by the AUMF. Therefore this raises a deeper issue – the normal ability of the executive to define US citizens as external enemies, and thus remove their constitutional protections. To examine this is to question the role of exceptionality in political and legal systems.

Both the Posner/Vermeule and Yoo defences of executive authority are couched in the idea of the 'positive' use of this authority. Yoo's argument on executive authority lacks balance precisely because it neglects any real examination of the negative connotations of his thesis. Nixon's use of unbounded presidential power for illegal purposes is framed by Yoo as a question of presidential 'privilege' – the subsequent extension (with negative consequences) of congressional authority over the executive.[67] Yoo does not make a connection between the executive authority afforded the president and Nixon's use of that authority for his own ends. In a similar fashion, Posner and Vermeule take a few core ideas from Carl Schmitt and then 'throw away the bones', dismissing the 'lens of Weimar historiography and politics'.[68]

The schizophrenic attitude towards the dangers and benefits of excessive executive authority is characteristic in both theses. The focus of this chapter is the concept of exceptions to legal systems – how a person can be extricated from these systems, and how the power to do so can be reconciled with the overarching concept of the rule of law. Key to the Obama administration's defence is that its ability to do so is consistent with the rule of law. If so, can the ability to externalise US citizens be reconciled with the rule of law?

The act of defining persons as enemies places them outside the constitutional legal system, but also relates them to that same system. Carl Schmitt and Giorgio Agamben offer different interpretations of the concept of exception. In Schmitt's thought, the exception defines the rule, and the ability to define the exception defines sovereignty: '[S]overeign is he who decides on the exception'.[69] In essence, the ability to suspend the rule of law defines sovereignty. In the US political system, the president unilaterally deciding to suspend the rule of law implies its sovereignty. But within the constitutional system, this power is in itself defined by the Constitution – the Constitution is itself sovereign. Therefore the question becomes whether the president is acting in a sovereign manner, or abiding by the Constitution. Is the president acting in accordance with powers delineated by the Constitution, or is he unilaterally expanding those powers? Agamben approaches sovereignty and exceptionality in a different manner. In *Homo Sacer*, Agamben defines the exception as persons removed from a legal system yet included within it by their relation to the system. Agamben relates this to *homo sacer*, a Roman legal concept that defined a person as sacred (and

Constitutional protections 137

prevented their sacrifice) yet simultaneously defined that any person that killed them could not be punished for homicide.[70] Agamben uses this concept to argue that persons are externalised (stripped of legal standing that would prevent them from being killed) but simultaneously internalised (in that the legal system incorporates them by relation). Agamben continues this with *State of Exception*, where he defines the mode of governance as stripping persons of legal standing in a manner similar to *homo sacer*.[71] Neither exception is in accordance with the rule of law as defined in the Constitution, but would appear to be explanations for the ability to define persons as enemies and hence kill them.

Is the use of targeted killings an exception in the sense posited by Schmitt? One logical chain, posited by critics, argues that the effect of targeted killing is exceptional. In relation to the killing of Anwar al-Awlaki, the ACLU argued that the executive branch, in response to a threat, stripped him of his due process rights in killing him.[72] By defining al-Awlaki as an 'enemy', the Obama administration was, in Schmitt's words, deciding 'in a situation of conflict what constitutes the public interest or interest of the state, public safety and order, le salut public, and so on'.[73] Agamben's critique relates to his concept of 'bare life', which he links to the decision to detain persons at Guantanamo Bay. In Agamben's framework, the stripping of rights from a person, as he conceives occurred at Guantanamo Bay, is exceptional.[74] The 'exception', therefore, is the unilateral right of the executive to define a US citizen as an enemy without prior judicial review or the production of evidence.

The *Al-Aulaqi* case can therefore be considered in two ways: one in which the executive unilaterally expanded its authority, and another in which it stripped al-Awlaki of legal protections. Yet neither of these approaches properly defines the executive's role in the al-Awlaki killing. The Obama administration's power in this instance was restricted to defining which legal system al-Awlaki belonged to – the internal, constitutional system or the external system of international law. Here one can define a key flaw in seeking to apply either Schmitt or Agamben's ideas to the question of targeted killings. Schmitt is concerned with internal political systems, not international legal regimes. Conversely, Agamben conceives of law in totality and does not appear to consider the division between an internal legal system and an external one, making no distinction between the standing of the Geneva Conventions or US criminal law.[75] Placing al-Awlaki in an external legal system (IHL) did not strip him of legal standing, but it did place him in a legal framework where the use of lethal force against him was legal. The power of definition is therefore not to strip rights, as Agamben would have it, or to suspend law in a Schmittian manner – it is to place persons in internal or external legal systems according to the law of the United States. Subsequent to placement of al-Awlaki within either system, the executive, so the argument goes, acted within powers given to it by Congress, via the AUMF, and therefore acted within its constitutional boundaries. In the case of al-Awlaki, the president's constitutional role as commander-in-chief, combined with the AUMF, gives the executive the ability to use military force against external enemies, to the extent legally empowered by Congress.[76] The targeted killing of al-Awlaki

138 *Constitutional protections*

was not, therefore, exceptional in the legal frameworks ascribed. While Schmittian exceptionality may be a feature of the US system in times of public emergency, this is inconsequential for the purposes of this argument – in the framework of Schmitt's arguments, the act of killing al-Awlaki was non-exceptional. The Obama administration's claimed authority is to place a person within a given legal framework and, unlike the Bush administration, it does not actively seek to restrict the rights available to that person within a framework, outside the usual course of legal process. Rather than stripping rights, the authority is placement. Agamben's critique is therefore insufficient to demonstrate that the Obama administration's defence is unconstitutional.

The depiction of the relationship between law and emergency power, as contained in the Posner/Vermeule thesis, as well as that of Yoo, may be correct, but it is not required by the Obama administration's defence of targeted killings. Neither the ideas of Schmitt nor those of Agamben on exception properly describe the type of legal circumstance as exists concurrent with the targeted killing programme. For Posner and Vermeule, the emergency requires that the executive act as it sees fit, which fits Schmitt's concept of sovereignty and exception: 'authority proves that to produce law it need not be based on law'.[77] This is echoed by Yoo. Agamben's critique of this exception is that it places persons outside the legal system by stripping them of legal privilege, in his terms reducing them to 'homo sacer', or 'bare life'. In Agamben's words, they become:

> [N]either prisoners nor persons accused, but simply 'detainees', they are the object of a pure de facto rule of a detention that is indefinite not only in the temporal sense but in its very nature as well, since it is entirely removed from the law and from judicial oversight.[78]

But this extralegal status stands in contrast to that depicted by the Schmittian Posner/Vermeule thesis, and the legally justified lawmaking of Yoo's crisis presidents. The question of legal protection and standing therefore forms an impasse in the debate.

Agamben's position is based on a definition of a person's status that ignores the process by which it is reached. In defining persons as enemies, both the Bush and Obama administrations made them potentially subject to two sets of law. Rather than stripping detaines of legal status, the Bush administration simultaneously applied two competing sets of law to them, which resulted in their indeterminate status. Nasser Hussain developed a theory of 'hyperlegality', which is important to consider here. He argues that 'what we are witnessing in current policy and programs is not a withdrawal of law but what I call a hyperlegality ... the increasing use of classifications of persons in the law, and ... the use of special tribunals and commissions'.[79] Hussain does not consider the interaction between domestic and international juridicial systems. Rather than removing status from persons, the Obama administration seeks to place them within specific legal frameworks, but uses the same authority – to define enemies – to do

Constitutional protections 139

so. The Posner/Vermeule thesis holds that, regardless, law should be sacrificed for security. The emergence of this dual application of law is problematic for their thesis, because 'security' was produced by the Bush administration by the excessive application of law rather than by its reduction. This also challenges Yoo's concept of executive power, because the law, as applied, does not completely derive from the Constitution. While US law allows for the domestic introduction of international legal instruments, this does not change the purpose of international law.

The Bush administration created the effect of 'bare life' by combining two contrasting legal systems and applying them to the same person. These two forms of law available to the executive have vastly diverging ends, as well as means; yet the ability of the executive to simultaneously implement these juridicial regimes creates a system that Agamben considers bare life, but is in fact hyperlegal. This dual-law system is the direct result of a convergence of legal and political circumstances, but creates a legal solution that can systematically strip citizens, in a legal fashion, of their constitutional rights and, in the case of Anwar al-Awlaki, their life. The powers of the executive derive not from placing persons outside the law, but from its ability to select, in a constitutional manner, which of two competing legal regimes should apply to a citizen that it defines as an enemy.

For Posner and Vermeule, as well as Yoo, the Constitution allows for the legal expansion of presidential power in times of emergency. For Posner and Vermeule, this makes rational sense; for Yoo, this is as the Founding Fathers intended. What all three understand is that the exercise of these emergency powers does not fundamentally alter the system itself. This, however, relies on a very distinct idea of war as a time-limited emergency and, furthermore, as an external phenomenon. The Obama administration's claimed authority rests on its ability to define persons as enemies, which this chapter has so far argued is not an extension of authority or predicated on emergency. Furthermore, this authority is 'normal', not exceptional. Although it is difficult to see how any legal restriction could be placed on the executive to prevent it defining enemies, what role should the courts play, if any, subsequent to such a determination?

Knowledge and warfare: legal oversight in times of terror

Thus far this chapter has argued two main points: first, the executive's ability to use targeted killings against persons is predicated on its ability to define them as an enemy and to externalise them from the constitutional system of law. Second, its ability to do so is not an emergency extension of executive power, nor does it create an exception. The question then turns to the legal oversight of this process. The central plank of Posner and Vermeule's thesis is that the legal system lacks the expertise to provide oversight of the executive in a time of emergency. This is compounded by the *Al-Aulaqi* v. *Obama* decision that contained these principles and held the use of targeted killings to be a question of political doctrine. Posner and Vermeule base their position on the fact that definable first-order

140 *Constitutional protections*

effects should take precedence over theoretical second-order ones: '[T]he temptation for civil libertarians is then to abandon substance in favour of sophisticated second-order arguments about the government's decision-making processes and its long term-institutional consequences'.[80] However, since Posner and Vermeule made this argument, the executive branch has targeted and killed a US citizen, without what critics consider providing due process, bringing these second-order arguments sharply into focus.[81] The effect of these cumulative decisions is to restrict the ability of the courts to provide oversight and redress to US citizens identified by the executive as enemies. From the perspective of political and legal realism, these statements and arguments fit with the Latin saying *inter arma enim silent leges*, commonly translated as 'in times of war, the laws fall silent'. However, the Obama administration's defence of targeted killings requires that its ability to define persons as enemies operates within the rule of law. The persistent nature of the US targeted killing programme makes positions antithetical to the rule of law untenable.

The legal debates surrounding the status of 'enemy combatants' involve three intertwined sets of legal arguments. First, there is the role of law in defining persons as enemies, which this thesis argues does not exist; second, there is the role of law in reviewing the definition of persons as enemies; and third, the role of law in defining what can, and cannot, be done to a person defined as an enemy. Key to understanding the difference in the role of the courts between these three concepts is the role of knowledge in conjunction with the constitutional limits placed on the courts in the form of the political question doctrine. The political question doctrine originates in *Marbury* v. *Madison*.[82] However, the modern interpretation derives primarily from tests outlined in the Supreme Court's opinion in *Baker* v. *Carr*:

> The factors to be considered by the court in determining whether a case presents a political question are: 1. Is there a textually demonstrable constitutional commitment of the issue to a coordinate political department (i.e. foreign affairs or executive war powers)? 2. Is there a lack of judicially discoverable and manageable standards for resolving the issue? 3. The impossibility of deciding the issue without an initial policy determination of a kind clearly for non judicial discretion. 4. The impossibility of a court's undertaking independent resolution without expressing lack of the respect due coordinate branches of government. 5. Is there an unusual need for unquestioning adherence to a political decision already made? 6. Would attempting to resolve the matter create the possibility of embarrassment from multifarious pronouncements by various departments on one question?[83]

Some question whether any particular defined doctrine exists,[84] and Rachel Barkow argues that the Supreme Court overexerted itself and largely abandoned the principle.[85] However, the deference of courts in subsequent years is well documented.

Constitutional protections 141

One key argument for limiting the role of lawyers and judicial review of executive decisions, including the decision to define a person as an enemy, is that the courts lack the ability to acquire the knowledge required to make a judgment on that decision.[86] A second argument for limiting the role of the courts is that the courts do not have the constitutional authority to review the decisions of the executive branch or Congress, except where their actions transgress the Constitution. This goes back decades; Louis Henkin questioned whether such a doctrine existed or was even necessary in 1976:

> The cases which are supposed to have established the political question doctrine required no such extraordinary abstention from judicial review; they called only for the ordinary respect by the courts for the political domain. Having reviewed, the Court refused to invalidate the challenged actions because they were within the constitutional authority of President or Congress.[87]

The Guantanamo Bay legal debates demonstrate the legitimate role of the courts in post hoc review of the executive's designation of a person. Either through writs of habeas corpus or the use of Combatant Status Review Tribunals, the legal system has a function in challenging the executive's designation of a person. Problematically, and as outlined in the *Al-Aulaqi* decision, the courts can only do so when persons are either detained by the executive or present themselves in court. Furthermore, the key problem is the assessment of the executive's decision, which is fundamentally rooted in an assessment of secret intelligence – information that cannot be made publicly available. The use of this information is also tied to the executive's decision about what action to take against a person. The ability of the courts to adjudicate this matter requires an examination of the political question doctrine. Lastly, Eric Holder's defence of targeted killings, which outlined the executive's attitude to due process constraints, remains important here. Defending the practice in total, Holder argued that due process did not necessarily require legal review. Targeted killings limit the courts' ability to challenge or review a designation by the executive, but Holder's defence is only relevant to the authority of the executive to define a person as an enemy. If anything, the problem lies with the expansive power afforded the executive by Congress, which limits the ability of the judiciary to intervene in a constitutional manner. Fundamentally, this is the result of the changing nature of warfare.

A primary criticism of the targeted killing programme is that it violates basic standards of due process. Even if one accepts the Obama administration's claims in defence of the targeted killing programme (that these acts are directed at known terrorists external to the United States and beyond the reach of any state), this situation is still troublesome. The core question is whether lawyers and the judiciary have a role in overseeing war. Posner, Vermeule and Yoo all argue that the Office of the President is best placed to judge and act in such a war, and all three deride the concept of leashing the executive in a time of war. Therefore,

142 *Constitutional protections*

the legitimacy of the judiciary in setting limitations on presidential ambitions in a time of war is the key issue. The concept of war contained within Posner and Vermeule's thesis is such that this is an impossibility. The Obama administration's defence, however, requires that the judiciary fulfil its traditional constitutional role as a check on the other branches of government. Even though one can disregard the majority of Posner and Vermeule's argument as irreconcilable with the empirical reality of the conflict, as opposed to their theoretical idea of war, one of their key observations is not so easily dismissed. As they state: '[O]ne of our central points is that we, as lawyers, do not know enough about the underlying variables to be able to express an informed opinion; nor do the administration's vociferous critics, in many cases'.[88] This echoes the argument in the *Al-Aulaqi* v. *Obama* decision, which sets out the grounds for considering the case political:

> As the D.3. Circuit recently explained, cases involving national security and foreign relations 'raise issues that 'frequently turn on standards that defy judicial application' or 'involve the exercise of a discretion demonstrably committed to the executive or legislature.'... Unlike the political branches, the Judiciary has 'no covert agents, no intelligence sources, and no policy advisors ... to assess the nature of battlefield decisions,'' ... or to 'define the standard for the government's use of covert operations in conjunction with political turmoil in another country,'... These types of decisions involve 'delicate, complex' policy judgments with 'large elements of prophecy,' and 'are decisions of a kind for which the Judiciary has neither aptitude, facilities, nor responsibility.[89]

Taken together, these two arguments question the ability of the judiciary and courts system to ever second-guess the executive. The US political question doctrine holds that the court cannot review matters that are essentially political questions. This same logic appears in the 2006 SCI ruling on targeted killings:

> the decision, made on the basis of the knowledge of the military profession, to perform a preventative act which causes the deaths of terrorists in the area. That decision is the responsibility of the executive branch. It has the professional-security expertise to make that decision.[90]

In all three cases two abilities to acquire knowledge are compared: that of the judiciary and that of the executive (incorporating its professional military). In all three, the judiciary's lack of knowledge and ability to acquire it form the crux of arguments that posit deference to the executive branch. The SCI ruling is not binding in the United States, but serves as an important foil because unlike the Posner/Vermeule thesis, and the political question doctrine outlined in *Al-Aulaqi v Obama*, the SCI ruling formulates a defence of judicial review despite this critical lack of knowledge:

Constitutional protections 143

The task of interpreting law is in the hands of the Court.... The question which the Court must ask itself is not whether the executive branch's understanding of the law is a reasonable understanding; the question which the court must ask itself is whether it is the correct understanding.... The expertise in interpreting the law is in the hands of the Court.[91]

Although all three interpretations incorporate the lack of judicial knowledge in their decisions, they do so for different reasons, and different conclusions are reached. This is important, because the logic of the SCI ruling runs directly against that of the Posner/Vermeule thesis. What is important to differentiate here is the different uses of knowledge – and the claims made as to the possibility of that use – between these three differing arguments. The *Al-Aulaqi* decision, it must be remembered, was made before the death of al-Awlaki. This is what is intended by the judge's choice of words, which abrogated responsibility for a decision based on lack of knowledge (and furthermore, inability to pass judgment). Similarly, the SCI judgment defers to the executive in the first instance, allowing it the freedom to choose whom to target and where. Where this differs from Posner and Vermeule is where they formulate the argument that judicial review is ineffective both a priori and after the fact:

[W]hen judges or academic commentators say that government has wrongly assessed the net benefits or costs of some security policy or other, they are amateurs playing at security policy, and there is no reason to expect that courts can improve upon government's emergency policies in any systematic way.[92]

This claim is highly suspect, particularly since it offers no defence against the basic argument contained within the SCI judgment that courts are best placed to review legal matters. Although Posner and Vermeule may indeed be correct that courts cannot formulate better security policy than government, this is based on the rule-of-thumb answer that government has more access to information than other institutions. This in itself relies on a belief in good judgement. Surveying presidential decision-making in foreign policy crises, Herek *et al.* identify seven symptoms of defective decision-making. Three of these refer directly to the acquisition or processing of information (poor information search, selective bias in processing information at hand, and failure to reconsider options in light of new information).[93] Although they find that presidential decision-making in crisis situations is variable, they note that poor information search rarely occurred in presidential decision-making (three occurrences in 19 crises).[94] Although this is not enough to state that such matters are critical to decision-making processes, it does suggest that the president tends to make decisions with the best information at hand. Given that the executive has access to more information than other potential decision makers, this structural feature would seem to weigh in favour of the president being better equipped to form policy in such situations. Nonetheless, that does not prevent post hoc judgement of such

144 *Constitutional protections*

matters. Similarly, the *Al-Aulaqi* decision was right in claiming that the court did not have the ability a priori to assess whether it was legal or not to place Anwar al-Awlaki on a targeted killing list, which resulted in his death; but this does not preclude post hoc analysis and legal review of the case. A judicial system that lacks post facto review of potentially illegal matters is toothless. In constructing their argument to denude the judiciary of its ability to restrain the executive, Posner and Vermeule also attack its ability to perform its basic function in society. Therefore there does appear to be legitimate scope for judicial review of a person's definition as an enemy, even where such a review occurs post-mortem. These questions of knowledge, however, do not address the second objection to legal oversight contained in the *Al-Aulaqi* decision – that of the political question doctrine.

The ability to review the executive's decisions and actions does not, however, equate to the ability to review its determination that a person is an enemy. The Obama administration's position regarding the Guantanamo Bay litigation demonstrates that it considers due process applicable to these decisions. The *Hamdan* decision gave US citizens the right to pursue habeas corpus writs in the federal system, which effectively re-includes US citizens in the constitutional system of the United States; concurrent with the *Boumediene* decision, this applies to US citizens under the de facto authority of the US government world-wide. Critics deride the use of military commissions and Combatant Status Review Tribunals; however, the latter give a due process method of challenging the determination of the executive. In this matter, whether these courts are arbitrary or not is irrelevant; the point stands that external enemies are given due process to challenge the executive's decision to determine them as such. Therefore, the executive acknowledges a form of due process for both internal and external enemies. There is, however, an important caveat to this with regards to targeted killings: this due process occurs when persons are physically returned to the system. In other words, for US citizens who have been externalised by the executive to recover their due process rights in regards to its decision to determine that they are enemies, they must first be captured or turn themselves over – as the *Al-Aulaqi* decision outlined.[95] The key requirement to identify persons as enemies is knowledge, and the executive does accept post hoc review of persons' status as enemies by the judiciary, which implies its capacity to assess the evidence on whether persons are, or are not, enemies. The question, therefore, turns to whether the courts have standing to review these determinations: which of the three executive actions related to targeted killings do the courts have standing to adjudicate on?

The successful writ of habeas corpus includes, or re-includes, persons in the constitutional system of the United States. Although this does not undo the executive's definition of persons as enemies, it does undo the executive's choice to define them as an external enemy. This is demonstrably possible post hoc, when persons are detained, but the previous section argued that it is extremely difficult for courts to determine a person's status prior to detention. A second problem is that of the political question doctrine – whether the courts have constitutional

Constitutional protections 145

standing to review the executive's definition of a person as an enemy, or whether such decisions fall outside the scope of the courts' constitutional authority. The US constitutional system differs from that of Israel because of the political question doctrine. Rachel Barkow, writing in 2002, charts the rise and fall of this doctrine prior to the subsequent decade encompassed by the War on Terror. At this point in time, Barkow contends, '[T]he Supreme Court's failure even to consider the political question doctrine reflects a broader trend in which the Court overestimates its own powers and prowess vis-à-vis the political branches'.[96] Subsequent to this period, the judiciary had deferred a number of times to the executive, and the dismissal of the *Al-Aulaqi* lawsuit on the grounds of the political question doctrine would point to its re-emergence in US legal and political culture. It is therefore significant to the issue of targeted killings.

Barkow's essay on the political question doctrine was written prior to the widespread US use of targeted killings. Her work cannot be read as an endorsement of such methods. It is used here because it is an eloquent and well-argued defence of the political question doctrine in total, rather than a defence of its applicability to the War on Terror. It serves as a useful link to the Posner/ Vermeule thesis, because the political question doctrine, in line with their arguments and the *Al-Aulaqi* decision, is a determining factor as to whether the courts can adjudicate on matters relating to targeted killings. The key difference between targeted killings and detentions is that targeted killings are non-reviewable; that is, unless a person can be removed from targeting lists, or the government otherwise constrained from using legal force against them *ex ante*, there is no possibility of review, except to declare the actions of the government illegal after a person has been killed. This *ex ante* constraint formed the key defence of the government's motion for dismissal of the *Al-Aulaqi* case:

> It is not the Government's contention here that any matter touching on foreign policy, national security, military, or intelligence affairs is non-justiciable, or that any overseas action – including the use of force – would be exempt from judicial review. Rather, it is the requests for declaratory and injunctive relief in this case that defendants contend are non-justiciable.[97]

The declaratory injunction sought in the *Al-Aulaqi* case is that Anwar al-Awlaki's name be removed from targeting lists *ex ante*. The essential problem in the case revolves around the ability of the executive to define a person as an enemy combatant, and whether it can do so to US citizens without outlining its criteria for doing so.[98] Before examining the ability of the courts to determine a citizen's combatant status, it is necessary to examine the political question doctrine in further detail. Barkow states that the first component of this doctrine, outlined in *Maybury* v. *Madison*, is that it is 'emphatically the province and duty of the judicial department to say what the law is'; but that this encompassing notion must be balanced with the *Maybury* decision's acknowledgement of 'the existence of certain questions that are wholly outside the purview of the courts'.[99] The courts have a role to play in adjudicating the scope of actions

146   *Constitutional protections*

taken by the executive pursuant to its identification of a person as an enemy, as the 2001–11 period of jurisprudence regarding enemy combatants demonstrates. But prior to this action, which in the *Al-Aulaqi* case was a targeted killing, one can identify two judgements fused together: first, that the executive judged al-Awlaki to be an external enemy; and second, that it judged the threat he posed significant enough to place him on a targeting list. Is either act a purely political matter? If not, could the courts adjudicate on either *ex ante*?

The difficulty comes in defining membership, particularly the criteria on which such a decision is based. The process of identifying members of terrorist networks is secret and within the executive's purview (the intelligence-collection agencies are all under the executive). But as Bradley and Goldsmith argue: 'it is crucial to distinguish between the power to detain someone with enemy combatant status and the processes for determining whether someone is an enemy combatant'.[100] The *Hamdi* decision introduced retroactive procedural protections for US citizens to guard against erroneous classification. In this sense, *Hamdi* legitimises the ability of the executive to define enemy combatants, even as it introduced procedural review of this process. The question of the executive's authority to define combatants was a fait accompli to this decision. The *Al-Aulaqi* decision ruled that the court lacked the means to determine the facts of the case a priori.[101] It is difficult to argue against the logic of the *Al-Aulaqi* decision, despite the reservations stated in the judgment:

> this Court recognizes the somewhat unsettling nature of its conclusion – that there are circumstances in which the Executive's unilateral decision to kill a U.S. citizen overseas is 'constitutionally committed to the political branches' and judicially unreviewable. But this case squarely presents such a circumstance.[102]

But this is in direct contrast to the position taken by the SCI on the matter:

> The position before us is intended to determine the permissible and the forbidden in combat which might harm the most basic right of a human being – the right to life. The doctrine of institutional non-justiciability cannot prevent the examination of that question.[103]

The SCI's words do not, however, refer to the same problem as the *Al-Aulaqi* decision. The SCI verdict refers to actions taken by the military pursuant to identifying persons as enemies. The case revolves around the permissibility of targeting enemies (combatants, civilians and those directly participating in hostilities), but the identification of a person as a potential enemy is not adjudicated on.

The problem is that a central political question – the identification of enemies – now makes a person liable for death. The *Quirin* decision removed the treason protections of the Constitution afforded to illegal combatants, but almost all non-conventional war is illegal in some manner. Henceforth, the identification of a person as party to a conflict makes them a legitimate target. It is difficult to see how a court could constrain the ability of the president, even outside the bounds of the AUMF, to define enemies of the United States. The *Hamdi* decision legalises the ability of the executive to define enemies, but affords US citizens due process. Attempts to circumvent this are detailed below.

The *ex ante* investigation of the targeted killing of a US citizen used the political question doctrine to establish that these acts remain within the purview of the executive. This is not necessarily illegal or immoral, as some have argued – the political question doctrine is an important feature of US law. This doctrine, however, would be hard to apply to retrospective investigations of such targeting. Regardless of the *ex ante* nature of debates surrounding the targeting of Anwar al-Awlaki in 2010, this theoretical Rubicon was crossed. The question, now open, is whether the courts will adjudicate on the matter. If the political question doctrine holds that the US court system cannot review the decision by the executive to kill a US citizen, it expands the power afforded the executive far beyond that envisaged in the Constitution. One proposed solution – for Congress to pass legislation either providing oversight for or prohibiting targeted killings[104] – is unsatisfactory, because it does not resolve the political question/due process dichotomy. Furthermore, McKelvey's suggestion connects the act of targeted killing with the act of enemy identification. The Obama administration's defence of targeted killings is predicated on the AUMF giving it authority for the act of targeted killing, while arguing that the authority to identify enemies derives from the president's role as commander-in-chief. In this sense, congressional oversight already exists – Congress can pass laws to restrict the scope of the AUMF. Even if the political question/due process dichotomy is non-resolvable, it is possible for Congress to restrict the use of this method in law.

The process by which an enemy is defined in a non-conventional conflict means that the definition of that enemy is inherently subjective. This section has argued that the grounds for identifying enemies is a political question, and that the process by which the knowledge is acquired to identify persons as enemies means that it is prohibitively difficult for the courts to adjudicate on this matter. However, the courts do have standing to judge on the outcome of this identification (the use of military force), and Congress does have the power to pass laws restricting the ability of the executive to use these methods. The use of lethal force in this manner brings into focus the relationship between citizen and state, which raises the key question of due process rights: can they offer US citizens any *ex ante* protection against the state?

If the civilian court system does have sufficient standing to review the US use of targeted killings, this runs counter to the Posner/Vermeule thesis, but not necessarily to the arguments set forth by Yoo. Although such a case has not occurred, the Obama administration's defence would require that it be able to take place, or at least be adjudicated on, were it to be consistent with its claim that it acts within its constitutional boundaries. One of the key features of the US constitutional system is due process – the remedy available to citizens against unlawful acts by the state. Is there any such due process available to citizens determined by the state to be enemies subject to targeted killings?

148 *Constitutional protections*

Attorney General Eric Holder's Northwestern University speech was clearly intended as a defence of the US targeted killing programme. It was sharply criticised both for this fact and for his reasoning within the speech itself.[105] The majority of Holder's speech concerns due process, as contained within the civil courts system, as well as in military commissions. Here, Holder walks a fine line, arguing that civilian criminal justice should be used to try terrorists, but also that the military commissions system is a form of due process. The effect of this is not only to defend the use of the civil courts system against persons who argue that al-Qaeda suspects should not have access to this system (Charles 'Cully' Stimson, speaking as then deputy assistant secretary of defense for detainee affairs had attacked top law firms for representing Guantanamo Bay detainees in 2007; the subsequent political storm led to his resignation),[106] but also to argue that military commissions are an appropriate form of due process (which is equally contentious). The question of military courts led to the passage of two Acts, the 2006 and 2009 Military Commissions Acts, both of which overlaid decisions reached in the Supreme Court. Holder's most contentious claim, however, was that: ' "[D]ue process" and "judicial process" are not one and the same, particularly when it comes to national security. The Constitution guarantees due process, not judicial process'.[107] To many legal experts, this parsing of due and judicial process was both wrong and predicated on straw man logical fallacies.[108] From the perspective of domestic constitutional law, it is difficult to understand such an action. However, in light of the administration's discourse on the War on Terror (including the discursive methods of preserving the non-illegality of its practice), as well as the dual application of constitutional law and IHL, this speech is remarkably cogent and well argued. This section will examine the pragmatic application of this dual-law system, how this does not render persons 'bare' as Agamben would have it, and then discuss the consequences of this speech. Holder's words connect the administration's discourse directly with the constitutional system of law in the United States. Some call this 'lawfare', both critically and in defence of the practice. This analysis looks outwards, at the subject, but the more important consideration is the effect that the use of a fighting method – targeted killings – has on the US political system. The Israeli context, by extending the scope of judicial oversight, allows for the preservation of judicial process. By relying on the 'emergency' and executive privilege, as Posner, Vermeule and Yoo argue, the US system does not.

The example of Israel is important because it provides a contrast to the results of the US legal and political system. The expansive claim made by the ISC in its 2006 case matched many features of the *Al-Aulaqi* decision regarding the inability of the court to determine, a priori, the case for or against a particular targeted killing. The difference, however, is that the ISC decision affirmed that targeted killings remained within the scope of the law. In effect, the ISC's judgment holds that it is supreme over both military and civil law, a situation in marked contrast to that of the United States. In the United States, the double application of law has been partly solved by the freedom afforded the executive to define enemies; yet this comes with the partial constraint of due process to be afforded US citizens. The nature of targeted killings meant that due process could not be given to citizens thus targeted, and so the Attorney General parsed 'judicial process' from 'due process'.

The key problem is that Holder's argument can be seen as legitimate in the case of executive determinations of enemies, but is illegitimate in regards to the decisions that the executive forms about persons determined to be enemies, as well as the actions taken pursuant to those decisions. Judicial process certainly forms part of the due process afforded citizens in the third case – as a remedy against the state's actions, or as a bar to its action. Similarly, what prevents the courts from forming *ex ante* decisions is the lack of knowledge that it has prior to a decision by the executive – but such knowledge is not lacking after the fact. The only method for the courts to function as part of the due process afforded citizens in the primary case – the determination of the executive that they are enemies – is by physical fact of capture. Holder is therefore partially right and partially misguided: the courts do have a role to play, but their function as part of due process changes at each step of the decisions required to conduct a targeted killing. Ultimately, unless the courts find reason to challenge the application of the AUMF to a US citizen, they cannot challenge the executive's use of targeted killings, but they can most certainly review the executive's actions in a given case.

The definitions given by the executive in its defence of targeted killings suffice to render instrumental criticism of them broadly irrelevant by reducing the debate to interpretations of words and phrases that have no fixed meaning. In a similar fashion, the use of targeted killings undercuts Yoo's core contention that the supreme authority of the executive was what the framers of the Constitution had in mind in the eighteenth century. Here, the question of targeted killings serves to illuminate the process by which the ability to define a person as party and subject to one set of law or another is a key feature of the US Constitution, something that the Article 3 protections sought to constrain in considerable detail.

Conclusion

The process by which persons are identified as enemies is key to understanding their relation to the constitutional system of the United States. The ability of the executive to define persons as enemies, traditionally constrained by the Article 3 treason provisions, has been expanded by the changing nature and definition of enemies, as well as by US case law. The erosion of these protections gives the president the ability to define which code of law persons belong to in the process of defining them as enemies.

The US use of targeted killings rests on the ability of the president to define persons as external enemies; without such ability, the executive loses its legal standing to use force against terrorist networks and other security threats. The Obama administration makes a specific claim about its ability to do so: that this ability is not only constitutional, but also in accordance with the rule of law.

150 *Constitutional protections*

Therefore, this chapter has examined this claim in relation to those of legal realists, and theorists of exceptionality within legal and political systems, and has argued that this claim was defensible. Furthermore, in examining US case law, this chapter has identified the 'problem' as being the expansive authority offered the executive by the AUMF. However, the laws that Congress passes are subject to review by the court system, and the executive must exercise its authority in accordance with the rule of law. Three key legal issues face the courts in the process of targeted killings: the identification of a person as an enemy, the judgement of the threat that a given person poses, and the measures used against them predicated on these two judgements. It is difficult to see how, on the basis of available knowledge, a court could rule on the identification and judgement of persons a priori; furthermore, the identification of persons as enemies is fundamentally a political question, and non-judiciable. The courts have demonstrated themselves fully capable and willing to rule on the third criterion – methods used against such persons. Fundamentally, the problem lies in the expansive authority afforded the executive by Congress, not an imperial presidency. This legitimacy, however, rests on congressional approval for war and the use of military force, which will be highly relevant to the arguments in the next chapter regarding the responsibility for the use of targeted killings.

The use of targeted killings against US citizens alters the relationship between the citizen and the state. This shift is the result of changing proclivity on the part of the executive to use military force against its own citizens, as well as the authority it has to do so under the AUMF. By identifying persons as belonging to al-Qaeda, the executive currently has the constitutional authority to kill them. What this underlines is that the changing nature of warfare, specifically war against non-conventional opponents, means that the authority that was once a means of identifying enemy nations and forces is now the authority to identify individual persons as enemies.

Notes

1 Jameel Jaffer, director of the ACLU's Center for Democracy speaking on South California Public Radio, 3 October 2011.
2 Holder, 'Northwestern University Speech'.
3 Eoin Carolan, *The New Separation of Powers: A Theory for the Modern State* (New York: Oxford University Press, 2009).
4 David J. Barron and Martin S. Lederman, 'The Commander in Chief at the Lowest Ebb: A Constitutional History', *Harvard Law Review* 121(3) (2008): 1095.
5 Most notably the detention cases such as *Hamdi* v. *Rumsfeld, Rasul* v. *Bush, Rumsfeld* v. *Padilla, Hamdan* v. *Rumsfeld* and *Boumediene* v. *Bush*.
6 Richard Jackson, 'Culture, Identity and Hegemony: Continuity and (the Lack of) Change in US Counterterrorism Policy from Bush to Obama', *International Politics* 48(2–3) (2011): 401–2.
7 Ron Paul, 'An Unconstitutional Killing: Obama's Killing of Awlaki Violates American Principles', *New York Daily News*, 2 October 2011.
8 Holder, 'Northwestern University Speech'; Koh, 'Obama Administration'.
9 Yoo, 'Assassination': 75.

Constitutional protections 151

10 Lindsay Kwoka, 'Trial by Sniper: The Legality of Targeted Killing in the War on Terror', *University of Pennsylvania Journal of Constitutional Law* 14(1) (2011): 325.

11 Ben McKelvey, 'Due Process Rights and the Targeted Killing of Suspected Terrorists: The Unconstitutional Scope of Executive Killing Power', *Vanderbilt Journal of Transnational Law* 44(5) (2011): 1383.

12 David Cole, 'An Executive Power to Kill?', *NYRB Blog*, 6 March 2012.

13 Koh, 'Obama Administration'; Yoo, 'Assassination'; Holder, 'Northwestern University Speech'.

14 Harold Hongju Koh, 'On American Exceptionalism', *Stanford Law Review* 55 (May 2003).

15 Anderson, 'Targeted Killing': 14.

16 McKelvey, 'Due Process Rights'.

17 Larson, 'Forgotten Constitutional Law of Treason'.

18 ACLU, 'ACLU Statement on Killing of Anwar Al-Aulaqi' (Washington, DC: American Civil Liberties Union, 30 September 2011).

19 Holder, 'Northwestern University Speech'.

20 Larson, 'Forgotten Constitutional Law of Treason': 873.

21 Larson, 'Forgotten Constitutional Law of Treason': 883.

22 Larson, 'Forgotten Constitutional Law of Treason': 894.

23 Larson, 'Forgotten Constitutional Law of Treason': 893–4.

24 *Kawakita* v. *United States*, 343 US 717 (1952).

25 *Ex Parte Milligan*, 71 US 2 (1866).

26 *Ex Parte Quirin*, 317 US 1 (1942).

27 *Ex Parte Milligan*.

28 *Ex Parte Quirin*.

29 Larson, 'Forgotten Constitutional Law of Treason': 897.

30 Bradley and Goldsmith, 'Congressional Authorization': 2111.

31 *In Re Territo*, 156 F. 2d 142 (1946).

32 *Ex Parte Milligan*.

33 Becker and Shane, 'Secret "Kill List"'.

34 Scott Shane, 'C.I.A. Is Disputed on Civilian Toll in Drone Strikes', *New York Times*, 11 August 2011.

35 George W. Bush, 'Order to the Secretary of Defense' (Washington, DC, 2002).

36 Holder, 'Northwestern University Speech'.

37 George P. Fletcher, 'Black Hole in Guantánamo Bay', *Journal of International Criminal Justice* 2(1) (2004).

38 Obama, 'Remarks by the President on National Security'.

39 Jeh Johnson, 'National Security Law'.

40 Radsan and Murphy, 'Due Process'.

41 Department of Defense, *Manual for Military Commissions United States*, 2010 edn (Washington, DC: DoD, 2010): II-15, Rule 204 (a).

42 National Defense Authorization Act for Fiscal Year 2012.

43 *Hedges* v. *Obama* (2013).

44 John Walker Lindh, also known as 'the American Taliban', was a US citizen who had joined the Taliban prior to the 9/11 attacks. Captured and detained in Afghanistan in 2001, he plea-bargained in 2002 and was sentenced to 20 years in prison.

45 In contrast to the Supreme Court's running battles with the executive branch over Guantanamo Bay, it has not yet considered the question of targeted killings. *Al-Aulaqi* v. *Obama* made it to the Federal District Court, but the ACLU/CCR did not appeal its dismissal to the Supreme Court.

46 *Al-Aulaqi* v. *Obama*: 80.

47 ACLU, 'Aulaqi v. Obama Complaint' (Washington, DC: American Civil Liberties Union, 2010): 5.

152 *Constitutional protections*

48 McKelvey, 'Due Process Rights': 1368–9.
49 Posner and Vermeule, *Terror in the Balance*.
50 Yoo, 'Assassination': 63–4.
51 Yoo, *Crisis and Command*.
52 Jenny S. Martinez, 'Process and Substance in the "War on Terror" ', *Columbia Law Review* 108(5) (2008); Daniel Solove, *Nothing to Hide: The False Tradeoff between Privacy and Security* (New Haven, CT: Yale University Press, 2011).
53 Obama, 'Remarks by the President on National Security'.
54 Posner and Vermeule, *Terror in the Balance*: 26–8.
55 Yoo, *Crisis and Command*: 402.
56 Holder, 'Northwestern University Speech'.
57 Giorgio Agamben, *State of Exception* (University of Chicago Press, 2005): 25–6.
58 Posner and Vermeule, *Terror in the Balance*: 42.
59 Yoo, *Crisis and Command*.
60 Posner and Vermeule, *Terror in the Balance*: 42.
61 Posner and Vermeule, *Terror in the Balance*: 142.
62 Yoo, *Crisis and Command*: 321.
63 Yoo, *Crisis and Command*: 321.
64 Posner and Vermeule, *Terror in the Balance*: Ch. 5.
65 Yoo, *Crisis and Command*: 331.
66 Yoo, *Crisis and Command*: 397.
67 Yoo, *Crisis and Command*: 383–5.
68 Posner and Vermeule, *Terror in the Balance*: 38.
69 Carl Schmitt, tr. George Schwab, *Political Theology: Four Chapters on the Concept of Sovereignty* (University of Chicago Press, 2005): 5.
70 Giorgio Agamben, *Homo Sacer: Sovereign Power and Bare Life* (Meridian Stanford, CA: Stanford University Press, 1998): 71–4.
71 Agamben, *State of Exception*.
72 ACLU, 'Aulaqi v. Obama Complaint'.
73 Schmitt, *Political Theology*: 6.
74 Agamben, *State of Exception*: 3–4. See also Judith Butler, 'Guantanamo Limbo: International Law Offers Too Little Protection for Prisoners of the New War', *Nation* 274(12) (2002).
75 Agamben, *State of Exception*: 3.
76 See Authorization for Use of Military Force.
77 Schmitt, *Political Theology*: 13.
78 Agamben, *State of Exception*: 3–4.
79 Nasser Hussain, 'Hyperlegality', *New Criminal Law Review* 10(4) (2007): 516.
80 Posner and Vermeule, *Terror in the Balance*: 274.
81 Savage, 'Secret US Memo'.
82 *Marbury* v. *Madison*, 5 US 137 (1803).
83 *Baker* v. *Carr*, 369 US 186 (1962).
84 Louis Henkin, 'Is There a "Political Question" Doctrine?', *Yale Law Journal* 85(5) (1976).
85 Rachel E. Barkow, 'More Supreme Than Court: The Fall of the Political Question Doctrine and the Rise of Judicial Supremacy', *Columbia Law Review* 102(2) (2002).
86 See test two outlined in *Baker* v. *Carr*.
87 Henkin, 'Is There a "Political Question" Doctrine?': 601.
88 Posner and Vermeule, *Terror in the Balance*: 158.
89 *Al-Aulaqi* v. *Obama*: 67.
90 *Public Committee against Torture in Israel* v. *Government of Israel*: 9.57.
91 *Public Committee against Torture in Israel* v. *Government of Israel*: 9.56.
92 Posner and Vermeule, *Terror in the Balance*: 31.

Constitutional protections   153

93 Gregory M. Herek, Irving L. Janis and Paul Huth, 'Decision Making During International Crises: Is Quality of Process Related to Outcome?', *Journal of Conflict Resolution* 31(2) (1987): 204–5.
94 Herek, Janis and Huth, 'Decision Making During International Crises': 216.
95 *Al-Aulaqi* v. *Obama*.
96 Barkow, 'More Supreme Than Court': 300.
97 *Al-Aulaqi* v. *Obama*, Document 29: 15.
98 ACLU, 'Aulaqi v. Obama Complaint': 5.
99 Barkow, 'More Supreme Than Court': 239.
100 Bradley and Goldsmith, 'Congressional Authorization': 2121.
101 *Al-Aulaqi* v. *Obama*: 79.
102 *Al-Aulaqi* v. *Obama*: 78.
103 *Public Committee against Torture in Israel* v. *Government of Israel*: 35.
104 McKelvey, 'Due Process Rights': 1377.
105 See, for example, Emily Bazelon, 'Not-So-Innocent Abroad', *Slate*, 6 March 2012; Steve Vladeck, 'Three More (Ambivalent) Reflections on the Holder Speech', *Lawfare*, 12 March 2012; Andrew Cohen, 'On "Targeted Killing" Speech, Eric Holder Strikes Out', *Atlantic Monthly*, 6 March 2012.
106 Neil A. Lewis, 'Official Attacks Top Law Firms over Detainees', *New York Times*, 13 January 2007.
107 Holder, 'Northwestern University Speech'.
108 Nathan Wessler, 'In Targeted Killing Speech, Holder Mischaracterizes Debate over Judicial Review', *ACLU*, 5 March 2012.

6 Normative principles of war

> Where all are guilty, no one is; confessions of collective guilt are the best possible safeguard against the discovery of culprits, and the very magnitude of the crime the best excuse for doing nothing.
>
> Hannah Arendt, *On Violence*[1]

Introduction

To defend the conduct of targeted killings, the Obama administration has made claims on something higher than the laws of war – the principles of the laws of war.[2] In practice, the Obama administration's defence of targeted killings works because it is able to rely on legal interpretations that enable it to define its own conduct as legal, irrespective of the similarity of these interpretations to those of the Bush administration. The Obama administration seeks to depict its conduct as ethical in order to distance itself from policies of the Bush administration, but also to highlight the supposed normality of its actions.

If the Obama administration's conduct is defensible in legal terms, why does it defend targeted killings in ethical terms? Again, legitimacy is the principle issue: by making moral claims, the Obama administration derives legitimacy from the moral force of these claims. By claiming that it abides by the principles of the laws of war, the Obama administration seeks to ground its defence of targeted killings in shared cultural values. By arguing that the United States' 'moral authority' is its 'strongest currency in the world', Barack Obama seeks to root his entire approach to national security in US 'values'.[3] This link between principles and values and the legal status of targeted killings is important because, as seen in Chapters 1 and 2, the Obama administration's reconciliations of its use of targeted killings with international law relies on a claim to abide by the principles of the laws of war. Outlining this reconciliation, Eric Holder used 'principles' in many ways. He spoke of the use of force 'in a manner consistent with applicable law of war principles', as well as outlining: 'any such use of lethal force by the United States will comply with the four fundamental law of war principles governing the use of force'.[4] In using the concept of principle, rather than instrumental law, Holder is affirming that the United States sees itself as conducting war in accordance with the principles of the laws of war.

Normative principles of war 155

The precise interaction of ethics and law in this context is unclear. The language of law remains the primary way of defining whether recourse to the use of force in international affairs is right or wrong, as well passing similar judgement on acts of violence in armed conflicts. Yet IHL is fundamentally rooted in the values and principles of the just war tradition.[5] One argument for engaging with ethics at the same time as law is that politicians rarely justify their actions in purely legal terms. Examining the discourse of the War on Terror reveals many more instances of 'It is lawful and right that …' (or similar) than 'It is lawful *therefore* right that …' as a form of argument. In making such claims, the Obama administration rejects moral realism, or the idea that war renders moral principles irrelevant.[6] In addition, the Obama administration is implicitly claiming that its actions adhere to the moral framework that underpins the Western way of war – just war ethics. Michael Walzer begins his investigation into the contemporary applicability of just war theory with the examination of realism and an important note of caution:

> Hypocrisy is rife in wartime discourse, because it is especially important at such a time to appear to be in the right. It is not only that the moral stakes are high; the hypocrite may not understand that; more crucially, his actions will be judged by other people, who are not hypocrites, and whose judgements will affect their policies towards him … we have no choice, I think, except to take his assertions seriously and put them to the test of moral realism.[7]

This junction of ethics and law is particularly relevant to present calls for accountability and transparency regarding the US use of targeted killings. It is in this context that I want to examine moral ways of thinking through the justification for violence, because it leads beyond the present impasse whereby the White House asserts that the president has all legal authority to use targeted killings; and there does not appear to be a way of challenging this claimed authority. One key wish of those seeking greater accountability for targeted killings is either a pre-strike legal review of the executive's decision, or legal review after the fact.[8] Prospects for either institution look dire, because neither the president nor Congress seem overly interested in creating a 'drone court' of any description.

Thinking through the vaunted 'principles of the laws of war' allows for a fresh perspective on what is otherwise a legal and political discussion. An elementary feature of just war theory is responsibility for the use of force and violence. It is this implicit engagement with the decision to use force that separates Walzer's moral realists from those who seek to engage with the moral consequences of violence. Accountability, after all, rests on the idea that someone, or something, can in theory be held responsible for a given action. It might be lawful to kill according to the law, but to kill in a manner where responsibility is not assignable to a person, while legal, contravenes the principle of moral responsibility that threads through the just war tradition. Military organisations are founded on the principle of command responsibility, and a chain of command

156 *Normative principles of war*

where responsibility is, at least in theory, assignable to a superior officer. Other organisations, such as the CIA, do not necessarily have in place such systems of assigning responsibility; or at least, these systems are not publicly disclosed. To understand the primacy of this concept, however, it is first necessary to look at just war theory itself.

Justice, law and war

Just war theory, the branch of ethics that tackles the specific issues associated with war and political violence, is an important dimension of the discussion on the use of drones and targeted killings. 'Killing by remote control', if not illegal, still raises many ethical questions.[9] Moreover, lawful actions can be held by some to be immoral – the use of military force is often a good case in point. From the opposite perspective, rebellions are usually unlawful by definition, but plenty of people argue that rebellion in the face of tyrannical governments is justifiable in moral terms. For its part, the Obama administration argues that this is not the case in its use of targeted killings – that these lethal actions are both lawful and ethical actions. This alignment is an important aspect of the Obama administration's defence, even though finding moral fault in the Obama administration's actions is unlikely to have a fraction of the consequences that, say, a Supreme Court ruling against the US government would.

The two branches of just war theory, *jus ad bellum* (regarding the resort to war) and *jus in bello* (regarding moral conduct within war), closely match the categories of international law relevant to war and armed conflict. The basic framework of just war theory is generally held to be the satisfaction of certain tests or criteria in order to ascertain whether an action is right or wrong. Differences regarding the basis on which said judgement is reached and the moral reasoning that leads to conclusions constitute the field of just war theory. The connection between the two branches of just war theory is important. Traditionally it has been held that soldiers waging war in a morally justifiable manner (conforming to the principles of distinction and proportionality, i.e. not intentionally killing civilians, and using as little force as necessary) are justified in doing so, even if the war is unjustified.[10] Recent 'revisionists' of the just war tradition have challenged this, notably David Rodin[11] and Jeff McMahan.[12] McMahan's account of the moral basis for justifiable killing has been particularly influential, notably because he argues that soldiers do not have the right to kill in an unjust war, although controversially he argues that the moral course of action is surrender.[13] The dialogue between authors such as Walzer, McMahan and latter-day defenders of the just war tradition such as Nigel Biggar[14] is important in that it allows us to think through the moral cost and consequences of war and, in doing so, encourages critical analysis of justifications offered for acts of violence.

In the context of this dialogue, targeted killings pose many moral questions, not least because 'on either the traditional view or the new revisionist approach there are moral boundaries to justifiable killing in war'.[15] For some, targeted killings are unjustifiable, but the debates about the moral boundaries reveal important differences. For example, even though there is something intuitively different about targeted killing, as opposed to more regular forms of killing in conventional wars, is there a particular moral difference in this way of killing? Drones, although a lawful means of waging war, cause considerable moral unease. Scholars have debated whether there is anything particularly novel about drones that might require a rethink of the way killing in war is justified.[16] But certainly, there are elements of killing from these platforms that appear new – for example, the idea of combatants being able to kill without any chance of themselves being harmed (an example of 'extreme asymmetry'[17] that would appear to undermine the mutually accepted risk of harm that Walzer considered integral to justifying violence in war).[18] Others, such as John Kaag and Sarah Kreps, point out the 'moral hazard' of employing these means, arguing that this lack of vulnerability might lead to less restraint on the resort to, or use of, force.[19] Drones, to some, reveal powerful moral critiques of the way in which states perceive human beings in moral terms, in the case of Grégoire Chamayou's 'necroethics',[20] whereas for others the problem that drones are thought to pose should be stood on its head: is it morally justifiable to *not* employ drones if they are indeed more precise than other available weapon platforms?[21]

The morality or immorality of targeted killings is a varied topic, but one principle objection to the Obama administration's conduct centres on accountability for targeted killings, and it is here that thinking through the concept and principle of responsibility in moral terms raises significant questions about the CIA's role in US targeted killings. The legal and ethical codes that govern the use of force in war require its responsible use. Legitimate acts in both IHL and just war theory require some form of calculation, which in turn implies decision, and thus responsibility stems from this decision. The inherently subjective nature of combat means that one allows soldiers certain flexibility in killing, particularly in close quarters, and this is embodied, on a personal level, in the concept of necessity. Reactions and accidents are a natural function of war and, as Clausewitz notes, the essential element of danger fundamentally alters the manner in which a soldier perceives the world and behaves.[22] What is important to note is that even in accidents a person or a group of persons can be held responsible for acts of violence. Responsibility-free warfare, in other words, would stand in stark contrast to our existing ways of thinking about the morality of war, even if misdeeds often go unpunished. In this sense, there is a difference between actions that a person could be held responsible for but go unpunished, and actions that nobody could justly be held responsible for.

President Obama's personal role in targeted killings appears to be an exercise in taking personal responsibility for the use of targeted killings.[23] At the same time, Obama is a single person, and unable to exercise close supervision of each and every act of violence. To some, the president's involvement is not enough.[24] Just war theory contains two key principles, individual responsibility and command responsibility, both of which hinge on the relationship between moral responsibility and voluntary actions or decisions. It is for this reason that the

158 *Normative principles of war*

literature on just wars principally concerns choices, sometimes theoretical ones, where particular courses of action are either praiseworthy or repugnant. In order to reach such judgements, however, someone has to be responsible for the use of force. Without the guiding principle of responsibility, the ethical structure of just war theory breaks down. So how best to engage with the concept of responsibility? In my opinion, engaging with the classes of responsibility found in Aristotle's *Nicomachean Ethics* is a good way of understanding the particular moral problems that the Obama administration's defence does not quite cover[25] – in particular, the problem of the CIA's use of signature strikes.

Accountability, responsibility and 'drone courts'

For some, political and legal accountability are vitally important. Philip Alston's critique of the US use of targeted killings focuses on the CIA and the Department of Defense, stating that 'neither operates with the degree of accountability officially envisaged under domestic law, and neither is in any meaningful way accountable for its actions in terms of the international legal obligations undertaken by the United States'.[26] Here, caution must be exercised, as Alston's use of 'accountability' differs (but is inherently related to) the term 'responsibility' as used in this chapter. Indeed, it is the difference between the two that makes it difficult for Alston's criticism to carry weight in the face of Holder's defence. Alston's concept of 'accountability' spans covert operations by the military as well as by the CIA.[27] The crux of Alston's argument is that if an act cannot be objectively examined, it is unaccountable and therefore illegitimate. Alston's initial line of inquiry – which specifically mentions Joint Special Operations Command (JSOC) – founders, and his attentions focus on the CIA: 'the bottom line is that intelligence agencies – particularly those that are effectively unaccountable – should not be conducting lethal operations abroad'.[28] The problem with such an argument is the instant rebuttal afforded by the process of 'double-hatting'. Alston cites this as a problem but, on a theoretical level, although the CIA is in charge of identifying and authorising targets, military operators fly the craft, and do so in a military capacity. Indeed, as Richard Whittle's history of the Predator drone points out, prior to 9/11 there were even mooted technological solutions to enable CIA officers to fire weapons from a drone, absolving military personnel from the decision to kill someone.[29]

Alston's argument is therefore about examining covert operations that involve lethal force. This relies on the assumption that responsibility is found in public accountability, which is not necessarily true. Public accountability may help foster responsibility, but a counterargument – that the US military fights in accordance with the laws and principles of war – allows organisations such as JSOC to be accountable and use force without such public accountability. Indeed, the requirements of operational security militate against the kind of public scrutiny that would accompany public accountability.

Accountability mechanisms are fundamentally intended to be a check on unconstrained political power.[30] Critical accounts of the lack of accountability for US targeted killings return to long-running problems for democracies: what kinds of covert activities are justifiable in liberal democracies? How can democratic control of secret exercises of power be assured? Some argue that the way the use of targeted killings has developed causes needless problems. For example, Micah Zenko writes that:

> U.S. targeted killings are needlessly made complex and opaque by their division between two separate entities: JSOC and the CIA. Although drone strikes carried out by the two organizations presumably target the same people, the organizations have different authorities, policies, accountability mechanisms, and oversight.[31]

Secrecy is a fundamental issue here, because without some degree of secrecy the intelligence activity required to conduct covert operations is impossible. Prior to the adoption of targeted killings as a major component of its counterterrorist policy, the United States had already grappled with many of these issues. For example, in addition to the congressional committees that exercise oversight of intelligence and military activities, the Foreign Intelligence Surveillance Court renders judgment on secret surveillance activities by intelligence and law enforcement agencies under the Foreign Intelligence Surveillance Act.[32] These institutions, which are meant to ensure accountability in secret, do not satisfy everyone. Notably, they have come under sustained attack recently due to public and journalistic outcry at surveillance activities detailed in material released by a former National Security Agency (NSA) contractor, Edward Snowden.[33]

The question is whether this perceived lack of accountability actually undermines the Obama administration's defence of its activities. One element of this is the lack of effective judicial review of targeted killings. Arguments that the United States needs a 'drone court' to review executive decisions before the conduct of a targeted killing are essentially calls for political change.[34] Contrary to these arguments, some see no need for a special court, or argue that existing systems of political accountability are sufficient to ensure political accountability for the use of force on behalf of the US state, or that such a court is plainly unworkable.[35] Even so, as Stephen Vladeck notes, the present general lack of after-the-fact accountability for actions of the US government means that 'victims of governmental overreaching in the conduct of national security policy will primarily have to turn to the political branches for redress, since retrospective judicial remedies will likely be unavailing'.[36] Is such a state of affairs inherently unjust? Certainly there is an argument that this is the case, but even if judicial accountability is unavailable, political accountability most certainly is – in the form of the democratic process. In moral terms, however, it is clear that responsibility for these actions has been accepted by a large number of relevant political figures and organisations. When the President of the United States sits down on a Tuesday and gives his assent to an act of violence, he can hardly be said to be ducking responsibility for these actions.

160   *Normative principles of war*

In terms of just war theory, the drone courts and accountability arguments mask a deeper problem: is the overall responsibility for targeted killings accepted by the president enough to satisfy the requirements of justifiable killing in war? In other words, is a problem to be found with the relationships between the individual decisions that direct acts of violence, the organisations that enable them and the president who takes overall responsibility? In answering this question, it is necessary to work from the ground up, so to speak, and examine the assignation of responsibility for acts of violence at the individual and corporate levels. The particular problem for the Obama administration is that its public defence of targeted killings requires it to defend something that on face value appears to be morally indefensible: signature strikes.

The moral problem of signature strikes

The many legal criticisms of the CIA's role in targeted killings usually relate back to the social concept of soldiers, or combatants, as socially acceptable agents of the state empowered to commit acts of violence on the state's behalf. The argument that I wish to make is twofold: first, that signature strikes, as a targeting method, could give rise to something that Aristotle would refer to as a 'non-voluntary' act – killing without responsibility; and second, that unlike with the military, we cannot be sure that the CIA is structured so that an individual in the organisation can be held responsible for such acts. In this argument, signature strikes are an example of distributed lethal action where individual persons within an organisation have rather less freedom of action or decision due to their placement within a bureaucratic entity. Signature strikes are not a class apart (many forms of killing in modern warfare require distributed action and decision-making), but they are an extreme example of this class of activity.

Moral responsibility – both individual and collective – for acts of violence and killing is the foundation on which just war theory is built. If we as humans did not care about killing, we would not have developed complex (and, to some, illogical) moral theories that outline the moral basis for killing one another. To be sure, accidents happen, as do non-combatant deaths that are the rationally accepted by-product of intentional action. The concept of moral responsibility is a significant aspect of ethics and moral philosophy, and is tied to the concept of free will.[37] Much of it concerns the basis on which we ascribe moral blame, or hold persons accountable for their actions. For this reason, the account of moral responsibility contained herein is one perspective on this particular issue.

Signature strikes pose a particular moral problem due to the issue of identification – in short, whether it is morally permissible to kill unknown persons. Knowledge, or at least some form of justifiable belief, is the basis for both decisions and actions that could be considered rational. Moral blame, or responsibility, is predicated on this kind of action as an act of free will because an 'agent's freedom is a necessary condition for the agent being morally responsible for the act'.[38] Aristotle links these two ideas to the concept of responsibility. In Aristotelian terms, responsibility – as we tend to think about it – occurs

Normative principles of war 161

in conjunction with voluntary acts – the decision to perform an act. Importantly, Aristotle differentiates between the negative, separating the concept of 'acts that are not voluntary' into involuntary and non-voluntary acts. Crucially, Aristotle includes the concept of ignorance in this distinction – a person's belief is a guide to whether their action can be held to be voluntary or involuntary. Furthermore, he includes the idea of guilt as differentiating involuntary acts (acts that cause the agent to feel pain) from non-voluntary acts (acts that do not inspire such feelings):

> Everything that is done by reason of ignorance is not voluntary; it is only what produces pain and repentance that is involuntary. For the man who has done something owing to ignorance, and feels not the least vexation at his action, has not acted voluntarily, since he did not know what he was doing, nor yet involuntarily, since he is not pained. Of people, then, who act by reason of ignorance he who repents is thought an involuntary agent, and the man who does not repent may, since he is different, be called a not voluntary agent; for, since he differs from the other, it is better that he should have a name of his own.[39]

From this, it is possible to distinguish between different acts and levels of responsibility: voluntary acts, which always incur responsibility; involuntary acts, which someone is held to account for; and non-voluntary acts, for which no responsibility exists. It is this last category that is inadmissible in the principles of the laws of war and just war theory. The reason for this is that when we think of responsibility in war, at least in moral terms, we usually look for some form of responsibility, even in the case of mistakes. Non-voluntary acts fall outside this way of thinking about moral responsibility.

The simplest model for analysing the justice or injustice of a course of action usually revolves around a single person making a decision based on a set of accepted evidence that characterises the moral problem. This does not have to be theoretical; Michael Walzer's work derived much of its power by drawing on historical examples of moral problems that echo in the world around us. This model, however, rarely suffices to describe military activity in the present day. In contemporary warfare, both knowledge and decisions can be transferred, particularly in crew-served weapons and indirect weapons. It is therefore important to examine the roles that these transfers have on responsibility. The next example is that of the two-person sniper team. Snipers work in pairs – a spotter relays key information to the sniper, who operates the rifle. If, on the basis of this information, the sniper fires on a target, both are responsible for the death of the targeted individual, even if the precise decision was the sniper's. Here, the transfer of critical targeting information from the spotter to the sniper makes them complicit in the act. Both of them are therefore making a voluntary act, and share responsibility, and the death of a civilian would be involuntary. This contrasts with the idea of a mortar team. When an indirect fire unit is asked to provide fire, it does so on the basis of transferred information, but does not have any effective choice

162 *Normative principles of war*

to restrain itself, except where it also possesses information that would constrain it (such as knowledge that a school is being targeted). Therefore, if a soldier were to call in an artillery strike that landed precisely, yet killed civilians, the artillery unit in question could not be held directly accountable – it would be the responsibility of the soldier relaying information and asking for the strike. Within the framework, the spotter's act would be voluntary, or involuntary if a non-permissible target were killed, whereas the mortar team's actions would be involuntary in both respects.

These theoretical examples are given to underline the important relationship between information, decision and responsibility. They are also included because they, in many ways, no longer represent the method by which targets are selected on the contemporary battlefield. This is a method highlighted by the use of remote craft, because UAV operators have no direct method of sensing the direct environment in which their craft is operating. What is important to understand is that UAV operators work within a decision framework that is entirely constructed of secondary-source information. Critics of the use of UAVs use this fact to cite that they are more liable to use force.[40] It is cited here to differentiate these operators from the example of the singular soldier, as cited earlier. UAV operators do, however, have access to some direct information, relayed by cameras on the UAV. In the context of discussions of personal and public identification found in Chapter 4, this constitutes public identifying knowledge, whereas the legitimacy of a target (in a targeted killing) is predicated on private identifying knowledge. This latter set of knowledge is constructed via intelligence collection and is thus secondary source. Furthermore, the process by which knowledge of their target is acquired is not necessarily centralised. It is the decentralisation of knowledge transfers that is important, because this is a key feature of the process by which persons are identified as targets in contemporary warfare, as well as in signature strikes. Although individuals may be able to acquire sufficient information to designate someone a target, they rely on multiple sources of information to identify persons as enemies and judge whether they represent a legitimate target.

The decentralised process of knowledge acquisition is important when we consider the question of misidentification. Returning to the concept of the artillery team, those operating the artillery piece would not have a choice but to fire when ordered, based on someone else's knowledge transfer. If they happened to know acquitting evidence, they might refuse an order, but otherwise the decision would not be theirs to make, and the responsibility would not be theirs to bear. This is again at work in the concept of suicide bombers. For instance, in the case of Jean Charles de Menezes, the police officers who shot and killed de Menezes had been told that he was a suicide bomber, but were cleared of responsibility on the basis of the information that they were acting on, which was transferred to them by a surveillance team. On arriving at the underground platform, they boarded a train at the direction of the surveillance team that had identified de Menezes as a suicide bomber. As the Independent Police Complaints Commission report states:

Normative principles of war 163

Charlie 2 and Charlie 12 then saw Hotel 3 grab him. They mistakenly believed that their own lives and those of others on the train were in danger and fired shots intending to kill the person they believed to be a suicide bomber.[41]

Importantly, in identifying an individual, a single source of information entered into a wider spread may misidentify them. This single source of knowledge may result in the death of an innocent, yet the transferor of that knowledge might not intend its use in this manner. A single incident of this, where information is misinterpreted, and when synthesised with many other sources of information, produces a result in which the transferors of information cannot be held responsible, nor can the person deciding to use force, because it is not their choice to make. Such an instance would confirm the critics of UAVs, but also widen this criticism to the whole mechanism of producing targeting solutions from multiple sources of information. In extreme situations, this could produce the effect of a non-voluntary act, since the person using the weapon platform is being told to fire from evidence available, whereas the persons providing evidence cannot be held directly to account because they do not provide the complete information for targeting.

It is in this sense that signature strikes present a particular problem in terms of just war theory. On the one hand, we can say that all the myriad individuals involved in assembling a set of data that identifies a person as a legitimate target have some form of hand in the actions that follow, even if they do not pull the trigger to release a missile as a result. On the other, the people responsible for actually killing someone likely have far less autonomy than we traditionally expect of morally responsible agents. Although not coerced, they have been provided with a world view (via accrued intelligence) that depicts a person as a legitimate target of attack. Yet the same could be said of many forms of military activity. Indeed, this kind of distributed and bureaucratic targeting is a feature of advanced militaries, which field weapon systems that require multiple agents to use. In this sense, the problem of distributed targeting and signature strikes is not the lack of individual responsibility, but the lack of the possibility of assigning responsibility to an individual. Were there no way of assigning moral responsibility to otherwise non-voluntary actions, members of military organisations could quite happily conduct multiple acts for which no one could be held truly responsible, either in a voluntary or involuntary manner. Yet non-voluntary acts cannot be accommodated within the framework of just war ethics, because the idea of moral conduct in war requires responsibility.

The revisionist account of individual moral responsibility would naturally find fault with the above. However, this same account would also struggle to account for moral conduct using contemporary military technology and tactical means of violence, given that these technologies implicitly reduce the moral agency of many individuals who are ultimately responsible for acts of violence. A lone individual could never know for sure that the information that they are basing decisions on (decisions that have life-or-death consequences) would be

164 *Normative principles of war*

morally justifiable. Contrary to the lone member of the armed forces, making choices through a Rawlsian 'veil of ignorance' based on agreed sets of known information, service personnel usually have to work 'in the blind', trusting that they are being told truth by others, and forming judgements on the basis of uncertainty. In this sense, a large set of military activity, not just things akin to signature strikes, would give rise to non-voluntary actions with lethal consequences. To understand how these do not violate the notion that justifiable action requires a form of responsibility, it is necessary to examine the social context of moral action. Military organisations contain a set of mechanisms that arbitrarily assign responsibility for the use of force – the chain of command, and command responsibility. The problem for the CIA is that we cannot be sure that these exist in the same form or shape.

Moral responsibility and chains of command

Ultimately, the core principle of the laws and ethics of war is that someone, or something, be held to account for the use of force. As Walzer argues, regardless of the distinction between absolute and utilitarian philosophy, '[W]ere there no guilt involved, the decisions they [political leaders] make would be less agonizing than they are'.[42] The hierarchical military command structure contains a process of arbitrarily assigning responsibility, regardless of information transfers and decisions in the form of command responsibility. Regardless of the internal structure of the CIA, its agents are not held to the same standards. In particular, the CIA is not bound by the UCMJ (the United States' body of military law), meaning that it is less constrained than the military.[43]

To prevent the commission of non-voluntary uses of force, either responsibility for the use of force can be arbitrarily assigned or the process of decision and information transfer can be controlled in such a manner that this problem does not arise. The US military contains three sets of 'firebreaks' built into its culture and structure. These are arbitrary rule sets, although rules of engagement (ROEs) are constructed with international law compliance in mind. In effect, these three rule sets assign responsibility in an arbitrary manner, but also ensure that responsibility is assigned. Whether or not these responsibility assignments are 'fair' is another matter entirely. Rather, the presence of these arbitrary rule sets within military structures forecloses the possibility of non-voluntary acts being committed, because even if such an act occurs, these rule sets transfer responsibility to a person who can be held accountable for the act. The link between decisions and knowledge requires the presence of some form of 'firebreak' for both in order to eliminate the possibility of unassigned non-voluntary acts. Alternatively, a higher-order responsibility 'firebreak' serves – command responsibility.

Returning to McNeal's work on UAV targeting, there is a clear decision firebreak in the military's use of ROEs.[44] These rule sets outline specific items of knowledge that are either visually confirmed or must be checked with superiors. ROEs restrict the ability of the individual to make an independent decision. Conformity of targeting in accordance with the ROEs which results in an illegitimate

Normative principles of war 165

act may be the decision of the individual, but since the decision has been shaped by this set of rules and procedures, responsibility is shared with the person or persons outlining the ROEs. Where a military sets over-permissive ROEs, or ones that are in contravention of the laws of war, the military itself bears the responsibility for this. As Grunawalt writes: '[O]ur rules of engagement are also the principal mechanism of ensuring that U.S. military forces are at all times in full compliance with our obligations under domestic as well as international law'.[45]

Due to this, military organisations setting ROEs that contravene international law also bear responsibility for doing so if soldiers follow these rules and commit acts illegal under IHL. This organisational responsibility does not, however, remove responsibility from the individual for committing such crimes. The ROEs therefore prevent the decision component of an action from contributing to a non-voluntary act. The problem, therefore, lies in the transfer of information.

ROEs represent a 'decision' firebreak as well as a 'knowledge' firebreak at the level of targeting. It is difficult, however, to determine the possibility of a similar type of firebreak in operation regarding the knowledge required to identify a person. Military intelligence follows patterns to standardise collection and usage, with standardised measures and tests for analysis and interpretation. But identifying persons in the context of signature strikes could rely on volumes of fragmentary information, such as telephone numbers acquired from captured mobile phones. The process of identifying terrorist networks and their members within the broader population entails the use of such evidence, and its constant accrual. Standards that prevent the use of such information would cripple the ability of intelligence analysts to identify targets. In theory, therefore, there exists no firebreak for information provided in good faith.

Identification of an opponent is an integral feature of warfare. Without such an opponent, Clausewitz's 'duel on a larger scale' could not take place.[46] In *Intelligence and War*, John Keegan states that '[F]rom the earliest times, military leaders have always sought information of the enemy, his strengths, his weaknesses, his intentions, his dispositions'.[47] But for Keegan, 'knowledge of the enemy' (the book's subtitle) is restricted to a set of knowledge about the enemy. What the US use of targeted killings brings into sharp relief is the importance of knowledge that enables the very identification of the enemy; in some ways this is a precursor to the knowledge that Keegan speaks of, while in others it is intermingled.

Conventional warfare fought by pitched battle allows for as close to bivalent opponent identification as possible within the bounds set by human rationality. The laws, ethics and conduct of warfare have always allowed for a gap between act and intent. Because the conduct of war is a stressful activity, individual participants are often placed under conditions in which they cannot be expected to make judgements as a normal person in a non-life-threatening position would. Differentiations between friend and foe, combatant and non-combatant, and legitimate target and illegitimate target are all exclusive of their opposite

166 *Normative principles of war*

number. Yet at the same time, chance, accident and friction are axiomatic to the conduct of war and prevent its simplification.[48] Any practitioner of war knows that, in practice, knowledge is incomplete; yet a number of our legal standards require what is, in many cases, theoretically perfect knowledge. This occurs at every level. The theory of effects-based operations envisioned the use of force to create second- or third-order effects. Rather than directly affect an opponent or operating environment, the aim was to shape it via reactions to the use of force. This approach was rejected by General Mattis and the US military due to the levels of knowledge that it required in order to be effective: 'its use has created unrealistic expectations of predictability and a counterproductive information appetite in American headquarters. It requires unattainable levels of knowledge about the enemy exercising its independent will'.[49] Conventional battles, however, generally occurred either in the field – removed from civilian presence – or as sieges, which constitute a special category. This physical removal allows for one key bivalent distinction – between combatants and non-combatants – to be achieved a priori. In practice, this distinction sometimes broke down, for instance with friendly units accidentally firing on one another. Both these near-bivalent identifications are made possible by mutuality – adherence to the conventions of warfare that for rational reasons removed war from urban environments (because fighting in such areas was extremely problematic) and required both parties to identify one another.

When conventionality breaks down, so does the possibility of bivalent identification of enemies. In Vietnam, US forces attempted to impose bivalence on a warzone. They faced the problem of fighting irregular forces, the Vietcong, who did not remove themselves from the civilian population or identify themselves as combatants. The willingness to fight under these conditions, a feature of what Schmitt calls 'partisan warfare', indicated that mutuality of warfare had broken down – neither side could agree to the terms on which they fought, and both sought to impose their terms on the other. As Schmitt states, it is a war:

> where new methods evolve daily for overwhelming and outwitting the enemy. Modern technology produces ever stronger weapons and means of annihilation, ever better means of transport and methods of communication, both for the partisans and for the regular troops who fight them. In the vicious circle of terror and counter-terror, the combat of the partisan is often simply a mirror-image of the partisan battle itself.[50]

Here, one US attempt to impose its form of warfare comes in the form of the free-fire zone. In this instance, US forces would clear physical zones around their bases to create free-fire zones. Whether this action is morally justified or not (or constitutes a war crime, as some have argued) is not the focus of this discussion. Telford Taylor argued this in 1971, which Waldemar Solf contested.[51] Systems of target deconfliction, such as 'kill boxes' are not predicated on the assumption that any person is an enemy. These targeting methods work by excluding friendly military units from a given area so that identified military

Normative principles of war 167

targets can automatically be considered hostile, and friendly fire casualties can be reduced.

US forces created free-fire zones to create physical zones into which anyone not identified as friendly could be considered a legitimate target. In effect, the creation of free-fire zones is the attempt to force bivalent distinctions on an irregular war; however, since US forces could not be sure that civilians were not among those in the free-fire zones, this practice relied on a logical fallacy. In essence, non-conventional warfare requires the identification of persons as enemies, as well as the identification of those persons under the rules governing the laws and ethics of war. The first process requires that arbitrary restraints on the transfer of information are unworkable, and thus a knowledge 'firebreak' cannot be established.

The lack of the possibility of a knowledge 'firebreak' creates the possibility of systemic production of violence without the possibility of refusal on the part of the individual, and without the responsibility on the part of the persons selecting the target. Therefore signature strikes, reliant as they are on the identification of individuals, cannot be considered compliant with the principles of the laws of war without some form of 'responsibility firebreak'. The military, however, contains a very robust method of assigning responsibility in such situations – the chain of command and command responsibility.

The outcome of command responsibility differs between organisational military structures. For example, Doty and Doty argue that the US Navy has historically relieved OF5/OF6 officers of command to a greater degree than the US Army has.[52] The principle of responsibility, however, remains the same, even though the authors note that the Army employs a more decentralised organisational structure than does the Navy, due to the nature of capital ship warfare and contemporary land warfare. As Matthew Moten notes: '[T]he Army's professional military ethic is not codified'.[53] But he does note that it is visible in key documents such as Field Manual 1, which states that '[W]hile the use of force is sometimes necessary for the common good, the authority to wield it carries a responsibility of the greatest magnitude'.[54] This has long standing: William Parks demonstrates that 'from the very outset of this nation [America], there was imposed upon the military commander the duty and responsibility for control of the members of his command'.[55] This responsibility means that officers can be held to account for the actions taken by persons beneath them.

This concept of command responsibility has legal ramifications. Parks argues that the post-World War II tribunals 'concluded that responsibility for control of a unit existed with command of that unit'.[56] The decisions reached in the *Yamashita*, *Von Leeb* and *List* trials connect command authority and excision of executive power with responsibility. This is connected in the US Army's FM-27, Section II, 501, which details responsibility for Acts of Subordinates:

> Such a responsibility arises directly when the acts in question have been committed in pursuance of an order of the commander concerned. The commander is also responsible if he has actual knowledge, or should have

168   *Normative principles of war*

knowledge, through reports received by him or through other means, that troops or other persons subject to his control are about to commit or have committed a war crime and he fails to take the necessary and reasonable steps to ensure compliance with the law of war.

Here there is scope for debate, which is opened up by the *Medina* precedent, in which the trial judge limited command responsibility to where the commander possessed 'actual knowledge'.[57] The *Medina* trial hinged on the question of whether Captain Medina should have inferred from basic principles that a war crime was occurring, and therefore controlled his troops. This is a derogation from the *Yamashita* standard, and the principles of FM-27. Does this open up the possibility of responsibility-free war crimes by use of assimilated data? The difference lies in the type of warfare being conducted. The nature of commands given in order to conduct targeted killings differs from those that arguably resulted in the deaths of many civilians at Son My. Furthermore, the nature of the mode of warfare is clear to the officers involved. Officers in command of UAVs may satisfy themselves that a target is valid, but at the same time they know implicitly that the type of warfare that is being conducted prevents the absolute knowledge required by instrumental IHL, and therefore they bear the responsibility for the consequences. McNeal's investigations of collateral damage estimation and mitigation prove this.[58] While collateral damage figures may be disputed, the process by which collateral damage estimates are collated, and by which senior military and political figures are bound in responsibility to these acts, appears straightforward.[59] In short, although the use of targeted killings may be constrained by ROEs, the nature of this method of using force is such that no constraints can be placed on the use and transfer of information involved. Despite this, the presence of a chain of command can ensure that responsibility for any such action can be assigned to someone within it.

The key feature of the US military is that it consists of a hierarchical chain of command that works in such a clear-cut fashion. Responsibility for an order can be determined from the level of cadet to the President of the United States, acting as commander-in-chief. This chain of command is open and transparent, and an integral component of the military. The same cannot be said of the CIA. For this reason, the use of signature strikes (or similar targeting methods) by the US military is different, in a moral sense, to their use by the CIA. Whereas the US military forecloses the possibility of non-voluntary acts with its social structure of arbitrarily assigning responsibility, the CIA does not, at least not to the same degree.

Shadow wars and the CIA

Once we consider assigning responsibility as a key problem, this allows for a technical criticism of the CIA. One of the key problems is the lack of information: the baseline interpretation of a lack of evidence. Philip Alston interprets this to mean that the CIA cannot be judged to be acting legitimately, and that it

Normative principles of war 169

is for the Obama administration to prove otherwise. This, in itself, cannot be taken to prove the illegitimacy of the Obama administration's use of targeted killings, but it does demonstrate a divergence between the claims made in defence of targeted killings and the government's reliance on the CIA to carry some of them out. Secrecy is no barrier to the use of force, as Alston assumes. However, and this is key, the CIA cannot be assumed to have the same command responsibility chain as the military. This in itself is not sufficient to consider the Obama administration's reliance on the CIA as being in contravention of the claims that it makes. Instead, it is the combination of the CIA and the use of signature strikes that presents problems. As previously noted (see p. 164), the only concept categorically preventing the commission of non-voluntary uses of force with signature strikes is the military's chain of command. Because this is not present in the CIA, and because we cannot be sure what management structure exists, the CIA's use of signature strikes is inconsistent with the Obama administration's claim to be abiding by the principles of the laws of war.

Philip Alston is highly critical of the CIA's role in targeted killings. He presents a convincing argument on the lack of oversight available to determine accountability in the CIA.[60] Alston's argument, however, relies on external and internal checks regarding an agency that he acknowledges has little transparency. Here, again, the problem of criticising or justifying covert action is made. Alston concludes that, in addition to oversight failures, 'a combination of the political question doctrine, the state secrecy exemption, and a reluctance to prosecute, ensure that the courts have indeed allowed the CIA to fall into a convenient legal grey hole'.[61] Yet the terms on which he bases his criticism, although legitimate, are essentially contestable – they cannot be used to invalidate the claims of the Obama administration on their own. Alston's criticism of the CIA is, in a sense, top-down: the functions of oversight that reach down to check the actions of those beneath are not functioning. This in part reflects his analytical model, which is rooted in international law. The problem with such an approach is that it makes a demand of the US government – that it act in a certain manner (that all governments must positively demonstrate oversight) – and, furthermore, makes demands that are impossible of clandestine agencies. An oversight approach to clandestine operations necessarily works from incomplete knowledge, a thirst for which can never be slaked. However, using the decision, information and responsibility model of analysing targeting decisions, one can examine the CIA in light of the military's experience – in particular, the method by which they can be considered to assign responsibility for uses of force. The oversight process, which can lead to judicial review, is indeed important, but the principle of responsibility in the act is something that can be judged. If the CIA is found wanting in this regard, the Obama administration's claims may be invalidated.

In regards to the decision to use force, Philip Alston considers that it is up to the United States to prove that its use of targeted killings is discriminate.[62] Conversely, Gregory McNeal argues that his research demonstrates that the US methodology of targeting with UAVs is discriminate, and it is therefore up to

170   *Normative principles of war*

critics to prove otherwise. This argument is problematic, and the two are effectively arguing past one another. Alston's argument is that the United States is legally bound to prove that its targeting is discriminate, which it is not. Yet to apply McNeal's research findings to the CIA's use of targeted killings, even though it does use military personnel, is problematic. The key argument that McNeal makes is that the US military's attitude and command structure, which underpin its targeting, also constrain and govern its use of UAVs. This cannot be directly transposed to the CIA, because this would mean assuming that a culture and hierarchy exist in a civilian intelligence agency. Even though the CIA has used lethal force, and has demonstrated an aversion to using lethal force after the Church Committee, the targeting restrictions of the US military cannot be assumed to be transposed to that organisation. One can assume some form of responsible management structure and legal oversight, but one cannot assume the presence of command responsibility in the manner that exists in the military.

McNeal's evidence is drawn from military sources operating as part of a military command chain, and therefore is fundamentally different in both law and organisational make-up from the CIA. Even if we accept essentially contested factors (such as the applicability of war, *lex specialis*, necessity and proportionality), we cannot know the targeting criteria or ROEs. Are secret targeting criteria enough to invalidate the use of the CIA? There is a parallel that provides a comparison: JSOC. JSOC, like the CIA, is a 'black box'. Although we can get fragmentary reports of its activities, we can never be sure of obtaining a complete picture. But differences exist: although both organisations maintain 'black box' budgeting, whereby large amounts are authorised by Congress but not made public, the budget for the National Intelligence Program is entirely opaque, with only the sum funding for the United States' intelligence community being made publicly available.[63] This is important, because it means that general knowledge of funding for the conduct of targeted killing programmes is unknown. This stands in contrast to military funding. Although the military contains a similar 'black box', the force structure of JSOC is broadly available to the public, as is its general number of operators and their relevant missions and speciality. Therefore, although both are secluded from public oversight, the availability of information on US Special Operations Command is far greater than that available to its CIA counterparts. We cannot, however, know its targeting criteria. Even with JSOC, we cannot assume that the same ROEs apply to covert operations as normal ones. This presents a problem for those interested in precise targeting, but from the principle of responsibility we know that JSOC is integrated into the chain of command. Although we cannot know JSOC's missions or targeting criteria, we can know that responsibility for the use of force lies with an officer between JSOC operators and the President of the United States. We know this because of the chain of command and its robust application in military culture. We cannot be sure of this fact with the CIA.

The United States uses two forms of targeting for targeted killings: personality strikes and signature strikes. In the former, a person is identified by personal information and identified as belonging to a terrorist network. This

Normative principles of war 171

identification and link is considered, in the US model, sufficient to legitimise them as a target. If they are significant enough to warrant action, they may be killed. In this case, both the US military and the CIA are legitimate in using such a method, because there is a manner of defining persons' identities, and thus their status as enemies and belligerents. Signature strikes, however, work from using patterns of public information to approximate identity – location, presence in an area, and so on. Whereas personality strikes use fuzzy logic to ascertain personal identity, and thus belligerency, signature strikes use fuzzy logic to assess combatant status but cannot accurately identify a person as belonging to a network. Both methods rely on decentralised intelligence collection and are thus liable to produce uses of non-voluntary force.

Key here is the question of identity – in conventional warfare combatant characteristics could identify someone as an enemy; in non-conventional warfare, the link between public identity (combatant characteristics) and private identity (membership of a belligerent group) is no longer axiomatic. Persons can no longer be assumed to belong to an enemy group, and thus an enemy, by value of their combatant characteristics. The use of a signature strike against a person identified by combatant characteristics using decentralised intelligence collection could give rise to a non-voluntary use of force. Although we cannot know the practices of either organisation, or the standards by which they target persons, JSOC would be legitimate in using signature strikes by virtue of its chain of command and the principle of command responsibility. Regardless of the practice of double-hatting, it appears that the persons involved in using force for targeted killings are military, but the persons defining targets are not. This is important, because the CIA does not have the same chain of command that the military has, nor can one be sure that it contains the same arbitrary assignations of responsibility for the use of force. In short, the CIA lacks a responsibility 'firebreak', and cannot be assumed to have one.

The term 'firebreaks' is used to denote real-world solutions to philosophical problems and paradoxes. These are arbitrary methods that provide workable methods for overcoming deeper problems. In the case of targeting, it is determinable that the targeting process, particularly that with the identification required in non-conventional warfare, does not contain the certainty requirement of bivalent identification in IHL or just war theory. This problem is overcome by the use of a 'decision firebreak' – the ROEs, which restrict the ability of soldiers to use force. However, a similar 'information firebreak' cannot be effectively implemented, due to the decentralised method of information collection. The absence of both types of firebreak would be problematic, but the command responsibility contained within the military's chain of command, even under the *Medina* rather than *Yamashita* principle of knowledge, suffices to allocate responsibility for any ordered act. As UAV strikes and other methods of targeted killings form ordered acts, persons can be held to account.

The chain of command is axiomatic to the US military and other similarly structured military forces. As noted previously (see p. 168), it contains a set of assumptions that derive from the professional identity of the military, as well as

172 *Normative principles of war*

their legal responsibilities. The *Medina* case alters, partially, the legal responsibilities, but it does not change the professional values of the services. Furthermore, the UCMJ allows for the prosecution of war crimes committed by service personnel. The CIA is treated here as an unknown entity for precisely the reason that it is a covert organisation. Although reports exist about its structure, including the 'double-hatting' of staff, this organisation cannot be assumed to use the same command structure as the military, nor are its personnel subject to the UCMJ. These two facts preclude considering the CIA in the same way as the military and, combined, mean that the 'responsibility firebreak' is not present in the CIA. Although this does not invalidate it as an actor using force, it means that when the CIA uses 'signature strikes', there is the distinct possibility of it committing non-voluntary uses of force. Therefore it is not the CIA alone, or the practice of 'signature strikes', that is problematic for the Obama administration's defence of targeted killings; it is the combination of the two. The CIA's use of signature strikes is incompatible with the principles of the laws of war, due to the fact that they may commit non-voluntary uses of force.

In light of the above examination, is the Obama administration's claim to adhere to the principles of the laws of war legitimate or illegitimate? Much rests on this issue. Throughout this book, the methodology of allowing for uncertainty, both in liminality and discourse, has demonstrated that many of the criticisms of the US use of targeted killings are not logically sound. The arguments of persons such as Mary Ellen O'Connell and Philip Alston are predicated on normative assumptions of what war is, or should consist of, that diverge from the interpretations offered by the Obama administration. However, this book has demonstrated that in order to defend itself against the criticisms made on the basis of necessity, proportionality, utility and legality (international and domestic), the Obama administration has had to make a particular claim – that the US use of targeted killings is in accordance with the principles of the laws of war, which in turn derive from the ethical code of just war theory.

The Obama administration does not have to make this claim. It did so to differentiate itself from the Bush administration. The claims made by the Obama administration in order to do this are, in most cases, difficult to disprove a priori. This section has identified a key inconsistency with this – the CIA's use of signature strikes. This chapter started from a simple premise – that the use of force had to have some form of immediate responsibility. This is separate from overall responsibility, which is held by the executive in any regard; rather, what this chapter has concerned itself with is the concept that a non-voluntary use of force was illegitimate at all times. This is different from an involuntary use of force, which could be accorded from a lack of knowledge. Decentralised intelligence collection processes are a possible source of non-voluntary uses of force, because this process effectively removes the ability of operators of a given weapon platform to decide whether to attack a target, and dissipates the concept of responsibility inherent in the transfer of knowledge that targets a person. The only way in which such methods could be considered permissible is via the arbitrary assignation of responsibility found in the concept of command

Normative principles of war 173

responsibility. Even the derogated form of command responsibility found in the United States subsequent to *Medina* contains the essential element of assigning responsibility to senior officers for the activities of their immediate subordinates. Within the US military's chain of command any act or use of force, legitimate or illegitimate, can be immediately assigned as the responsibility of a given officer. Regardless of the covert nature of JSOC, this command responsibility and chain of command can be considered to hold true. Within the CIA, this cannot be held true.

When conducted by the CIA, US targeted killings cannot, prima facie, be held to be within the principles of the laws of war. Decentralised intelligence collection requires the assurance of a robust chain of command in order to accord with these principles. Because the CIA cannot be considered to have this, actions taken by the agency cannot be held, on a basic philosophical level, to be in accordance with the principles of the laws of war. In the majority of cases, the claims made by the Obama administration are plausible – in terms of necessity, proportionality and intent. The principles of the laws of war are unforgiving, and the basic principle that force is used responsibly – that non-voluntary acts are impermissible – is one of them. As a superpower, and member of the UNSC, there is nothing to stop the United States from making a blunt assertion of realism in the conduct of its targeted killing campaign. However, although the CIA and signature strikes are inconsistent with the Obama administration's defence, it is entirely possible for the Obama administration to use targeted killings and remain within the legal and ethical frameworks that govern and constrain the conduct of war.

Political externalities and US values

The possible and probable outcomes of the Obama administration's defence can be termed 'political externalities' to a certain way of rationalising violence. They are, in truth, more than that. One of the key facets of the Obama administration's defence is something entirely indefinable: values. As John Brennan stated: '[W]e're better than that. We're better than them. We're Americans'.[64] The same words are echoed time and again in the speeches that constitute the Obama administration's defence of its national security policy:

> Our most sacred principles and values – of security, justice and liberty for all citizens – must continue to unite us, to guide us forward, and to help us build a future that honors our founding documents and advances our ongoing – uniquely American – pursuit of a safer, more just, and more perfect union.[65]

It is difficult to conceive of a higher call upon the values of the United States than President Obama's words in reference to its founding documents – the Declaration of Independence, the Constitution and the Bill of Rights: 'if we cannot stand for our core values, then we are not keeping faith with the documents that

174   *Normative principles of war*

are enshrined in this hall'.[66] Yet these values cannot be tested in a manner similar to law and ethics. In a similar fashion, this book has noted a number of criticisms of targeted killings that are essentially policy choices. Taken together, these political externalities and value questions do not invalidate the claims of the Obama administration, but they do demonstrate that a position defensible in terms of law and ethics does not mean adherence to the values it espouses and, furthermore, it is likely to have serious future consequences.

The power to define persons as enemies is axiomatic to the president's role as commander-in-chief of the armed forces. Congress, too, can define enemies – it has the constitutional authority to declare war. The Obama administration's authority to act on its designations relies on the AUMF, which is power given to the executive by Congress. Furthermore, the courts have demonstrated that they do have a role to play in reviewing executive decisions, particularly those involving US citizens. There is nothing stopping the courts from taking a review function, as some have argued they should,[67] but it has also been argued that it is extremely difficult to envision a role for the courts in approving decisions to act. In short, the president is constitutionally capable of acting in the manner that Barack Obama does. That does not, however, mean that he should.

The United States was founded on the principle that sovereign authority is separated into checks and balances. Furthermore, it was founded at a time when political enemies were either defined by physical fact (presence on a battlefield or presence within an organised armed group) or were accorded the protections encoded in Article 3 of the Constitution. Since then, the changing operational nature of war and conflict means that belligerency can be assessed either by physical fact or by identity – the question of whether an individual can be identified as belonging to an amorphous group. Strict adherence to the law, in particular, means that the latter question of identity gives the president the ability, through the act of identification, to define a person as a political enemy without the protections afforded by the Constitution.

The problem that this poses is that there is no word to describe the authority and power that it affords the president. President Obama is neither a tyrant nor a dictator; nor can his presidency be considered '[I]mperial',[68] because he does not display the characteristics of an emperor. The convergence of legal precedent and congressional authority gives a non-sovereign entity within the constitutional system the power to kill a citizen without check or review. Furthermore, this power is exercised not through the military, but through unaccountable intelligence agencies. There is no 'originalist' reading of the Constitution in this sense, because the framers and Founding Fathers could never have imagined transnational terrorist networks or weapons of mass destruction. What Obama does as president is, in this sense, define the values of the system as it functions in the twenty-first century. Given the possibilities tabled, such as enhanced congressional oversight, or post hoc judicial review, choosing the value of secrecy will define the Office of the President, not just the man. As Michael Hayden put it: '[D]emocracies do not make war on the basis of legal memos locked in a D.O.J. safe'.[69]

Normative principles of war 175

The relationship between the citizen and the state is important, but so too is the United States' role in the world. The United States' acceptance of a targeted killing policy barely a decade after its strong condemnation of Israel for operating a similar policy sets a standard – the legitimisation of transnational force against individuals.

Peter Singer argues that the adoption of robotic systems is changing the political calculations on the use of force.[70] An important area of further research will be the effect that the continued implementation of autonomous and robotic warfare systems has on the political calculations for the use of force. UAVs can deliver the same effect as manned aircraft, but the risk of deploying them is far lower. Indeed, they appear to be preferable even though they are statistically more susceptible to failure than are their manned equivalents.

The question of boundaries is once more relevant – technology is likely to proliferate, and other states are likely to use it. The standards set by the United States tell the rest of the world that it is okay to kill persons presenting threats in third-party states. The US justification for this relies on the implicit belief that the United States acts in good faith, but the manner in which it legitimises these acts opens legal space for others to follow. Attempts at future-casting for potential candidate-states that might perform this lack basis in fact and evidence. There are, however, plenty of powerful states with both the economic power and technical capability to develop such technology, and there are plenty of states that consider themselves threatened by non-state actors in other states. Where the United States goes, some may follow.

Conclusion

The executive's claim that it adheres to the principles of the laws of war is inconsistent with the use of the CIA to conduct targeted killings, particularly signature strikes. This claim is highly significant, because it justifies many of the discursive terms used by the administration to justify the targeted killing programme. Many of the criticisms applied to drone warfare could equally be made about other forms of warfare that rely on decentralised methods of target acquisition. However, the requirement to individuate opponents, as well as classify them as targets, prevents the formation of a knowledge firebreak, in line with the ROEs' decision firebreak. Thus the only method for these operations to conform with the principles of the laws of war is to ensure that a command structure is in place that prevents non-voluntary uses of force. The command structure does this by arbitrarily assigning responsibility to the senior officer, thus transforming non-voluntary acts into involuntary ones. This difference is unlikely to matter to critics such as Alston, O'Connell and Tiedemann, but it undermines the primary claim made by the administration in its defence of targeted killings. If it continues to claim that its targeted killing campaign is in accordance with the principles of the laws of war while using the CIA instead of the military, then it is guilty of hypocrisy.

176 *Normative principles of war*

Notes

1 Hannah Arendt, *On Violence* (London: Allen Lane, 1970): 65.
2 Holder, 'Northwestern University Speech'; Koh, 'Obama Administration'.
3 Obama, 'Remarks by the President on National Security'.
4 Holder, 'Northwestern University Speech'.
5 Gary D. Solis, Solis, *Law of Armed Conflict*: 18.
6 Walzer, *Just and Unjust Wars*: 3–4.
7 Walzer, *Just and Unjust Wars*: 20.
8 Amos N. Guiora and Jeffrey S. Brand, 'Establishment of a Drone Court: A Necessary Restraint on Executive Power', in *Legitimacy and Drones: Investigating the Legality, Morality and Efficacy of UCAVs*, edited by Steven J. Barela (Farnham, England and Burlington, VT: Ashgate, 2015); Stephen I. Vladeck, 'Targeted Killing and Judicial Review', *The George Washington Law Review Arguendo* 82 (2014).
9 See Bradley J. Strawser, ed., *Killing by Remote Control* (Oxford University Press, 2013).
10 Walzer, *Just and Unjust Wars*: 127.
11 David Rodin, *War and Self Defense* (Oxford University Press, 2002).
12 Jeff McMahan, *Killing in War* (Oxford University Press, 2009).
13 Jeff McMahan, *Killing in War*: 50.
14 Nigel Biggar, *In Defence of War* (Oxford University Press, 2014).
15 Bradley J. Strawser, 'Introduction: The Moral Landscape of Unmanned Weapons', in *Killing by Remote Control*, edited by Bradley J. Strawser (New York, NY: Oxford University Press, 2013): 6.
16 Asa Kasher and Avery Plaw, 'Distinguishing Drones: An Exchange', in *Killing by Remote Control*, edited by Bradley J. Strawser (New York, NY: Oxford University Press, 2013).
17 Uwe Steinhof, 'Killing Them Safely: Extreme Asymmetry and its Discontents', in *Killing by Remote Control*, edited by Bradley J. Strawser (New York, NY: Oxford University Press, 2013).
18 Walzer, *Just and Unjust Wars*: 34–7.
19 Kaag and Kreps, *Drone Warfare*.
20 Chamayou, *Theory of the Drone*: 146–7.
21 Bradley Jay Strawser, 'Moral Predators: The Duty to Employ Uninhabited Aerial Vehicles', *Journal of Military Ethics* 9(4) (2010): 342–68.
22 Clausewitz, *On War*: Book 1, Ch. 4.
23 Becker and Shane, 'Secret "Kill List"'.
24 Particularly when mistakes are made. See Adam Entous, Damian Paletta and Felicia Schwartz, 'American, Italian Hostages Killed in CIA Drone Strike in January', *The Wall Street Journal*, 23 April 2015.
25 Aristotle, *The Nicomachean Ethics* (Oxford University Press, 2009): Book 3.
26 Alston, 'CIA and Targeted Killings': 284.
27 Alston, 'CIA and Targeted Killings': 285.
28 Alston, 'CIA and Targeted Killings': 445.
29 Richard Whittle, *Predator: The Secret Origins of the Drone Revolution* (Picador, 2015): 224.
30 Andreas Schedler, 'Conceptualising Accountability', in *The Self-Restraining State: Power and Accountability in New Democracies*, edited by Andreas Schedler, Larry Diamond and Marc F. Plattner (London: Lynne Rienner Publishers, 1999).
31 Micah Zenko, 'Transferring CIA Drone Strikes to the Pentagon' (Report, Washington, DC: Council on Foreign Relations Press, April 2013).
32 Foreign Intelligence Surveillance Act (1978).
33 Glenn Greenwald, *No Place to Hide: Edward Snowden, the NSA, and the U.S. Surveillance State* (New York, NY : Metropolitan Books/Henry Holt, 2014).

Normative principles of war 177

34 Guiora and Brand, 'Establishment of a Drone Court'.
35 Bloomberg Editorial Board, 'Why a "Drone Court" Won't Work' *Bloomberg View*, 18 February 2013.
36 Stephen I. Vladeck, 'The New National Security Canon', *American University Law Review* 61(5) (2012): 1329.
37 Christopher Cowley, *Moral Responsibility* (Abingdon, UK: Routledge, 2014): 7–8.
38 Cowley, *Moral Responsibility*: 8.
39 Aristotle, *Nicomachean Ethics*: Book 3.
40 O'Connell, 'Seductive Drones': 139.
41 Independent Police Complaints Commission (IPCC), *Stockwell One: Investigation into the Shooting of Jean Charles De Menezes at Stockwell Underground Station on 22 July 2005* (Report, London: IPCC, 2007): 137.
42 Walzer, *Just and Unjust Wars*: 326.
43 Elizabeth Sepper, 'The Ties That Bind: How the Constitution Limits the CIA's Actions in the War on Terror', *New York University Law Review* 81(5) (2006): 1809.
44 McNeal, 'Are Targeted Killings Unlawful?': 328–31.
45 Richard J. Grunawalt, 'The JCS Standing Rules of Engagement: A Judge Advocate's Primer', *Air Force Law Review* 42 (1997).
46 Clausewitz, *On War*: 83.
47 Keegan, *Intelligence in War*: 9.
48 Clausewitz, *On War*: 138–40.
49 James N. Mattis, 'USJFCOM Commander's Guidance for Effects-based Operations', *Parameters* 38 (2008): 22.
50 Carl Schmitt, 'Theory of the Partisan': 19–20.
51 Waldemar Solf, 'A Response to Telford Taylor's Nuremberg and Vietnam: An American Tragedy', *Akron Law Review* 5(1) (1972).
52 Joe Doty and Chuck Doty, 'Command Responsibility and Accountability', *Military Review* 92(1) (2012): 35–6.
53 Matthew Moten, *The Army Officers' Professional Ethic: Past, Present, and Future* (Carlisle, PA: Strategic Studies Institute, U.S. Army War College, 2010): 1.
54 US Army, *Field Manual 1* (Washington, DC: US Army, 2005): Sections 1–52.
55 William H. Parks, 'Command Responsibility for War Crimes', *Military Law Review* 62 (Fall 1973): 5.
56 Parks, 'Command Responsibility': 83.
57 Matthew Lippman, 'The Evolution and Scope of Command Responsibility', *Leiden Journal of International Law* 13(1) (2000): 154.
58 Gregory S. McNeal, 'Targeted Killing and Accountability', *Georgetown Law Journal* 102(3) (2014); McNeal, 'Are Targeted Killings Unlawful?'.
59 McNeal, 'Are Targeted Killings Unlawful?': 329–30.
60 Alston, 'CIA and Targeted Killings'.
61 Alston, 'CIA and Targeted Killings': 88.
62 Alston, 'CIA and Targeted Killings'.
63 White House, *National Intelligence Program Federal Budget Fiscal Year 2012* (Washington, DC: White House, 2012).
64 Brennan, 'Ethics and Efficacy'.
65 Holder, 'Northwestern University Speech'.
66 Obama, 'Remarks by the President on National Security'.
67 Jameel Jaffer, 'Judicial Review of Targeted Killings', *Harvard Law Review Forum* 126(6) (2013).
68 This term was used by David Cole in reference to Arthur Schlesinger Jr's 1970s book, *The Imperial Presidency*. See David Cole, 'Are We Stuck with the Imperial Presidency?', *New York Review of Books*, 7 June 2012; Arthur M. Schlesinger, *The Imperial Presidency* (Boston: Houghton Mifflin, 2004).

178 *Normative principles of war*

69 Quoted in Becker and Shane, 'Secret "Kill List"'. It should be noted that in this instance Hayden, working for the Republican presidential candidate, was likely trying to score political points, but the statement is important.
70 Singer, *Wired for War*. Singer also argues that the use of UAVs undermines political restraints on war; see Singer, 'Do Drones Undermine Democracy?'.

7   Conclusion

> If the defendant was justifiable in doing what he did, every citizen of the United States would, in time of war, be equally exposed to a like exercise of military power and authority.
>
> *Smith* v. *Shaw*, 1815[1]

> He who fights with monsters should be careful lest he thereby become a monster. And if thou gaze long into an abyss, the abyss will also gaze into thee.
>
> Friedrich Nietzsche[2]

The contemporary debate surrounding the use of targeted killings is unlikely to be resolved by the assurances of the Obama administration. Words are, however, important. The manner in which the Obama administration justifies its use of targeted killings in legal and ethical terms is shown in this book to have implications for the frameworks of law and ethics that are used to legitimate warfare. The Obama administration's defence of targeted killings is largely consistent with its legal and ethical claims. However, the use of signature strikes by the CIA is inconsistent with some of the claims that the Obama administration makes. This intersection between a covert civilian agency and a particular targeting method is liable to produce what this book characterises as the non-voluntary use of force (the use of force without responsibility), which is antithetical to both the laws of war and the principles of warfare, as well as the ethics of war. This is, admittedly, a technical point, and involuntary uses of force – for which blame is assignable – occur as a matter of routine in warfare. The lack of punishment for such acts is, however, a subjective matter. What this book argues is that this technical matter – the non-voluntary use of force – highlights the need for military command structures where weapons systems are used that rely on multiple sources of information for targeting.

The key problem with the debates surrounding the US use of targeted killings were the varying normative assumptions regarding the legality, ethics and utility of these acts. Furthermore, this involves key areas that are essentially contested concepts – the status of terrorists, ideas such as military necessity, and normative ethical assumptions regarding the use of force. The Obama administration's defence of the use of targeted killings is that they are legal,

180 *Conclusion*

ethical and in accordance with US values. Testing this defence requires engaging with the legal and ethical frameworks that can be tested: constitutional law, international law and just war ethics. As a counter to a key problem encountered in the debate surrounding targeted killings, it is necessary to test propositions of the Obama administration by giving the administration's defence the benefit of the doubt.

The central claim of targeted killing supporters is that the use of military force is necessary. In Chapter 3, I engaged with the counterarguments, which posit that law enforcement methods should take precedence in countering terrorism. However, there are territories in which terrorists operate where the criminal justice paradigm does not function and the law enforcement paradigm is therefore inapplicable. The arguments for military necessity cite that terrorist networks are able to operate in these areas, and therefore the Obama administration's claim that it has to act cannot be countered with the evidence available. Even though state-building is a viable alternative, I argued that the cost of state-building, combined with the variability of results, does not invalidate the Obama administration's claim. Military force therefore has some degree of utility and therefore there is a plausible reason for using force – disrupting terrorist networks. Therefore, this book has argued that the Obama administration's claim is valid within the areas that it currently uses targeted killings.

The conduct of the United States' targeted killing programme differs from that of others. The essentialist critique of targeted killings – that these acts are wrong in themselves, or that the use of UAVs is illegal and unethical – relies on a different normative assumption of the validity of force, or does not have enough evidence. The evidence does not support the contention that the US use of targeted killings is indiscriminate; however, it does suggest that it kills a significant number of civilians, contrary to the claims of the CIA and others. The evidence does, however, suggest that these strikes are killing a significant number of terrorists and associated militants. The exact effect of these strikes is unknown, but the numbers of persons killed suggest that the Obama administration's claim that these strikes disrupt al-Qaeda and associated networks appears valid, and therefore satisfies the criteria for necessity and utility.

Is the use of force against individuals legitimate? As noted, it is possible to determine that the use of force against individuals has been legitimated during the twentieth century, contrary to the assumptions of some supporters who consider it to be axiomatic to warfare. The use of force against civilians is very difficult to justify; however, terrorists and guerrillas represented a liminal status – neither illegitimate nor legitimate by definition, yet able to be legitimated by discourse. Defining persons as enemies, in a political and military sense, is key to the process of legitimating targets. Examining the US example, the ability of the US president to define an enemy is key, as is the constitutional legitimacy to use force.

The international legal regimes that govern the use of force are extremely important in legitimating its use but are also highly interpretable. Chapter 4 examined the legal cases for and against the use of targeted killings and found

Conclusion 181

that legal theorists who argue that targeted killings are illegal on principle in international law rely on a very strict interpretation of the law that ignores its interpretability. However, the interpretations of law that are required to legitimise targeted killings expand the concept of self-defence and validate the targeting of wide networks of terrorists. The key political outcome of this legitimisation is that it expands the scope for states to define enemies in international law and use force against them.

A key criticism of the US use of targeted killings is that these acts are unconstitutional. Chapter 5 examined the constitutionality of targeted killings by examining whether the president needed to expand his authority or operate in a sovereign manner in order to define persons as enemies and use force against them. The strictest test of this is whether the president had the ability to do this with US citizens, as recently occurred with the killing of Anwar al-Awlaki. The ability of the president to define a person as an enemy is a product of the US legal system, and by defining citizens as belonging to a belligerent organisation, the president has the authority to use force against them, but the ability to do so is derived from the AUMF. Examining theorists of exception Carl Schmitt and Giorgio Agamben, it is arguable that the president did not need to act in a sovereign manner in order to do this. Lastly, even though the courts could not act to restrain targeted killings, there is an open question of whether they can review such acts.

Finally, this book examined the ethical justification for the use of force. This is especially important, because the Obama administration's legal justifications for the use of force rely on the principles of the laws of war. Chapter 6 of this book examined the concept of responsibility and argued that the use of means that could result in non-voluntary uses of force were outside the boundaries of the ethics of just war theory. It then examined two different topics that are held to be unethical: the CIA's use of force and the use of signature strikes. It found that neither practice breaks with just war ethics individually, but that the combination of the two – the CIA's use of signature strikes – could give rise to non-voluntary uses of force and is therefore inconsistent with the defence for targeted killings offered by the Obama administration. Lastly, it is necessary to point out that justifications for the use of force in terms of law and ethics can produce outcomes that are inconsistent with the value system professed by the Obama administration and, furthermore, the political consequences are significant. This is not sufficient to invalidate the claims of the Obama administration, but they represent significant challenges to the justification of such acts and underline the seriousness of the use of force. Ultimately, the use of targeted killings is a choice. Security might not require the sacrifice of the rule of law and adherence to just war ethics, but it comes at an indefinable cost to values.

Notes

1 *Smith* v. *Shaw*, 12 Johns. 257 (1815).
2 Friedrich Wilhelm Nietzsche, *Beyond Good and Evil: Prelude to a Philosophy of the Future* (London: Constable, 1997): Ch. 4, 146.

Bibliography

Ackerman, Spencer, 'Rare Photographs Show Ground Zero of the Drone War', *Wired*, 12 December 2011, www.wired.com/2011/12/photos-pakistan-drone-war.

Ackerman, Spencer, 'Obama's New Defense Plan: Drones, Spec Ops and Cyber War', *Wired*, 5 January 2012, www.wired.com/2012/01/pentagon-asia-strategy.

Agamben, Giorgio, *Homo Sacer: Sovereign Power and Bare Life* (Meridian Stanford, CA: Stanford University Press, 1998).

Agamben, Giorgio, *State of Exception* (University of Chicago Press, 2005).

ACLU, 'Key OLC Memoranda Relating to Interrogation, Detention, Rendition and/or Surveillance' (Washington, DC: American Civil Liberties Union, 2009).

ACLU, 'Aulaqi v. Obama Complaint' (Washington, DC: American Civil Liberties Union, 2010).

ACLU, 'ACLU Statement on Killing of Anwar Al-Aulaqi' (Washington, DC: American Civil Liberties Union, 30 September 2011).

Alston, Philip, 'Report of the Special Rapporteur on Extrajudicial, Summary or Arbitrary Executions' (UN General Assembly, Human Rights Council, 2010).

Alston, Philip, 'The CIA and Targeted Killings Beyond Borders', *Harvard National Security Journal* 2 (2011).

Amann, Diane M., 'Guantanamo', *Columbia Journal of Transnational Law* 42 (2003).

Amnesty International, 'Guantánamo Detainees: The Legal Black Hole Deepens', *Amnesty* (Report, Amnesty International, London, 2003).

Anderson, Kenneth, 'Targeted Killing in US Counterterrorism Strategy and Law', in *Legislating the War on Terror*, edited by Benjamin Wittes (Washington, DC: Brookings Institution Press, 2009).

Anderson, Kenneth, 'Efficiency *in Bello* and *Ad Bellum*: Making the Use of Force Too Easy?', in *Targeted Killings: Law and Morality in an Asymmetrical World*, edited by Claire Finkelstein, Jens D. Ohlin and Andrew Altman (Oxford University Press, 2012).

Aquinas, St Thomas, tr. Kenneth E. Comp Alrutz, *War and Peace* (Washington, DC: University Press of America, 1982).

Arendt, Hannah, *On Violence* (London: Allen Lane, 1970).

Aristotle, *The Nicomachean Ethics* (Oxford University Press, 2009).

Arquilla, John and David Ronfeldt, 'Cyberwar Is Coming!', *Comparative Strategy* 12(2) (1993).

Arquilla, John and David Ronfeldt, *The Advent of Netwar* (Santa Monica, CA: RAND, 1996).

Arquilla, John and David Ronfeldt, *Networks and Netwars: The Future of Terror, Crime, and Militancy* (Santa Monica, CA: RAND, 2001).

Bibliography 183

Augustine, St, tr. Marcus Dods, *The City of God* (Peabody, MA: Hendrickson Publishers, 2009).

Ayub, Fatima and Sari Kouvo, 'Righting the Course? Humanitarian Intervention, the War on Terror and the Future of Afghanistan', *International Affairs* 84(4) (2008).

Badey, Thomas J., 'US Counter-Terrorism: Change in Approach, Continuity in Policy', *Contemporary Security Policy* 27(2) (2006).

Banks, William C. and Peter Raven-Hansen, 'Targeted Killing and Assassination: The US Legal Framework', *University of Richmond Law Review* 37 (2002).

Barkow, Rachel E., 'More Supreme Than Court: The Fall of the Political Question Doctrine and the Rise of Judicial Supremacy', *Columbia Law Review* 102(2) (2002).

Barron, David J. and Martin S. Lederman, 'The Commander in Chief at the Lowest Ebb: A Constitutional History', *Harvard Law Review* 121(3) (2008).

Bar-Zohar, Michael, *Spies in the Promised Land: Iser Harel and the Israeli Secret Service* (Boston: Houghton Mifflin, 1972).

Bazelon, Emily, 'Not-So-Innocent Abroad', *Slate*, 6 March 2012, www.slate.com/articles/news_and_politics/jurisprudence/2012/03/eric_holder_s_speech_on_targeted_killings_was_incredibly_unsatisfying_.html.

Becker, Jo and Scott Shane, 'Secret "Kill List" Proves a Test of Obama's Principles and Will', *New York Times*, 29 May 2012.

Benjamin, Medea, *Drone Warfare: Killing by Remote Control* (New York and London: OR Books, 2012).

Bergen, Peter and Paul Cruickshank, 'Revisiting the Early Al Qaeda: An Updated Account of Its Formative Years', *Studies in Conflict & Terrorism* 35(1) (2012).

Bergen, Peter and Katherine Tiedemann, 'The Year of the Drone: An Analysis of U.S. Drone Strikes in Pakistan, 2004–2010' (Washington, DC: New America Foundation, 2010).

Biggar, Nigel, *In Defence of War* (Oxford University Press, 2014).

Blair, Dennis C., 'Drones Alone Are Not the Answer', *New York Times*, 14 August 2011.

Blair, J. Anthony and Ralph H. Johnson, 'The Current State of Informal Logic', *Informal Logic* 9(2) (1987).

Blank, Laurie, 'Targeted Strikes: The Consequences of Blurring the Armed Conflict and Self-Defense Justifications', *William Mitchell Law Review* 38(5) (2012).

Bloomberg Editorial Board, 'Why a "Drone Court" Won't Work' *Bloomberg View*, 18 February 2013.

Blum, Gabriella and Philip Heymann, 'Law and Policy of Targeted Killing', *Harvard National Security Journal* 1 (2010).

Boccaletti, Stefano, Vito Latora, Yamir Moreno, Martin Chavez and D.-U. Hwang, 'Complex Networks: Structure and Dynamics', *Physics Reports* 424(4) (2006).

Bodin, Jean, tr. Julian H. Franklin, *On Sovereignty: Four Chapters from the Six Books of the Commonwealth* (Cambridge University Press, 1992).

Bolt, Neville, David Betz and Jaz Azari, *Propaganda of the Deed 2008: Understanding the Phenomenon* (London: Royal United Services Institute for Defence and Security Studies, 2008).

Bowden, Mark, *Black Hawk Down: A Story of Modern War* (London: Bantam Press, 1999).

Bowden, Mark, *Killing Pablo: The Hunt for the World's Greatest Outlaw* (Penguin, 2002).

Bowen, Wyn Q. and David H. Dunn, *American Security Policy in the 1990s: Beyond Containment* (Aldershot, UK: Dartmouth, 1996).

184 *Bibliography*

Boyle, Michael J., 'The Costs and Consequences of Drone Warfare', *International Affairs* 89(1) (2013).

Boys, James D., 'What's So Extraordinary About Rendition?', *International Journal of Human Rights* 15(4) (2011).

Bradley, Curtis A. and Jack L. Goldsmith, 'Congressional Authorization and the War on Terrorism', *Harvard Law Review* 118(7) (2005).

Brennan, John O., 'Strengthening Our Security by Adhering to Our Values and Laws' (Speech, Harvard Law School, Cambridge, MA, 16 September 2011).

Brennan, John O., 'The Ethics and Efficacy of the President's Counterterrorism Strategy' (Speech, Woodrow Wilson International Center for Scholars, Washington, DC, 30 April 2012).

Brown, Neville, 'Climate, Ecology and International Security', *Survival* 31(6) (1989).

Buley, Benjamin, *The New American Way of War: Military Culture and the Political Utility of Force* (Abingdon, UK: Routledge, 2007).

Bull, Hedley, *The Anarchical Society: A Study of Order in World Politics,* 3rd edn (Basingstoke: Palgrave, 2002).

Bureau of Investigative Journalism, 'Covert War on Terror: The Data', *Bureau of Investigative Journalism* (2015), www.thebureauinvestigates.com/category/projects/drones/drones-graphs.

Bush, George W., 'Address to the Nation on 9/11' (Speech, The White House, Washington, DC, 11 September 2001).

Bush, George W., 'Address to a Joint Session of Congress' (Speech, US Capitol Building, Washington, DC, 21 September 2001).

Bush, George W., 'Military Order of November 13, 2001 Detention, Treatment, and Trial of Certain Non-Citizens in the War against Terrorism', *Federal Register* (Washington, DC: Executive Office of the President, 2001): 57833.

Bush, George W., 'Order to the Secretary of Defense' (Washington, DC, 2002).

Bush, George W., 'President Discusses Creation of Military Commissions to Try Suspected Terrorists' (Speech, White House, Washington, DC, 6 September 2006).

Bush, George W., *Decision Points* (London: Virgin, 2010).

Butler, Judith, 'Guantanamo Limbo: International Law Offers Too Little Protection for Prisoners of the New War', *Nation* 274(12) (2002).

Buzan, Barry, 'Rethinking Security after the Cold War', *Cooperation and Conflict* 32(1) (1997).

Buzan, Barry, 'Will the "Global War on Terrorism" be the New Cold War?', *International Affairs* 82(6) (2006).

Bybee, Jay S., *Standards of Conduct for Interrogation under 18 USC [Sections] 2340–2340a: Memorandum for Alberto R. Gonzales, Counsel to the President* (Washington, DC: Office of the Assistant Attorney General, 2002).

Bybee, Jay S., *Memorandum for John Rizzo, Acting General Counsel of the Central Intelligence Agency: Interrogation of Al Qaeda Operative* (Washington, DC: US Department of Justice, Office of Legal Counsel, 1 August 2002).

Byman, Daniel, 'Do Targeted Killings Work?', *Foreign Affairs* 85 (2006).

Byman, Daniel, *A High Price: The Triumphs and Failures of Israeli Counterterrorism* (New York: Oxford University Press, 2011).

Callwell, Charles E., *Small Wars: Their Principles and Practice*, 3rd edn (Lincoln: University of Nebraska Press, 1996).

Carey, Tim and Marcus de Búrca, 'Bloody Sunday 1920: New Evidence', *History Ireland* 11(2) (2003).

Bibliography 185

Carolan, Eoin, *The New Separation of Powers: A Theory for the Modern State* (New York: Oxford University Press, 2009).

Carpenter, Charli, 'Latest Data on Drone Deaths', *Lawyers Guns and Money* (2010), www.lawyersgunsmoneyblog.com/2010/11/latest-data-on-drone-deaths.

Cassese, Antonio, 'Expert Opinion on Whether Israel's Targeted Killing of Palestinian Terrorists Is Consonant with International Humanitarian Law', *Public Committee Against Torture* et al. v. *Government of Israel* et al. (Israeli High Court of Justice, 2007).

Cebrowski, Arthur K. and John J. Garstka, 'Network-Centric Warfare: Its Origin and Future', *US Naval Institute Proceedings* (1998).

Chamayou, Grégoire, *A Theory of the Drone* (New York: The New Press, 2014).

Chepesiuk, Ron, *The Bullet or the Bribe: Taking Down Colombia's Cali Drug Cartel* (Westport, CT: Praeger, 2003).

Chertoff, Michael, 'War v. Crime: Breaking the Chains of the Old Security Paradigm', in *Confronting Terror: 9/11 and the Future of American National Security*, edited by Dean Reuter and John Yoo (New York, NY: Encounter Books, 2011).

Cheney, Richard, 'Speech to the American Enterprise Institute' (Speech, Washington, DC, 21 May 2009).

Cheney, Richard B. and Liz Cheney, *In My Time: A Personal and Political Memoir* (London: Threshold, 2011).

Chesney, Robert, 'Who May Be Killed? Anwar Al-Awlaki as a Case Study in the International Legal Regulation of Lethal Force', *Yearbook of International Humanitarian Law* 13 (2010).

Chick, Kristen, 'CIA Director Says Al Qaeda on the Run as a Leader Killed in US Drone Strike', *Christian Science Monitor*, 18 March 2010.

Christopher, Russell, 'Imminence in Justified Targeted Killing', in *Targeted Killings: Law and Morality in an Asymmetrical World*, edited by Claire Finkelstein, Jens D. Ohlin and Andrew Altman (Oxford University Press, 2012).

Church Committee, 'United States Senate Select Committee to Study Governmental Operations with Respect to Intelligence Activities', *AARC* (Assassination Archives and Research Center, 1975).

Clausewitz, Carl von, tr. Michael Howard and Peter Paret, *On War* (London: Everyman's Library, 1993).

Clausewitz, Carl von, *On War* (Oxford University Press, 2007).

Cloud, David S., 'Civilian Contractors Playing Key Roles in U.S. Drone Operations', *Los Angeles Times*, 29 December 2011.

Cohen, Andrew, 'On "Targeted Killing" Speech, Eric Holder Strikes Out', *Atlantic Monthly*, 6 March 2012, www.theatlantic.com/national/archive/2012/03/on-targeted-killing-speech-eric-holder-strikes-out/254000.

Coker, Christopher, *Ethics and War in the 21st Century* (London: Routledge, 2008).

Coker, Christopher, *War in an Age of Risk* (Cambridge, UK: Polity Press, 2009).

Colbert, Stephen, *The Colbert Report* (TV Programme, 6 March 2012).

Cole, David, 'An Executive Power to Kill?', *NYRB Blog*, 6 March 2012, www.nybooks.com/blogs/nyrblog/2012/mar/06/targeted-killings-holder-speech.

Cole, David, 'Are We Stuck with the Imperial Presidency?', *New York Review of Books*, 7 June 2012.

Condron, Sean, *Operational Law Handbook* (Charlottesville, VA: The Judge Advocate General's Legal Center and School, US Army, 2011).

Cook, Kendra, 'The Silent Force Multiplier: The History and Role of UAVs in Warfare', *Aerospace Conference, 2007 IEEE* (2006).

186 Bibliography

Corn, Geoffrey and Eric Jensen, 'Transnational Armed Conflict: A "Principled" Approach to the Regulation of Counter-Terror Combat Operations', *Israel Law Review* 42(1) (2010).

Costello, John, *The Pacific War* (New York: Quill, 1982).

Cowley, Christopher, *Moral Responsibility* (Abingdon, UK: Routledge, 2014).

Creveld, Martin Van, *Technology and War: From 2000 BC to the Present* (New York, NY: Free Press, 1991).

Croft, Stuart, 'British Jihadis and the British War on Terror', *Defence Studies* 7(3) (2007).

Cronin, Audrey, *Ending Terrorism: Lessons for Policymakers from the Decline and Demise of Terrorist Groups* (London: IISS, Adelphi Papers vol. 394, 2008).

Cronin, Audrey Kurth, *How Terrorism Ends: Understanding the Decline and Demise of Terrorist Campaigns* (Princeton University Press, 2009).

Dammer, Harry R., Erika Fairchild and Jay S. Albanese, *Comparative Criminal Justice Systems*, 3rd edn (Belmont, CA: Wadsworth/Thomson Learning, 2006).

Dandeker, Christopher, *Surveillance, Power and Modernity: Bureaucracy and Discipline from 1700 to the Present Day* (Cambridge: Polity, 1990).

Danner, Allison M., 'Defining Unlawful Enemy Combatants: A Centripetal Story', *Texas International Law Journal* 43 (2007).

Danner, Mark, 'US Torture: Voices from the Black Sites', *The New York Review of Books* 56(6) (2009).

De Londras, Fiona, 'Guantánamo Bay: Towards Legality?', *The Modern Law Review* 71(1) (2008).

Department of Defense, *Manual for Military Commissions United States*, 2010 edn (Washington, DC: DoD, 2010).

Department of Defense General Counsel, *Department of Defense Law of War Manual* (Washington, DC: Department of Defense, 2015).

Department of Justice Office of Legal Counsel, 'Memorandum for the Attorney General Re: Applicability of Federal Criminal Laws and the Constitution to the Contemplated Lethal Operations against Shaykh Anwar al-Aulaqi' (Memo, 16 July 2010).

Dillon, Michael and Julian Reid, *The Liberal Way of War: Killing to Make Life Live* (London: Taylor & Francis, 2009).

DiPrizio, Robert, *US Humanitarian Interventions in the Post-Cold War Era* (Baltimore, MD: Johns Hopkins University Press, 2002).

Divoll, Vicki, 'Targeted Killings: Who's Checking the Executive Branch?', *The Los Angeles Times*, 25 March 2012.

Dolan, Anne, 'Killing and Bloody Sunday, November 1920', *Historical Journal* 49(3) (2006).

Dore, Philip, 'Greenlighting American Citizens: Proceed with Caution', *Louisiana Law Review* 72 (2011).

Doty, Joe and Chuck Doty, 'Command Responsibility and Accountability', *Military Review* 92(1) (2012).

Downes, Claire, '"Targeted Killings" in an Age of Terror: The Legality of the Yemen Strike', *Journal of Conflict and Security Law* 9(2) (2004).

Dunlap Jr, Charles, 'Law and Military Interventions: Preserving Humanitarian Values in 21st Conflicts' (Presentation, Humanitarian Challenges in Military Intervention Conference, Harvard University, 29 November 2001).

Dunlap Jr, Charles, 'Does Lawfare Need an Apologia?', *Case Western Reserve Journal of International Law* 43 (2010).

Bibliography 187

Dunn, David H., 'Bush, 11 September and the Conflicting Strategies of the "War on Terrorism"', *Irish Studies in International Affairs* 16 (2005).

Edwards, Adam and Peter Gill, *Transnational Organised Crime: Perspectives on Global Security* (New York: Routledge, 2003).

Edwards, Paul M., *Korean War Almanac* (New York: Facts On File, 2008).

Eichensehr, Kristen, 'On Target? The Israeli Supreme Court and the Expansion of Targeted Killings', *Yale Law Journal* 116 (2007).

Elden, Stuart, 'Contingent Sovereignty, Territorial Integrity, and the Sanctity of Borders', *SAIS Review* 26(1) (2006).

Elledge, Matthew, *The Global War on Terrorism: A Policy of Containment* (Fort Leavenworth, Kansas: United States Army Command and General Staff College, 2003).

Elliott, David W. P., *The Vietnamese War: Revolution and Social Change in the Mekong Delta, 1930–1975* (Armonk, NY: M. E. Sharpe, 2003).

Ellis, John, *The Social History of the Machine Gun* (Baltimore, MD: Johns Hopkins University Press, 1986).

Elsea, Jennifer K. and Michael John Garcia, 'Enemy Combatant Detainees: *Habeas Corpus* Challenges in Federal Court', *Congressional Research Service*, 3 February 2010.

Entous, Adam, Siobhan Gorman and Matthew Rosenberg, 'Drone Attacks Split US Officials', *The Wall Street Journal*, 4 June 2011.

Entous, Adam, Siobhan Gorman and Julian E. Barnes, 'U.S. Relaxes Drone Rules', *Wall Street Journal*, 26 April 2012.

Entous, Adam, Damian Paletta and Felicia Schwartz, 'American, Italian Hostages Killed in CIA Drone Strike in January', *The Wall Street Journal*, 23 April 2015.

Farley, Benjamin R., 'Targeting Anwar Al-Aulaqi: A Case Study in US Use of Force Justifications', *American University National Security Law Brief* 2(1) (2011).

Farrell, Theo, *The Norms of War: Cultural Beliefs and Modern Conflict* (Boulder, CO: Lynne Rienner Publishers, 2005).

Fava, Giovanni Claudio, 'Report on the Alleged Use of European Countries by the CIA for the Transportation and Illegal Detention of Prisoners' (European Parliament, 2007).

Finn, Peter and Anne E. Kornblut, 'Guantanamo Bay: Why Obama Hasn't Fulfilled His Promise to Close the Facility', *Washington Post*, 24 April 2011.

Fletcher, George P., 'Black Hole in Guantánamo Bay', *Journal of International Criminal Justice* 2(1) (2004).

Freedman, Lawrence, 'The Coming War on Terrorism', in *Superterrorism: Policy Responses*, edited by Lawrence Freedman (Oxford: Blackwell, 2002).

Freedman, Lawrence, *Deterrence* (Cambridge: Polity Press, 2004).

Frost, Mervyn, *Towards a Normative Theory of International Relations: A Critical Analysis of the Philosophical and Methodological Assumptions in the Discipline with Proposals Towards a Substantive Normative Theory* (New York: Cambridge University Press, 1986).

Fukuyama, Francis, *The End of History and the Last Man* (London: Hamilton, 1992).

Fukuyama, Francis, *State-Building: Governance and World Order in the 21st Century* (Ithaca, NY: Cornell University Press, 2004).

Gaddis, John L., *Strategies of Containment: A Critical Appraisal of American National Security Policy During the Cold War* (New York, NY: Oxford University Press, 2005).

Gaddis, John L., *George F. Kennan: An American Life* (New York, NY: Penguin Press, 2011).

Gallie, Walter B., 'Essentially Contested Concepts', *Proceedings of the Aristotelian Society* (Harrison & Sons, 1955).

188   Bibliography

Gallup, 'Muslim Americans: Faith, Freedom, and the Future', *Gallup* (Poll, 2011).

Garfield, Richard M. and Alfred I. Neugut, 'The Human Consequences of War', in *War and Public Health*, edited by Barry S. Levy and Victor W. Sidel (New York, NY: Oxford University Press, 2008).

Gearson, John, 'The Nature of Modern Terrorism', *Political Quarterly* 73 (2002).

Gearson, John, 'Deterring Conventional Terrorism: From Punishment to Denial and Resilience', *Contemporary Security Policy* 33(1) (2012).

Gennep, Arnold van, *Les Rites De Passage. Etitude Systematique Des Rites* (1909).

Gleditsch, Nils Petter, Peter Wallensteen, Mikael Eriksson, Margareta Sollenberg and Håvard Strand, 'Armed Conflict 1946–2001: A New Dataset', *Journal of Peace Research* 39(5) (2002).

Gonzales, Albert R., 'Remarks at the University of Chicago Law School', *Chicago Journal of International Law* 7 (2006).

Google, 'Your Interview with the President, 2012', *Google* (2012), www.youtube.com/watch?v=eeTj5qMGTAI.

Goolsby, Rebecca, 'Combating Terrorist Networks: An Evolutionary Approach', *Computational and Mathematical Organization Theory* 12(1) (2006).

Grant, Thomas D., 'Defining Statehood: The Montevideo Convention and Its Discontents', *Columbia Journal of Transnational Law* 37(2) (1998).

Greenwald, Glenn, 'America's Drone Sickness', *Salon*, 19 April 2012.

Greenwald, Glenn, *No Place to Hide: Edward Snowden, the NSA, and the U.S. Surveillance State* (New York, NY : Metropolitan Books/Henry Holt, 2014).

Greenwood, Christopher, 'International Humanitarian Law and the Tadic Case', *European Journal of International Law* 7 (1996).

Greenwood, Christopher, 'International Law and the "War against Terrorism"', *International Affairs* 78(2) (2002).

Grey, Stephen, *Ghost Plane: The Inside Story of the CIA's Secret Rendition Programme* (London: Hurst, 2006).

Grondin, David, 'The Other Spaces of War: War Beyond the Battlefield in the War on Terror', *Geopolitics* 16(2) (2011).

Grotius, Hugo, *On the Law of War and Peace* (Whitefish, MT: Kessinger, 2004).

Grunawalt, Richard J., 'The JCS Standing Rules of Engagement: A Judge Advocate's Primer', *Air Force Law Review* 42 (1997).

Guerin, Orla, 'Pakistani Civilian Victims Vent Anger over US Drones', *BBC News*, 3 November 2011, www.bbc.co.uk/news/15553761.

Guiora, Amos, 'Targeted Killing as Active Self-Defense', *Case Western Reserve Journal of International Law* 36(2) (2004).

Guiora, Amos N. and Jeffrey S. Brand, 'Establishment of a Drone Court: A Necessary Restraint on Executive Power', in *Legitimacy and Drones: Investigating the Legality, Morality and Efficacy of UCAVs*, edited by Steven J. Barela (Farnham, England and Burlington, VT: Ashgate, 2015).

Gunaratna, Rohan and Aviv Oreg, 'Al Qaeda's Organizational Structure and Its Evolution', *Studies in Conflict and Terrorism* 33(12) (2010).

Habermas, Jurgen, *Legitimation Crisis* (Boston: Beacon Press, 1975).

Haulman, Daniel L., *US Unmanned Aerial Vehicles in Combat, 1991–2003* (Air Force Historical Research Agency, 2003).

Hehir, Aidan, 'The Myth of the Failed State and the War on Terror: A Challenge to the Conventional Wisdom', *Journal of Intervention and Statebuilding* 1(3) (2007).

Bibliography 189

Helman, Gerald B. and Steven R. Ratner, 'Saving Failed States', *Foreign Policy* 89 (Winter 1992/1993).

Hendrickson, Ryan, 'War Powers in the Obama Administration', *Contemporary Security Policy* 31(2) (2010).

Henkin, Louis, 'Is There a "Political Question" Doctrine?', *The Yale Law Journal* 85(5) (1976).

Herek, Gregory M., Irving L. Janis and Paul Huth, 'Decision Making During International Crises: Is Quality of Process Related to Outcome?', *Journal of Conflict Resolution* 31(2) (1987).

Herman, Edward S. and Noam Chomsky, *Manufacturing Consent: The Political Economy of the Mass Media* (New York, NY: Pantheon Books, 1988).

Heuser, Beatrice, *The Evolution of Strategy* (Cambridge University Press, 2010).

Hoffman, Bruce, 'The Changing Face of Al Qaeda and the Global War on Terrorism', *Studies in Conflict and Terrorism* 27(6) (2004).

Hoffman, Bruce, 'The Myth of Grass-Roots Terrorism: Why Osama Bin Laden Still Matters', *Foreign Affairs* 87 (2008).

Hoffman, Bruce, 'The Leaderless Jihad's Leader: Why Osama Bin Laden Mattered', *Foreign Affairs* 90 (2011).

Hoffman, Paul, 'Human Rights and Terrorism', *Human Rights Quarterly* 26(4) (2004).

Holder, Eric, 'Northwestern University Speech' (Speech, Northwestern University School of Law, Chicago, IL, 5 March 2012).

Howard, Michael, *War and the Liberal Conscience* (London: Hurst, 2008).

Human Rights Watch, 'Black Hole: The Fate of Islamists Rendered to Egypt' (Report, Human Rights Watch, 2005).

Human Rights Watch, 'Letter to President Obama: Targeted Killings by the US Government' (Letter, Human Rights Watch, 2011).

Hunter, Thomas Byron, 'Targeted Killing: Self-Defense, Preemption, and the War on Terrorism', *Journal of Strategic Security* 2(2) (2009).

Hunter, Thomas, *Targeted Killing: Self-Defense, Preemption, and the War on Terrorism* (Booksurge, 2009).

Huntington, Samuel P., 'The Change to Change: Modernization, Development, and Politics', *Comparative Politics* 3(3) (1971).

Hussain, Nasser, 'Hyperlegality', *New Criminal Law Review* 10(4) (2007).

Ignatieff, Michael, *Virtual War: Kosovo and Beyond* (London: Chatto & Windus, 2000).

IISS, *The Military Balance: 2012* (London: The International Institute for Strategic Studies, 2012).

Independent Police Complaints Commission (IPCC), *Stockwell One: Investigation into the Shooting of Jean Charles De Menezes at Stockwell Underground Station on 22 July 2005* (Report, London: IPCC, 2007).

International Court of Justice, 'Advisory Opinion on the Legality of the Threat or Use of Nuclear Weapons', 1996 ICJ 226.

'International Criminal Court Article 98: Agreement between the United States of America and Afghanistan', *Department of State* (Treaty, Washington, DC, 20 September 2002).

Issacharoff, Samuel and Richard H. Pildes, 'Targeted Warfare: Individuating Enemy Responsibility', *New York University Law Review* 88(5) (2013).

Jackson, Richard, 'Culture, Identity and Hegemony: Continuity and (the Lack of) Change in US Counterterrorism Policy from Bush to Obama', *International Politics* 48(2–3) (2011).

190   *Bibliography*

Jackson, Robert H., *Quasi-States: Sovereignty, International Relations, and the Third World* (Cambridge University Press, 1990).

Jackson, Robert H. and Carl G. Rosberg, 'Why Africa's Weak States Persist: The Empirical and the Juridical in Statehood', *World Politics* 35(1) (1982).

Jaffer, Jameel, 'Judicial Review of Targeted Killings', *Harvard Law Review Forum* 126(6) (2013).

Jenks, Chris 'Law from Above: Unmanned Aerial Systems, Use of Force, and the Law of Armed Conflict', *North Dakota Law Review* 85(3) (2010).

Johnson, Jeh, 'Speech to the Heritage Foundation' (Speech, Heritage Foundation, Washington, DC, 18 October 2011).

Johnson, Jeh, 'National Security Law, Lawyers and Lawyering in the Obama Administration' (Speech, Yale Law School, New Haven, CT, 22 February 2012).

Johnson, Patrick B. and Anoop K. Sarbahi, 'The Impact of US Drone Strikes on Terrorism in Pakistan', *International Studies Quarterly* 0 (2016) (first published online 4 January 2016).

Johnson, Stuart E. and Martin C. Libicki, eds, *Dominant Battlespace Knowledge* (Washington, DC: National Defense University, 1996).

Jones, Reece, 'Sovereignty and Statelessness in the Border Enclaves of India and Bangladesh', *Political Geography* 28(6) (2009).

Kaag, John and Sarah Kreps, *Drone Warfare* (Cambridge, UK and Malden, MA: Polity, 2014).

Kahana, Ephraim, *Historical Dictionary of Israeli Intelligence* (Lanham, MD: Scarecrow Press, 2006).

Kahn, David, *The Codebreakers: The Story of Secret Writing* (New York: Macmillan, 1967).

Kaldor, Mary, *New and Old Wars: Organized Violence in a Global Era* (Stanford University Press, 1999).

Kannof, Abraham U., 'Dueling Nationalities: Dual Citizenship, Dominant & Effective Nationality, and the Case of Anwar Al-Aulaqi', *Emory International Law Review* 25(3) (2011).

Kaplan, Robert, 'The Coming Anarchy: How Scarcity, Overpopulation, Tribalism and Disease Are Rapidly Destroying the Social Fabric of the World', *Atlantic Monthly*, February 1994.

Karnow, Stanley, *Vietnam: A History* (New York, NY: Viking, 1991).

Kasher, Asa and Avery Plaw, 'Distinguishing Drones: An Exchange', in *Killing by Remote Control*, edited by Bradley J. Strawser (New York, NY: Oxford University Press, 2013).

Keegan, John, *Intelligence in War: Knowledge of the Enemy from Napoleon to Al-Qaeda* (London: Pimlico, 2004).

Kenney, Michael, *From Pablo to Osama: Trafficking and Terrorist Networks, Government Bureaucracies, and Competitive Adaptation* (Pennsylvania State University Press, 2007).

Kilcullen, David and Andrew Exum, 'Death from Above, Outrage Down Below', *New York Times*, 17 May 2009.

Kimmage, Daniel, 'Al-Qaeda Central and the Internet' (Washington, DC: New America Foundation, 2010).

Klaidman, Daniel, *Kill or Capture: The War on Terror and the Soul of the Obama Presidency* (New York, NY: Houghton Mifflin Harcourt, 2012).

Klein, Aaron J., *Striking Back: The 1972 Munich Olympics Massacre and Israel's Deadly Response* (New York: Random House, 2005).

Bibliography 191

Koh, Harold Hongju, 'On American Exceptionalism', *Stanford Law Review* 55 (2003).

Koh, Harold Hongju, 'The Obama Administration and International Law' (Speech, Annual Meeting of the American Society of International Law, Washington, DC, March 25 2010).

Koh, Harold Hongju, 'The Lawfulness of the U.S. Operation Against Osama bin Laden', *Opinio Juris*, 19 May 2011, http://opiniojuris.org/2011/05/19/the-lawfulness-of-the-us-operation-against-osama-bin-laden.

Kramer, Cheri, 'The Legality of Targeted Drone Attacks as U.S. Policy', *Santa Clara Journal of International Law* 9 (2011).

Krauthammer, Charles, 'Barack Obama: Drone Warrior', *Washington Post*, 1 June 2012.

Kretzmer, Daniel, 'Targeted Killing of Suspected Terrorists: Extra-Judicial Executions or Legitimate Means of Defence?', *European Journal of International Law* 16(2) (2005).

Krisch, Nico, 'International Law in Times of Hegemony: Unequal Power and the Shaping of the International Legal Order', *European Journal of International Law* 16(3) (2005).

Kucinich, David, 'Letter to President Obama' (Letter, Washington, DC: Congress of the United States, 12 June 2012).

Kwoka, Lindsay, 'Trial by Sniper: The Legality of Targeted Killing in the War on Terror', *University of Pennsylvania Journal of Constitutional Law* 14(1)(2011).

Lamb, Robert D., *Ungoverned Areas and Threats from Safe Havens* (Washington, DC: Office of the Under Secretary of Defense for Policy, 2008).

Larson, Carlton F. W., 'The Forgotten Constitutional Law of Treason and the Enemy Combatant Problem, *University of Pennsylvania Law Review* 154 (2005).

Lewis, Michael W., *Submission to Subcommittee Hearing: 'Drones II'* (Washington, DC: U.S. House of Representatives Committee on Oversight and Government Reform Subcommittee on National Security and Foreign Affairs, 2010).

Lewis, Neil A., 'Red Cross Finds Detainee Abuse in Guantánamo', *Washington Post*, 29 November 2004.

Lewis, Neil A., 'Official Attacks Top Law Firms over Detainees', *New York Times*, 13 January 2007.

Lieber, Francis, *General Orders No. 100* (Washington, DC: Government Printing Office, 1898).

Lim, Dawn and Noah Shachtman, 'Air Force Tells Reporters: You're Not Welcome at Our Drone Base Anymore', *Wired*, 29 November 2011, www.wired.com/2011/11/press-kept-out-of-drone-base/all/1.

Lind, William S., Colonel Keith Nightengale (USA), Captain John F. Schmitt (USMC), Colonel Joseph W. Sutton (USA) and Lieutenant Colonel Gary I. Wilson (USMCR), 'The Changing Face of War: Into the Fourth Generation', *Marine Corps Gazette* (1989).

Lippman, Matthew, 'The Evolution and Scope of Command Responsibility', *Leiden Journal of International Law* 13(1) (2000).

Lippmann, Walter, *Public Opinion* (New York, NY: Harcourt, 1922).

Loane, Geoff, *ICRC Report on the Treatment of Fourteen 'High Value Detainees' in CIA Custody* (Washington, DC: International Committee of the Red Cross, 2007).

Long, Austin, *On 'Other War': Lessons from Five Decades of RAND Counterinsurgency Research* (Santa Monica, CA: RAND, 2006).

Luban, David, 'Lawfare and Legal Ethics in Guantanamo', *Stanford Law Review* 60 (2007).

Luban, David, 'Liberalism, Torture, and the Ticking Bomb', in *Intervention, Terrorism, and Torture: Contemporary Challenges to Just War Theory*, edited by Steven P. Lee (Dordrecht: Springer, 2007).

192 Bibliography

Lukaszewicz, Thomas B., *Joint Doctrine and UAV Employment* (Newport, RI: Naval War College, 1996).

Luttwak, Edward, 'A Post-Heroic Military Policy: The New Season of Bellicosity', *Foreign Affairs* 75(4) (1996).

Lynn, John A., 'Discourse, Reality, and the Culture of Combat', *International History Review* 27(3) (2005).

McCrisken, Trevor, 'Ten Years On: Obama's War on Terrorism in Rhetoric and Practice', *International Affairs* 87(4) (2011).

McKelvey, Ben, 'Due Process Rights and the Targeted Killing of Suspected Terrorists: The Unconstitutional Scope of Executive Killing Power', *Vanderbilt Journal of Transnational Law* 44 (2011).

McKitrick, Jeffrey, James Blackwell, Fred Littlepage, George Kraus, Richard Blanchfield, and Dale Hill, 'The Revolution in Military Affairs', *Air War College Studies in National Security: Battlefield of the Future* 3 (1995).

McMahan, Jeff, *Killing in War* (Oxford University Press, 2009).

McMahan, Jeff, 'Targeted Killing: Murder, Combat or Law Enforcement?', in *Targeted Killings: Law and Morality in an Asymmetrical World*, edited by Claire Finkelstein, Jens D. Ohlin and Andrew Altman (Oxford University Press, 2012).

McNeal, Gregory S., 'Are Targeted Killings Unlawful? A Case Study in Empirical Claims without Empirical Evidence', in *Targeted Killings: Law and Morality in an Asymmetrical World*, edited by Claire Finkelstein, Jens D. Ohlin and Andrew Altman (Oxford University Press, 2012).

McNeal, Gregory S., 'Targeted Killing and Accountability', *Georgetown Law Journal* 102(3) (2014).

Mahnken, Thomas G., *Technology and the American Way of War* (New York, NY: Columbia University Press, 2008).

Makarenko, Tamara, 'The Crime-Terror Continuum: Tracing the Interplay between Transnational Organised Crime and Terrorism', *Global Crime* 6(1) (2004).

Maritain, Jacques, 'The Concept of Sovereignty', in *In Defence of Sovereignty*, edited by Wladyslav Stankiewicz (New York: Oxford University Press, 1969).

Martinez, Jenny S., 'Process and Substance in the "War on Terror"', *Columbia Law Review* 108(5) (2008).

Mattis, John, 'Assessment of Effects Based Operations', *Memorandum for US Joint Forces Command* 14 (2008).

Maxwell, Mark, 'Rebutting the Civilian Presumption: Playing Whack-a-Mole without a Mallet?', in *Targeted Killings: Law and Morality in an Asymmetrical World*, edited by Claire Finkelstein, Jens D. Ohlin and Andrew Altman (Oxford University Press, 2012).

Meessen, Karl M., 'Unilateral Recourse to Military Force against Terrorist Attacks', *Yale Journal of International Law* 28 (2003).

Melzer, Nils, *Targeted Killing in International Law* (Oxford University Press, 2008).

Melzer, Nils, 'Interpretive Guidance on the Notion of Direct Participation in Hostilities under International Humanitarian Law', *ICRC* (Geneva: ICRC, 2009).

Mendelsohn, Barak, 'Al-Qaeda's Franchising Strategy', *Survival* 53(3) (2011).

Menjívar, Cecilia, 'Liminal Legality: Salvadoran and Guatemalan Immigrants' Lives in the United States', *American Journal of Sociology* 111(4) (2006).

Menkhaus, Kenneth J., 'Governance without Government in Somalia: Spoilers, State Building, and the Politics of Coping', *International Security* 31(3) (Winter 2006/07).

Michaelsen, Scott and Scott C. Shershow, 'Beyond and Before the Law at Guantánamo', *Peace Review* 16(3) (2004).

Bibliography 193

Michalski, Milena and James Gow, *War, Image and Legitimacy: Viewing Contemporary Conflict* (Abingdon, UK: Routledge, 2007).

Miller, Abraham H. and Nicholas A. Damask, 'The Dual Myths of "Narco-Terrorism": How Myths Drive Policy', *Terrorism and Political Violence* 8(1) (1996).

Miller, Greg, 'Under Obama: An Emerging Global Apparatus for Drone Killing', *Washington Post*, 27 December 2011.

Miller, Greg, 'At CIA, a Convert to Islam Leads the Terrorism Hunt', *Washington Post*, 25 March 2012.

Miller, Greg, 'CIA Seeks New Authority to Expand Yemen Drone Campaign', *Washington Post*, 19 April 2012.

Miller, Greg, 'Legal Memo Backing Drone Strike That Killed American Anwar Al-Awlaki Is Released', *Washington Post*, 23 June 2014.

Miller, Greg and Julie Tate, 'CIA Shifts Focus to Killing Targets', *Washington Post*, 2 September 2011.

Moloney, Ed, *A Secret History of the IRA* (W. W. Norton, 2002).

Morley, Jefferson, 'Petraeus and the Signature of U.S. Terror', *Salon*, 19 April 2012, www.salon.com/2012/04/19/petraeus_and_the_signature_of_u_s_terror.

Morselli, Carlo, C. Giguère and K. Petit, 'The Efficiency/Security Trade-Off in Criminal Networks', *Social Networks* 29(1) (2007).

Moss, Kenneth B., *Undeclared War and the Future of U.S. Foreign Policy* (Baltimore, MD: Johns Hopkins University Press, 2008).

Moten, Matthew, *The Army Officers' Professional Ethic: Past, Present, and Future* (Carlisle, PA: Strategic Studies Institute, U.S. Army War College, 2010).

Mothana, Ibrahim, 'How Drones Help Al Qaeda', *New York Times*, 13 June 2012.

Murphy, Martin N., *Somalia: The New Barbary?: Piracy and Islam in the Horn of Africa* (London: Hurst, 2011).

Murphy, Sean D. 'The Doctrine of Preemptive Self-Defense', *Villanova Law Review* 50(3) (2005).

Näsström, Sofia, 'The Legitimacy of the People', *Political Theory* 35(5) (2007).

Neumann, Peter R., *Old and New Terrorism* (London: Polity Press, 2009).

Neumann, Peter, Ryan Evans and Rafaello Pantucci, 'Locating Al Qaeda's Center of Gravity: The Role of Middle Managers', *Studies in Conflict and Terrorism* 34(11) (2011).

New America Foundation, 'Pakistan Survey', *New America Foundation* (2014), https://web.archive.org/web/20141218004320/http://pakistansurvey.org.

Newman, David G., *Flying Fast Jets: Human Factors and Performance Limitations* (Farnham: Ashgate Publishing, 2014).

Newmann, William W., 'Reorganizing for National Security and Homeland Security', *Public Administration Review* 62 (2002).

Nietzsche, Friedrich Wilhelm, *Beyond Good and Evil: Prelude to a Philosophy of the Future* (London: Constable, 1997).

National Commission on Terrorist Attacks upon the United States (NCTAUS), *The 9/11 Commission Report: Final Report of the National Commission on Terrorist Attacks Upon the United States* (New York, NY and London: W. W. Norton, 2004).

Obama, Barack, 'Remarks by the President on National Security' (Speech, National Archives, Washington, DC, 21 May 2009).

Obama, Barack, 'Remarks by the President in Address to the Nation on the Way Forward in Afghanistan and Pakistan' (Speech, United States Military Academy, West Point, NY, 1 December 2009).

194   *Bibliography*

Obama, Barack, 'Executive Order 13492: Review and Disposition of Individuals Detained at the Guantánamo Bay Naval Base and Closure of Detention Facilities', *Federal Register* (Washington, DC: Executive Office of the President, 2009).

Obama, Barack, 'Nobel Peace Prize Acceptance Speech' (Speech, Oslo, Norway, 10 December 2009).

Obama, Barack, 'Remarks by the President at the "Change of Office" Chairman of the Joint Chiefs of Staff' (Speech, Ceremony Fort Myer, VA, 30 September 2011).

O'Connell, Mary Ellen, 'To Kill or Capture Suspects in the Global War on Terror', *Case Western Reserve Journal of International Law* 35 (2003).

O'Connell, Mary Ellen, 'The Legal Case against the Global War on Terror', *Case Western Reserve Journal of International Law* 36(2) (2004).

O'Connell, Mary Ellen, 'When Is a War Not a War: The Myth of the Global War on Terror', *ILSA Journal of International and Comparative Law* 12 (2005).

O'Connell, Mary Ellen, 'The Choice of Law against Terrorism', *Journal of National Security Law and Policy* 4 (2010).

O'Connell, Mary Ellen, 'Seductive Drones: Learning from a Decade of Lethal Operations', *Journal of Law, Information and Science* 21(2) (2011/2012).

O'Connell, Mary Ellen, 'Unlawful Killing with Combat Drones: A Case Study of Pakistan, 2004–2009', in *Shooting to Kill: Socio-Legal Perspectives on the Use of Lethal Force*, edited by Simon Bronitt *et al.* (Oxford and Portland, Oregon: Hart, 2012).

Ohlin, Jens D., 'Targeting Co-Belligerents', in *Targeted Killings: Law and Morality in an Asymmetrical World*, edited by Claire Finkelstein, Jens D. Ohlin and Andrew Altman (Oxford University Press, 2012).

Ohlin, Jens D., 'Targeted Killings Symposium: Jens David Ohlin Responds to Craig Martin', *Opinio Juris*, 4 June 2012, http://opiniojuris.org/2012/06/04/targeted-killings-symposium-jens-david-ohlin-responds-to-craig-martin.

Ohlin, Jens D., *The Assault on International Law* (Oxford University Press, 2015).

Omissi, David E., *Air Power and Colonial Control: The Royal Air Force, 1919–1939* (Manchester University Press, 1990).

Owens, William A., 'The Emerging U.S. System-of-Systems', *Strategic Forum* 63 February (1996).

Panetta, Leon, 'Director's Remarks at the Pacific Council on International Policy' (Speech, Pacific Council on International Policy, Los Angeles, CA, 18 May 2009).

Paret, Peter, Gordon Alexander Craig and Felix Gilbert, *Makers of Modern Strategy from Machiavelli to the Nuclear Age* (Oxford: Clarendon, 1986).

Parks, William H., 'Command Responsibility for War Crimes', *Military Law Review* 62 (Fall 1973).

Parks, William H., 'Lessons from the 1986 Libya Airstrike', *New England Law Review* 36(4) (2002).

Parks, William H., 'No Mandate, No Expertise and Legally Incorrect', *New York University Journal of International Law and Policy* 42(3) (2010).

Paul, Ron, 'An Unconstitutional Killing: Obama's Killing of Awlaki Violates American Principles', *New York Daily News*, 2 October 2011.

Peters, Gretchen, *Seeds of Terror: How Heroin Is Bankrolling the Taliban and Al Qaeda* (New York: Thomas Dunne, 2009).

Phillips, Sarah, 'What Comes Next in Yemen? Al-Qaeda, the Tribes, and State-Building' (Report, Washington, DC: Carnegie Endowment for Peace, 2010).

Plaw, Avery, *Targeting Terrorists: A License to Kill?* (Aldershot, England and Burlington, VT: Ashgate, 2008).

Bibliography 195

Plaw, Avery, Matthew Fricker and Brian Glyn Williams, 'Practice Makes Perfect?: The Changing Civilian Toll of CIA Drone Strikes in Pakistan', *Perspectives on Terrorism* 5(5–6) (2011).

Porter, Patrick, 'Long Wars and Long Telegrams: Containing Al-Qaeda', *International Affairs* 85(2) (2009).

Posen, Barry R., 'The Struggle against Terrorism: Grand Strategy, Strategy, and Tactics', *International Security* 26(3) (2002).

Posner, Eric and Adrian Vermeule, 'Accommodating Emergencies', *Stanford Law Review* 56 (2003).

Posner, Eric and Adrian Vermeule, *Terror in the Balance: Security, Liberty, and the Courts* (Oxford University Press, 2007).

Potter, E. B., *Nimitz* (Annapolis, MD: Naval Institute Press, 1976).

Preston, Stephen, 'Remarks on the Rule of Law' (Speech, Harvard Law School, Harvard, MA, 10 April 2012).

Priest, Diane, 'CIA Holds Terror Suspects in Secret Prisons', *Washington Post*, 2 November 2005.

Proulx, Vincent-Joël, 'If the Hat Fits, Wear It, If the Turban Fits, Run for Your Life: Reflections on the Indefinite Detention and Targeted Killing of Suspected Terrorists', *Hastings Law Journal* 56(5) (2005).

Raab, Jörg and H. Brinton Milward, 'Dark Networks as Problems', *Journal of Public Administration Research and Theory* 13(4) (2003).

Rabasa, Angel, *Ungoverned Territories: Understanding and Reducing Terrorism Risks* (Santa Monica, CA: RAND, 2007).

Radsan, Afsheen and Richard Murphy, 'Due Process and Targeted Killing of Terrorists', *Cardozo Law Review* 31 (2009).

Radsan, Afsheen and Richard Murphy, 'Measure Twice, Shoot Once: Higher Care for CIA Targeted Killing', *University of Illinois Law Review* 4 (2011).

Radsan, Afsheen and Richard Murphy, 'The Evolution of Law and Policy for CIA Targeted Killing', *Journal of National Security Law and Policy* 5 (2012).

Raghavan, Sudarsan, 'In Yemen, U.S. Airstrikes Breed Anger, and Sympathy for Al-Qaeda', *Washington Post*, 30 May 2012.

Raines, Joshua, 'Osama, Augustine, and Assassination: The Just War Doctrine and Targeted Killings', *Transnational Law and Contemporary Problems* 12 (2002).

Ramsden, Michael, 'Targeted Killings and International Human Rights Law: The Case of Anwar Al-Awlaki', *Journal of Conflict and Security Law* 16(2) (2011).

Rapp, Stephen J., 'U.S. Statement to the Assembly of States Parties of the International Criminal Court' (New York, NY: US Department of State, 2011).

Reporters Without Borders, 'Call For Better Media Access To Tribal Areas', *Reporters Without Borders*, 10 November 2009, http://en.rsf.org/pakistan-call-for-better-media-access-to-10-11-2009,34965.html.

Ricks, Thomas E., *Fiasco: The American Military Adventure in Iraq* (New York: Penguin Press, 2006).

Rid, Thomas, 'Deterrence Beyond the State: The Israeli Experience', *Contemporary Security Policy* 33(1) (2012).

Risen, James, 'U.S. to Hunt Down Afghan Drug Lords Tied to Taliban', *New York Times*, 9 August 2009.

Rodin, David, *War and Self Defense* (Oxford University Press, 2002).

Roggio, Bill, 'Senior al Qaeda, Taliban, and Allied Jihadist Leaders Killed in US Airstrikes in Pakistan, 2004–2015', *Long War Journal*, 11 June 2015, www.longwarjournal.org/pakistan-strikes-hvts.

196   *Bibliography*

Rostow, Walt W., *The Process of Economic Growth*, 2nd edn (Oxford: Clarendon Press, 1960).

Rotberg, Robert, *State Failure and State Weakness in a Time of Terror* (Washington, DC: Brookings Institution Press, 2003).

Roth, Kenneth, 'The Law of War in the War on Terror: Washington's Abuse of Enemy Combatants', *Foreign Affairs* 83 (2004).

Rubinstein, Ira S., Ronald D. Lee and Paul M. Schwartz, 'Data Mining and Internet Profiling: Emerging Regulatory and Technological Approaches', *The University of Chicago Law Review* 75 (2008).

Sadat, Leila N., 'Ghost Prisoners and Black Sites: Extraordinary Rendition under International Law', *Case Western Reserve Journal of International Law* 37 (2005).

Sageman, Marc, *Understanding Terror Networks* (Philadelphia: University of Pennsylvania Press, 2004).

Sageman, Marc, *Leaderless Jihad: Terror Networks in the Twenty-First Century* (Philadelphia: University of Pennsylvania Press, 2008).

Sageman, Marc and Bruce Hoffman, 'Does Osama Still Call the Shots?: Debating the Containment of Al Qaeda's Leadership', *Foreign Affairs* 87(4) (2008).

Sands, Philippe, *Torture Team: Uncovering War Crimes in the Land of the Free* (London: Penguin, 2009).

Saniotis, Arthur, 'Re-Enchanting Terrorism: Jihadists as "Liminal Beings"', *Studies in Conflict and Terrorism* 28(6) (2005).

Sarkees, Meredith R. and Franck W. Wayman, *Resort to War: A Data Guide to Inter-State, Extra-State, Intra-State, and Non-State Wars, 1816–2007* (Washington, DC: CQ Press, 2010).

Satterthwaite, Margaret L., 'Rendered Meaningless: Extraordinary Rendition and the Rule of Law', *The George Washington Law Review* 75 (2006).

Savage, Charlie, 'Secret US Memo Made Legal Case to Kill a Citizen', *New York Times*, 8 October 2011, www.nytimes.com/2011/10/09/world/middleeast/secret-us-memo-made-legal-case-to-kill-a-citizen.html.

Scahill, Jeremy, 'Washington's War in Yemen Backfires', *The Nation*, 5 March 2012.

Scahill, Jeremy, 'Speech at the International Drone Summit' (Speech, Washington, DC, 29 April 2012).

Scahill, Jeremy, 'Interview on National Public Radio', *NPR* (Interview, NPR Radio, 16 May 2012).

Scahill, Jeremy, 'Interview on MSNBC' (Interview, MSBNC, 2 June 2012).

Scahill, Jeremy, *Dirty Wars: The World is a Battlefield* (London: Serpent's Tail, 2013).

Schabas, William A., *An Introduction to the International Criminal Court* (Cambridge University Press, 2001).

Schabas, William A., 'Lex Specialis? Belt and Suspenders? The Parallel Operation of Human Rights Law and the Law of Armed Conflict, and the Conundrum of Jus Ad Bellum', *Israel Law Review* 40(2) (2007).

Schedler, Andreas, 'Conceptualising Accountability', in *The Self-Restraining State: Power and Accountability in New Democracies*, edited by Andreas Schedler, Larry Diamond and Marc F. Plattner (London: Lynne Rienner Publishers, 1999).

Scheffer, David, 'Lawfare and War Crimes Tribunal: Whose Lawfare Is It, Anyway?', *Case Western Reserve Journal of International Law* 43 (2010).

Schlesinger, Arthur M., *The Imperial Presidency* (Boston: Houghton Mifflin, 2004).

Schmitt, Carl, 'The Theory of the Partisan', *The New Centennial Review* 4(3) (1963).

Schmitt, Carl, *The Concept of the Political* (University of Chicago Press, 1996).

Bibliography 197

Carl Schmitt, tr. George Schwab, *Political Theology: Four Chapters on the Concept of Sovereignty* (University of Chicago Press, 2005).

Schmitt, Carl, tr. Jeffrey Seitzer, *Constitutional Theory* (Durham: Duke University Press, 2008).

Schmitt, Michael N., 'Humanitarian Law and Direct Participation in Hostilities by Private Contractors or Civilian Employees War', *Chicago Journal of International Law* 5 (2005).

Schondorf, Roy S., 'Extra-State Armed Conflicts: Is There a Need for a New Legal Regime?', *New York University Journal of International Law and Policy* 37(1) (2004–2005).

Sepper, Elizabeth, 'The Ties That Bind: How the Constitution Limits the CIA's Actions in the War on Terror', *New York University Law Review* 81(5) (2006).

Serle, Jack, 'Yemen Strikes Visualised', *Bureau of Investigative Journalism*, 29 March 2012, www.thebureauinvestigates.com/2012/03/29/yemen-strikes-visualised.

Shalikashvili, John M., *Joint Vision 2010* (Washington, DC: Chairman of the Joint Chiefs of Staff, 1995).

Shane, Scott, 'C.I.A. Is Disputed on Civilian Toll in Drone Strikes', *New York Times*, 11 August 2011.

Shane, Scott, David Johnston and James Risen, 'Secret US Endorsement of Severe Interrogations', *New York Times*, 4 October 2007.

Shane, Scott, Mark Mazzetti and Robert F. Worth, 'Secret Assault on Terrorism Widens on Two Continents', *New York Times*, 14 August 2010.

Shaw, Malcolm N., *International Law,* 5th edn (Cambridge University Press, 2003).

Shaw, Martin, *The New Western Way of War: Risk-Transfer War and Its Crisis in Iraq* (Cambridge, UK: Polity Press, 2005).

Singer, Peter, *The President of Good and Evil: The Ethics of George W. Bush* (London: Dutton, 2004).

Singer, Peter W., 'Outsourcing War', *Foreign Affairs* 84 (2005).

Singer, Peter W., *Wired for War: The Robotics Revolution and Conflict in the Twenty-First Century* (Penguin, 2009).

Singer, Peter W., 'Double-Hatting Around the Law: The Problem with Morphing Warrior, Spy and Civilian Roles', *Armed Forces Journal* 1 (2010).

Singer, Peter W., 'Do Drones Undermine Democracy?', *New York Times*, 21 January 2012.

Slaughter, Anne-Marie, Andrew S. Tulumello and Stepan Wood, 'International Law and International Relations Theory: A New Generation of Interdisciplinary Scholarship', *American Journal of International Law* 92(3) (1998).

Slaughter Burley, Anne-Marie, 'International Law and International Relations Theory: A Dual Agenda', *American Journal of International Law* 87(2) (1993).

Smith, Megan and James I. Walsh, 'Do Drone Strikes Degrade Al Qaeda? Evidence from Propaganda Output', *Terrorism and Political Violence* 25(2) (2013).

Smith, Rupert, *The Utility of Force: The Art of War in the Modern World* (London: Allen Lane, 2005).

So, Alvin Y., *Social Change and Development: Modernization, Dependency, and World-Systems Theories* (Newbury Park, CA: Sage Publications, 1990).

Solf, Waldemar, 'A Response to Telford Taylor's Nuremberg and Vietnam: An American Tragedy', *Akron Law Review* 5(1) (1972).

Solis, Gary D., *The Law of Armed Conflict: International Humanitarian Law in War* (New York, NY: Cambridge University Press, 2010).

198   Bibliography

Solove, Daniel, *Nothing to Hide: The False Tradeoff between Privacy and Security* (New Haven, CT: Yale University Press, 2011).

Spector, Ronald H., *After Tet: The Bloodiest Year in Vietnam* (New York: Free Press, 1993).

Staeheli, Paul W., 'Collapsing Insurgent Organizations through Leadership Decapitation: A Comparison of Targeted Killing and Targeted Incarceration in Insurgent Organizations' (Thesis, Naval Postgraduate School, Monterey, CA, 2010).

Statman, Daniel, 'Targeted Killing', *Theoretical Inquiries in Law* 5 (2004).

Stein, Yale, 'Any Name Illegal and Immoral', *Ethics and International Affairs* 17(1) (2003).

Steinhof, Uwe, 'Killing Them Safely: Extreme Asymmetry and Its Discontents', in *Killing by Remote Control*, edited by Bradley J. Strawser (New York, NY: Oxford University Press, 2013).

Steyn, Johan, 'Guantanamo Bay: The Legal Black Hole', *International and Comparative Law Quarterly* 53 (2004).

Stone, John, 'Al Qaeda, Deterrence, and Weapons of Mass Destruction', *Studies in Conflict and Terrorism* 32(9) (2009).

Strawser, Bradley Jay, 'Moral Predators: The Duty to Employ Uninhabited Aerial Vehicles', *Journal of Military Ethics* 9(4) (2010).

Strawser, Bradley J., 'Introduction: The Moral Landscape of Unmanned Weapons', in *Killing by Remote Control*, edited by Bradley J. Strawser (New York, NY: Oxford University Press, 2013).

Strawser, Bradley J., ed., *Killing by Remote Control* (New York, NY: Oxford University Press, 2013).

Suskind, Ron, *The One Percent Doctrine: Deep inside America's Pursuit of Its Enemies since 9/11* (London: Simon & Schuster, 2006).

Taft, William H., Patricia M. Wald and Sandra Day O'Connor, *US Policy toward the International Criminal Court* (Report, ASIL, 2009).

Taylor, Peter, *Brits: The War against the IRA* (London: Bloomsbury, 2001).

Tenet, George, *At the Center of the Storm: My Years at the CIA* (London: Harper Press, 2007).

Tilly, Charles, ed., *The Formation of National States in Western Europe* (Princeton University Press, 1975).

Tinetti, John, *Lawful Targeted Killing or Assassination: A Roadmap for Operators in the Global War on Terror* (Newport, RI: Naval War College, 2004).

Tipps, Dean C., 'Modernization Theory and the Comparative Study of National Societies: A Critical Perspective', *Comparative Studies in Society and History* 15(2) (1973).

Tyler, Tom R., *Legitimacy and Criminal Justice: International Perspectives* (New York, NY: Russell Sage Foundation, 2007).

Ullman, Richard H., 'Redefining Security', *International Security* 8(1) (1983).

Ulrich, Jonathan, 'The Gloves Were Never On: Defining the President's Authority to Order Targeted Killing in the War against Terrorism', *The Virginia Journal of International Law* 45 (2004).

United States Marine Corps, *Marine Corps Manual* (Washington, DC: U.S. Govt. Printing Office, 1940).

Urban, Mark, *Big Boys' Rules: The Secret Struggle against the IRA* (London: Faber, 1992).

US Army, *Field Manual 1* (Washington, DC: US Army, 2005).

Van De Velde, James R., 'The Impossible Challenge of Deterring "Nuclear Terrorism" by Al Qaeda', *Studies in Conflict and Terrorism* 33(8) (2010).

Bibliography 199

Vega-Redondo, Fernando, *Complex Social Networks* (Cambridge University Press, 2007).

Vladeck, Steve, 'Three More (Ambivalent) Reflections on the Holder Speech', *Lawfare*, 12 March 2012, www.lawfareblog.com/2012/03/more-on-the-holder-speech.

Vladeck, Stephen I., 'The New National Security Canon', *American University Law Review* 61(5) (2012).

Vladeck, Stephen I., 'Targeted Killing and Judicial Review', *The George Washington Law Review Arguendo* 82 (2014).

Wachtel, Howard A., 'Targeting Osama Bin Laden: Examining the Legality of Assassination as a Tool of US Foreign Policy', *Duke Law Journal* 55(3) (2005).

Wæver, Ole, 'Securitization and Desecuritization', *On Security* 66 (1995).

Wæver, Ole and David Carlton, *Identity, Migration and the New Security Agenda in Europe* (London: Pinter, 1993).

Walsh, Declan, 'Pakistani Parliament Demands End to U.S. Drone Strikes', *New York Times*, 20 March 2012.

Waldron, Jeremy, 'Justifying Targeted Killing with a Neutral Principle', in *Targeted Killings: Law and Morality in an Asymmetrical World*, edited by Claire Finkelstein, Jens D. Ohlin and Andrew Altman (2012).

Walzer, Michael, *Just and Unjust Wars: A Moral Argument with Historical Illustrations*, 3rd edn (New York: Basic Books, 2000).

Walzer, Michael, 'Terrorism and Just War' *Philosophia* 34 (2006).

Weber, Max, *Politics as a Vocation* (Philadelphia, PA: Fortress Press, 1972).

Wedgwood, Ruth, 'The International Criminal Court: An American View', *European Journal of International Law* 10(1) (1999).

Weigley, Russell F., *The American Way of War: A History of United States Military Strategy and Policy* (Bloomington: Indiana University Press, 1977).

Wessler, Nathan, 'In Targeted Killing Speech, Holder Mischaracterizes Debate over Judicial Review', *ACLU*, 5 March 2012, www.aclu.org/blog/national-security/targeted-killing-speech-holder-mischaracterizes-debate-over-judicial-review.

Wheeler, Nicholas J., *Saving Strangers: Humanitarian Intervention in International Society* (Oxford University Press, 2000).

Whetham, David, 'Ethics, Law and Conflict', in *Ethics, Law and Military Operations*, edited by David Whetham (Basingstoke, UK: Palgrave Macmillan, 2011).

White House, 'Executive Order 12333', *Federal Register* (Washington, DC: White House, 1981).

White House, *The National Security Strategy of the United States of America* (Washington, DC: White House, 2006).

White House, 'Executive Order 13470 Further Amendments to Executive Order 12333, United States Intelligence Activities', *Federal Register* (Washington, DC: White House, 2008).

White House, *National Intelligence Program Federal Budget Fiscal Year 2012* (Washington, DC: White House, 2012), www.whitehouse.gov/omb/factsheet_department_intelligence.

Whittle, Richard, *Predator: The Secret Origins of the Drone Revolution* (Picador, 2015).

Williams, Michael C., 'Words, Images, Enemies: Securitization and International Politics', *International Studies Quarterly* 47(4) (2003).

Wilner, Alex S., 'Targeted Killings in Afghanistan: Measuring Coercion and Deterrence in Counterterrorism and Counterinsurgency', *Studies in Conflict and Terrorism* 33(4) (2010).

200 Bibliography

Wilner, Alex S., 'Deterring the Undeterrable: Coercion, Denial, and Delegitimization in Counterterrorism', *Journal of Strategic Studies* 34(1) (2011).

Wolfendale, Jessica, 'The Myth of "Torture Lite"', *Ethics and International Affairs* 23(1) (2009).

Woods, Chris and Emma Slater, 'Arab Spring Brings Steep Rise in US Attacks in Yemen', *Bureau of Investigative Journalism*, 29 March 2012, www.thebureau investigates.com/2012/03/29/arab-spring-saw-steep-rise-in-us-attacks-on-yemen-militants.

Wright, Alan, *Policing: An Introduction to Concepts and Practice* (Devon, UK: Willan, 2002).

Wright, Lawrence, *The Looming Tower: Al-Qaeda and the Road to 9/11* (New York: Knopf, 2006).

X (George F. Kennan), 'The Sources of Soviet Conduct', *Foreign Affairs* 25(4) (1947).

Yin, Tung, 'Boumediene and Lawfare', *University of Richmond Law Review* 43 (2008).

Yoo, John, *Memo to Alberto Gonzales* (Washington, DC: US Department of Justice, Office of Legal Counsel, 1 August 2002).

Yoo, John, *War by Other Means: An Insider's Account of the War on Terror* (New York: Atlantic Monthly Press, 2006).

Yoo, John, *Crisis and Command: The History of Executive Power from George Washington to George W. Bush* (New York, NY: Kaplan, 2010).

Yoo, John, 'Assassination or Targeted Killings after 9/11', *New York Law School Law Review* 56 (2011).

Zenko, Micah, *Between Threats and War: U.S. Discrete Military Operations in the Post-Cold War World* (Stanford University Press, 2010).

Zenko, Micah, 'Transferring CIA Drone Strikes to the Pentagon' (Report, Washington, DC: Council on Foreign Relations Press, April 2013).

Zoellick, Robert, 'Congress and the Making of US Foreign Policy', *Survival* 41(4) (1999).

Cases, legislation and treaties

Al-Aulaqi v. *Obama*, 727 F. Supp. 2d 1 (DDC, 2010).

Al-Aulaqi v. *Panetta*, Civil Action No. 2012-1192 (DC 2014).

Authorization for the Use of Military Force (2001).

Baker v. *Carr*, 369 US 186 (1962).

Boumediene v. *Bush*, 553 US 723 (2008).

Ex Parte Milligan, 71 US 2 (1866).

Ex Parte Quirin, 317 US 1 (1942).

Foreign Intelligence Surveillance Act (1978).

Geneva Convention for the Amelioration of the Condition of the Wounded on the Field of Battle (Geneva, 22 August 1864).

Hamdan v. *Rumsfeld*, 548 US 557 (2006).

Hamdi v. *Rumsfeld*, 542 US 507 (2004).

Hedges v. *Obama*, No. 12-3176 (2d Cir. 2013).

In Re Territo, 156 F. 2d 142 (1946).

International Covenant on Civil and Political Rights (adopted 16 December 1966, entered into force 23 March 1976) 999 UNTS 171.

Johnson v. *Eisentrager*, 339 US 763 (1950).

Joint Resolution Concerning the War Powers of Congress and the President, Pub.L. 93–148.

Bibliography 201

Kawakita v. *United States*, 343 US 717 (1952).

Marbury v. *Madison*, 5 US 137 (1803).

National Defense Authorization Act for Fiscal Year 2012.

Public Committee against Torture in Israel v. *Government of Israel* (2006).

Rasul v. *Bush*, 542 US 466 (2004).

Rumsfeld v. *Padilla*, 542 US 426 (2004).

Smith v. *Shaw*, 12 Johns. 257 (1815). Quoted in Justice Scalia's dissent to the Hamdi decision, *Hamdi* v. *Rumsfeld*: 14.

Uniform Code of Military Justice, 64 Stat. 109, 10 US3. Chapter 47.

Index

accountability 158–9, 169
Afghanistan 33, 42, 46
Agamben, Giorgio 134, 136–9, 148
agency 161–3, 165, 171
al-Harithi, Abu Ali 3
al-Qaeda 1, 32–5, 41, 48, 53, 68, 80–2
Alston, Philip 4, 19, 42, 49, 74, 103, 158, 169
armed conflict 117
Arquilla, John 13
aulaqi v. *Panetta* 4, 106, 132, 137, 139, 141–6, 148
Authorization for the Use of Military Force (AUMF) 2, 31, 36, 53, 68, 123, 125, 128, 130, 137, 147, 149, 174
Awlaki, Anwar 3, 87, 89, 124–5, 128, 137, 147

Baker v. *Carr* 140
battlefields 106, 112–14, 129
Bin Laden, Osama 39, 51
Boumediene v. *Bush* 131–2, 144
Brennan, John 39–40, 69, 173
Bureau of Investigative Journalism, The 3
Bush administration 1, 42–4, 46, 48
Bush, George W. 34–6
Bybee, J.S. 43

Caroline doctrine 101
Central Intelligence Agency (CIA), The 2, 16, 36, 43–5, 49–53, 56, 157–60, 164, 168–73
Cheney, Dick 46
Church Committee, the 31, 50–1
civilian casualties 88–9
Clausewitz, Carl Von 6
Clinton, Bill 50
Colombia 14
command responsibility 57, 125, 155,

162–4, 167, 169–71, 173; *Medina* 168, 171–3; *Yamashita* 167–8, 171
containment 80–1
counter-insurgency 84, 86
counter-terrorism policy 36, 124
covert action 49, 52
crime-terror continuum 111
Cronin, Audrey Kurth 41

Damocles, Operation 13–14, 53
decision making 143, 165
detention 4, 43, 45, 135
deterrence 81
direct participation in hostilities (DPH) 107, 111
discourse 6
double-hatting 103, 158–9, 164, 170–1
drone courts 155
drones *see* unmanned aerial vehicles
drug trafficking 109
due process 3–4, 45, 48, 124, 130, 141, 147–8

enemies: defining 53, 73, 102, 126–30, 132–3, 136–7, 139, 146–7, 149; political 47, 126, 129
enhanced interrogation 32, 43, 46
Escobar, Pablo 14
Ex Parte Milligan 126–7
Ex Parte Quirin 40, 126–8, 132, 146
Executive Orders (EO): EO11905 51; EO12036 51; EO12333 5, 51–2, 98; EO13470 52; EO13492 46

fourth-generation warfare (4GW) 13
free-fire zones 166–7

governance 78
grievance 83–4

Index 203

Guantanamo Bay 4, 32, 45–6, 124, 127–32, 137, 141, 148

Habeas corpus 131, 144
Habermas, Jürgen 36
Hamdan v. *Rumsfeld 144*
Hamdi v. *Rumsfeld* 40, 130–1, 146–7
Heydrich, Reinhard 11
Hitler, Adolf 11
Holder, Eric 9, 40, 98, 99, 124, 130, 141, 155
hostilities 72

identity 108–9, 165
insurgents 14
intelligence 109, 165
International Criminal Court (ICC), the 116–17
international humanitarian law 10, 13, 31–2, 45, 49, 56, 68, 74, 88, 89, 90, 98–105, 107, 111, 113, 116–18, 130, 137, 155, 170
international human rights law 50, 99–100, 104, 107, 125
international law 21, 44, 68–71, 74, 97–101, 109, 115–16
internment of Japanese–Americans 135
Intifada 17–18
IRA 11, 16–17
Iraq 42, 86, 88
Ireland 16
Israel Defense Forces 16

Johnson v. *Eisentrager* 45
Joint Special Operations Command (JSOC) 158–9, 168, 170
judicial review 141
jurisdiction 144
just war tradition 155–6, 160–5, 171; revisionists 156

Kawakita v. *United States* 126
knowledge 107–9, 160, 162–3, 165–6
Koh, Harold 11, 39
Kosovo 55

law enforcement 44, 70, 75–9
lawfare 44
legitimacy 19, 35–6, 52, 84–8
liberty/security trade-off 133, 138–40, 142
Libya 105–6
liminality 47, 50, 73
Lindh, John Walker 131
logic 110–12, 166
Loughall 17

McNeal, Gregory 19, 164, 169
Marbury v. *Madison* 140, 145
media 86
Mehsud, Baitullah 90
Melzer, Nils 2, 73, 107
military 55–7
Military Commissions Act 2006 148
Military Commissions Act 2009 131–2, 148
military law 126–7, 164
moral hazards 157

National Defense Authorization Act 2012 131
necessity 10, 69
networks 12, 82–3, 90, 105–6, 109; membership of 102, 109
norms 22

Obama administration 1–2, 36; defence of targeted killings 37–9, 46–7, 67–8, 77, 97, 99, 124, 155, 172; speeches 4, 19–22, 37–9
Obama, Barack 157, 173
O'Connell, Mary Ellen 44, 75

Pakistan 3, 85–6
Patriot Act 124
Phoenix Program 15–16
political authority: Congress 2, 49, 137, 147, 174; constitutional 20, 123, 125, 136, 174; courts 73, 99, 140, 142, 144, 147; executive branch 2, 5, 31, 47–9, 123–9, 133, 135–9
political emergency 133–6, 139, 148
political question doctrine 139, 141, 143–5
Posner, Eric 133, 135, 138–9, 147
posse comitatus 130
Powers, Gary 54
Preston, Stephen W. 40–1
prisoners of war 126–8
Prosecutor v. *Duško Tadic* 104, 113
Public Committee against Torture in Israel v. *Government of Israel* 4, 18, 102, 106, 141, 146

Rasul v. *Bush* 131
rendition 43, 46
responsibility 52, 157, 160–5, 167, 170
Rommel, Erwin 11–12
rule of law 2, 7, 50, 136
rules of engagement 164–5, 168, 170–1
Rumsfeld v. *Padilla* 129–31

204 *Index*

Schmitt, Carl 47, 133, 136, 137–8
secrecy 159, 169
securitisation 33–5
security 35, 37
self defence 101, 115–16
sovereignty 75–9, 112, 115
Special Air Service, the 16–17
state authority 77–8
state building 69, 79
state failure 76–9
state of exception 134, 137
Supreme Court of Israel 18, 142–3, 146, 148

targeted killings 58; definition 2, 32, 102–3; and disruption 89–90; Israeli 4, 13–18, 85, 102–6; judgements 55; necessity 80; signature strikes 53–4, 57–8, 111–12, 160, 162, 172; utility 70, 87–90
targeting 58, 114–15
technology 8–9, 158, 175
territory 113–14, 128, 175
terrorists 14, 32
Tilly, Charles 33
treason 47, 126–7

UK 16

UN 115; charter 115–16; Security Council 98, 115–16, 173
ungoverned space 76
Uniform Code of Military Justice, the 126, 132, 164
unmanned aerial vehicles (UAVs) 53–6, 87, 158, 162, 175

Vermuele, Adrian 133, 135, 138–9, 147
Vietnam War 15–16
violence 7, 9–11

Walzer, Michael 155
war 5, 68–74, 109, 124, 132, 134–5
war on drugs 14
war powers 2, 40, 48–51, 125, 135
War Powers Resolution 50
warfare 6–8; asymmetric 11, 54–5; conventional 10, 47, 58, 113, 165–6; network-centric 12; post-heroic 55; unconventional 11, 165–6
warzones 3; *see also* battlefields
Wrath of God 15, 112

Yamamoto, Isoroku 9–12
Yemen 88
Yoo, John 31, 43, 50, 72–5, 124, 133–4, 138–9, 147